LESSONS *in* LOVE

LESSONS
in LOVE

THE TRANSFORMATION OF
SPIRIT THROUGH INTIMACY

GUY CORNEAU

Translated from the French by Nanette Bilodeau

Henry Holt and Company

New York

Henry Holt and Company, Inc.
Publishers since 1866
115 West 18th Street
New York, New York 10011

Henry Holt® is a registered
trademark of Henry Holt and Company, Inc.

Published in Canada by Fitzhenry & Whiteside Ltd.,
195 Allstate Parkway, Markham, Ontario L3R 4T8.
First published in French as *N'y a-t-il pas d'amour heureux?*
by Editions Robert Laffont, Paris, 1997.

Library of Congress Cataloging-in-Publication Data
Corneau, Guy.
Lessons in love: the transformation of spirit through
intimacy / Guy Corneau.—1st ed.
          p.   cm.
Includes bibliographical references.
ISBN 0-8050-6024-3 (hardcover: alk. paper)
1. Love.   2. Intimacy (Psychology).   3. Man-woman relationships.
          4. Jungian psychology.   I. Title.
BF175.5.L68C67   1999   98-20668
158.2—dc21   CIP

Henry Holt books are available for special promotions
and premiums. For details contact: Director, Special Markets.

First Edition 1999

Designed by Michelle McMillian

Printed in the United States of America
All first editions are printed on acid-free paper. ∞

1   3   5   7   9   10   8   6   4   2

LESSONS IN LOVE

To my parents for their love and generosity

To my sisters for their friendship

*To Marie-Ginette and to all the women who
have contributed to my difficult birth*

To Life, cradling us all so graciously on her bosom

Contents

Acknowledgments

My thanks go foremost to my partner in life, Marie-Ginette Landry, who believed in this project from the start and did everything possible to ensure its completion.

I thank Christiane Blondeau, my esteemed assistant, for managing the office while I was writing, for preparing the first draft of the manuscript, and for meticulously supervising the final product.

My agent, Marie-Claude Goodwin, who negotiated the contracts with Éditions de l'Homme and Robert Laffont. I owe her my sincere appreciation.

My gratitude goes to Joëlle de Gravelaine, director of the Robert Laffont *Réponses* series, for treating me with such respect and friendship, also to James de Gaspé Bonar, then editor at Éditions de l'Homme, for his unshakable faith in my work.

My admiration goes to Jean Bernier, whose guiding hand and

faith in my work restored my self-confidence at a time when I was in a slump.

I thank many others who accompanied me on this long journey. Céline Bietlot and Shandra Lord, whose assistance was heaven-sent. Hélène Deschesnes and Nicole Plamondon, first and final readers, respectively, deserve my special gratitude for their enthusiastic reactions to my ideas.

My thanks go equally to my colleague and friend Jan Bauer for her stimulating ideas, as well as to Robert Blondin, Tom Kelly, Pierre Lessard, Marie-Lise Labonté, Danièle Morneau, Louis Plamondon, Camille Tessier, and each and every member of my family for their ongoing encouragement. The support of my Belgian "caravan"— Thomas D'Ansembourg, Louis Parez, Pol Marchandise, Bettina de Pauw, Régine Parez, Alexiane Gillis, Liliane Gandibleu, Véronique Boissin, and Pierre-Bernard Velge—was also very important to this project.

Last but not least, my eternal gratitude goes to all those who have frequented my office and attended my talks and seminars. Your contributions and input—parts of yourself freely given— bring life and meaning to this book.

The verb to love weighs a ton.
Not to love weighs even more.

FELIX LECLERC

Introduction

Tea for Two . . .

"Tea for two and two for tea, me for you and you for me. . . ." I stole my first kiss from a girl singing that song. Oh! It was just a peck really. It happened in the woods near my childhood home. I must have been fourteen years old. My heart beat madly. The song, the yearning, scent of the damp forest, the smile of my beloved. . . . It all blended so perfectly.

I was young and spreading my wings. Nothing could stop me. My eager heart threw me into the arms of girls in whom I would find a home. It was all so easy. Believing in the ruse that everything would be all right if I just met the right partner. But love played its own trick on me. Today, I am forty-five years old, live alone, and have no children. I have a partner, but we live in separate apartments.

I thought love would make my life easier. Instead, it proved to be an endless complication. I've known several women and have even attempted commitment at times. Yet the partners I really loved were afraid of me. And the women who really loved me were those I fled. My naive enthusiasm met with the pitfalls of day-to-day living, jealousy, and betrayal. While I spent years trying to love at all costs, I also lived a decade with my heart closed—determined to love yet not to love . . . out of spite and fear of further suffering.

As I saw in myself an intense and shining lover, generous and sensitive, committed and responsible, I also saw someone with an axe to grind toward women. Deep within, I encountered the avenger, the coward, and the liar—an army of characters I did not recognize and have preferred not knowing. Admittedly, those characters are there, now forcing me to couch my judgments of others, as I recognize my own capacity for light and darkness.

As time went by, I discovered that my loving was a way of filling the void I felt inside. I wore my heart on my sleeve because I did not know what to do with it. I wanted a woman to take over my life so that I wouldn't have to live it myself. I needed to understand it all. So, I plunged into the recesses of my childhood to identify the origin of my problems. I also delved into the lives of my partners and listened to my patients for clues.

I gradually understood that love is this powerful cohesive force, flinging us haphazardly one on top of the other through desire and pain. Now I know that this force is about confronting ourselves as well as others. Through love's obstacles, we embark upon self-discovery. By wounding us, making us vulnerable and working us over, so to speak, love prepares us to receive it in all its splendor, making us more humble and open to happiness.

Today, my heart sings again. My inner journey has restored me, brought me peace. For me, love has become an inner state, not dependent on a partner. But I also know that maintaining and reinventing this state is a labor of love itself. But could there be a nobler or more urgent task than the renewal of human love?

Love at War

War has broken out in the land of love. Why is there such war when all we want is happiness? Why do we fight with the people we love the most? Does this war serve a purpose? Who declared it? Can anything be gained? And finally, how can we end it?

The fact is that no matter what the pretext, all wars are territorial. Wars break out when two countries claim sovereignty over the same land, or when the borders between two independent states are poorly defined or have become blurred over time. In the case where clear boundaries are established and respected, there is no confusion and no conflict.

Now in a society undergoing a total upheaval in its definition of roles and boundaries, the challenge is equally considerable. Such uncertainty promotes widespread conflict particularly as it affects families and couples. Indeed, because the roles defined by our patriarchal culture are being questioned, because we dare to ask what is a father, mother, man, woman, heterosexual, homosexual, it was to be expected that an open conflict would wind up affecting the domain of emotional relationships between men and women.

In a way, we could say we needed this conflict to break away from the outdated patterns that predetermined our lives. War brings men and women to the boiling point. Just as nature needs intense heat in order to dissociate certain amalgamates and to create new molecules, so it is on the physical and psychological levels. In this instance, the new molecules created are those of mutual support and equality between men and women.

But every crisis poses a risk. For the Chinese, the word *crisis* means both opportunity and danger. We could say that crisis offers a dangerous potential for change, taking advantage of an opening to create a new kind of intimacy between men and women. The danger would be for both sexes to dwell on incessant griping with each other.

Happiness Is . . .

When I give seminars on intimacy, I often begin by asking the audience if they know at least one happy couple. Most raise their hands. Three couples? Only about ten people in a group of five hundred respond. Five couples? Rarely is a hand raised.

Astonishing statistics! Is the couple an illusion or even a form of masochism? Almost everyone gives it a try in the hope of finding that ever-elusive bliss. Much like the dangling carrot, the hope of finding happiness with someone keeps driving us on. Will we ever find it?

Like the psychoanalyst Jan Bauer, I tend to think that intimacy between men and women has never really existed,[1] despite a few isolated cases. It is not as if happiness once were a reality suggesting that previous generations had succeeded where we so miserably fail. No! The phenomenon of the happy couple—intimacy between men and women—lies ahead . . . waiting to be invented. This is not an affirmation of failure, but rather a process of creating something new. We are all apprentices.

Inventing Intimacy

The intent of this book is to examine the challenge of intimacy between men and women as we near the third millennium. There are many difficulties on this journey . . . problems I will reflect upon. I do not pretend to propose a magic formula for conjugal bliss. Not only do I not have one, but I do not really believe one exists. Rather than devise strategies or systems that would make the journey easier, I will attempt to unlock the meaning behind the problems. In bringing certain patterns to light, making them visible and recognizing them, the hope is that they can be transcended.

At the outset, this book situates the crisis jarring today's couples in the context of a teetering patriarchy. We move on to a clarification of some theories that will be used throughout the book, such as the formation of the ego, parental complexes, self-esteem, and animus and anima archetypes. Then, in what could be called sections one and two, we will examine father-daughter and mother-son relationships, since they are the direct source of conditioning in the dynamic between the sexes. In fact, the deficiencies of the past largely explain the predicaments of the present. Here, we see how the father's negligence produces the "woman who loves too much" and how maternal smothering produces the "man who's afraid to love." We will also discuss the inner conflict imposed on the "good boy" in his attempt to find the capacity to love and on the "good girl" in her effort to claim a sense of initiative. I will also include some thoughts on "the role of the mother," since I realized how much my book *Absent Fathers, Lost Sons*[2] could have disturbed some mothers, particularly single parents.

In the third section, we are ready to talk about love. Chapter 9, "Love in Distress," speaks of the problems couples face when they flounder in repetitive behaviors. It explains why men suffer from what could be called in jest "the noose syndrome" and why women suffer from the "lasso syndrome." Chapter 10, "Love in Joy," discusses the current intimacy challenge and offers some possible answers to help us out of the crisis. It raises issues and suggests some attitudes for building a viable couple.

The book has a chapter on "Intimacy with Oneself," since it seems to me that today's new issue is: How can one be intimate with another if there is no intimacy with oneself? The love relationship presents not only a magnificent opportunity to work on oneself but can also serve as a bridge for communion with another person and with the universe.

My principal focus in this book is heterosexual relationships, but I hope that homosexual couples can also identify with the content and find it useful, since the couple experience poses surprising similarities, regardless of sexual orientation. Also, it should be noted that the classic father-daughter and mother-son bonds are relative. It is obvious that in the game of love, a man does not always choose a woman who resembles his mother; she can just as easily combine some traits of the father. In the same way a woman can fall in love with a man who resembles her mother psychologically.

Psychological Musing Is Not Dogma

I do not pretend to possess the truth. For me, truth is what works in one's own reality. And it always relates to a larger context. The Pueblo Indians saw themselves as the sons and daughters of the Sun God, to whom they gave daily worship. They believed that if they neglected their religious practices, the sun would refuse to rise. Such a belief gave meaning to their existence and inspired them to live in close communion with nature. Robbing them of this belief would make them ill. Such was the psychological truth of their reality at the time, but one that would work rather poorly today. Every human needs a guiding principle or myth to give life meaning. What is important here is not that this concept or worldview be objective or verifiable, but that it generate the enthusiasm required to continue to progress on the road of life.

That is the kind of truth I am seeking, a psychological truth allowing us to look at couple dynamics from a new angle, a truth that would lend meaning to our problems and encourage us to go on living and loving. So, use this book, won't you, as a research tool. Take what's important to you, that with which you identify, and leave the rest.

Love at Peace

Today love has become a battlefield, and I do not know of any sure way to escape it. I only know from experience that introspection on a regular basis—looking at what is happening inside, observing one's actions without judgment, forgiving oneself, one's parents, and everyone who shares our lives—becomes a source of serenity giving rise to great joy. Somehow, suffering releases its grip on us, and life becomes a lot more livable.

Coming into this freedom involves doing our housecleaning. It means we have to wage a war of love, to conquer something important. It means battling against confusion to gain the right to be oneself. Between the Devil and God, between spirituality and materialism, between feminine and masculine values, a path is there, allowing us to walk on firm ground, close to the earth. Rooted in all our senses, with gladness of heart and peace of spirit, we may come to know the joy of sharing in the great universal community. We are not born to be beasts of sex, hopeless lovers, or ascetic recluses. We are invited to live in dignity as human beings.

This book is full of tears, insights, cries, and laughter. It was guided by a spirit of love and peace. May you discover this fountain and quench your thirst on life's journey.

LESSONS *in* LOVE

I

Love at War

SOFA TACTICS

The Woman

He has just come in from work and is sitting on the sofa, tired but content. After removing his shoes he yawns and stretches. He has a lot to tell you this evening, continuing even as you head to the kitchen for some wine. He's wearing the shirt you like so much. In fact, you picked it out for him because it gives him a mischievous air. He takes life so seriously! You love these times, when he's relaxed and lets himself go in conversation. Being tired helps of course. You don't find the subject particularly interesting, but at least he's talking to you. He's relating.

While he talks, you advance toward the sofa, feeling lustful and sensual. You have a spontaneous urge to kiss him right there, just to celebrate the moment. For once you will initiate foreplay, instead of him all the time—a responsibility he complains about bitterly.

He's watching you from the corner of his eye. He smiles and takes the glasses of wine and sets them on the table. He responds to your first kiss with visible pleasure. But the more you insist, the worse it gets. You definitely sense that he's uneasy. You feel his whole body stiffening, as if refusing any further involvement. He's still smiling, but his face is frozen. He has stopped talking and reaches for his wine.

He is visibly uneasy and you can't figure out why. Or maybe you do, and you don't like what you're beginning to understand. The truth is that when you initiate foreplay, it never goes very far. It's never the right time, and he may even say he has a headache! You would think he's a little boy afraid of his mother. But you're not his mother, and want nothing to do with her. But oh how you'd love to send her little darling back to her all wrapped up and labeled "damaged goods."

The Man

She comes home from work before you, and her scent has already filled the whole apartment, blending with the warmth of the late afternoon sun coming through the open windows. She asks you if you'd like some wine, and you answer *why not?* You love it when she's in a good mood and caters to your every need and whim. At times like these, life is beautiful. You feel lucky to be pampered in so many special ways.

While she goes to the kitchen, you talk about everything and anything just to make her laugh, because you know she likes your chatter. As you are talking, you suddenly feel the urge to make love to her. Ah . . . if she would only make the first move (which she almost never does), you would eat her right up! But what luck, there she is offering herself to you—fantasy has become reality. But something's wrong. Is the intensity exaggerated? Such passion upsets you. It's as if her life depended on it, as if her need for love were so great that no man would ever be able to satisfy it.

She has set her glass on the table and cuddles up, kissing you. Now she wants to hear you say *I love you*. Oh no! Not that again. She always wants you to say *I love you*. You should make a tape recording so she could listen to it all day long. The situation is beginning to get on your nerves. Where does this need for affection come from, a need so great that you dare not get too close for fear of being swallowed up? "Didn't have a father!" is her repeated excuse. Really! "Didn't have a father!" As if *you* ever had one.

After the fourth kiss, you stretch out an arm to get your glass. You hope your uneasiness has gone unnoticed, but knowing her intuition, you can never be sure. Spilling your wine on the rug might be a solution, but on second thought you decide to go to the bathroom to compose yourself and stall for time.

The Woman

Well, there he is running away again, but this time you won't run after him. You've had enough. Enough of this male indifference. Enough of acting like a nice girl. Enough of making his favorite meals and fulfilling his bedroom fantasies in exchange for the affection never given. Your anger begins to mount and you decide to keep quiet. What you want to say seems too awful, too vicious.

Five minutes ago you wanted to kiss him, but now you want to get even. If only he'd come out of the bathroom.

The Man

As you stall in the bathroom, you reproach yourself for your attitude. After all, she did all that to please you. If you followed her initiative for once. . . . If you gave her the love she expects, it would end the petty war of the past few days. So you return to the living room, full of good intentions.

You find her distant, cold, snappy, all huddled up at the end of the sofa. Your good intentions have just been dissolved. "If it's war she wants, that's what she'll get," you think. You won't be manipulated! Besides, ever since she's been in therapy and begun to assert herself, it seems that the problems have only increased. Nothing gets by her.

Then, as she starts one of her tirades on commitment, your blood curdles. You swallow a bit of wine to calm down, but it tastes like vinegar. Yes, vinegar, of course, vinegar! In a flash, you seem to have grasped the heart of the problem. She's a sour pickle! Everything she touches tastes like vinegar. Another ruined evening, and you have only one thought in mind: to leave.

You try to interrupt to tell her, but she takes the words right out of your mouth: "I suppose you want to leave again. Perhaps you think I'm disturbed, but isn't it really that I'm disturbing? Nuance, my dear! Besides, do you honestly think other women are different? Do you really believe you'll ever find the ideal woman? Look at yourself!"

The Burden of a Dream

And so it begins again! The waltz of blame and accusations. The tone will escalate. Doors will slam. Somebody will leave and return. There will be a few screams, a few tears, bitterness on both sides, contrition, a little kiss, and, on a good night, there will be makeup sex! And in a few days, it will start over again.

I know, you're probably thinking that this only happens in your living room. Sorry to disappoint you, it happens everywhere! Of course, you will add your personal touch. Sometimes, it's two men on the sofa . . . sometimes two women. Often it is the female partner who refuses to be approached. In some cases, there will be physical violence. But in general the scenario does not vary much. Sometimes you'd think that human love relationships follow a predetermined program.

She says that she's ready for a man who is capable of commitment. She wants *him* to give her what Daddy never could. But the burden of such expectation scares him, particularly because he has no idea what intimacy is, either with others or with himself. He understands power, fame, mechanics, and ideas. But emotions are something else. He lacks the main ingredient in this love recipe, the ingredient *she* claims to have. As a result, he feels worthless at the emotional level.

He feels guilty for not responding to her lifelong dream and knows he cannot adequately fit the expected role. *She's* unhappy for not being able to make him happy no matter how much she tries to help him to become the prince charming of her dreams. *He* feels controlled, manipulated, forced to be what he's not. He felt the same confusion around his mother, who also wished to turn him into her prince. It's a replay of the same dream. *She* has the same grip on him, without even realizing it.

She doesn't realize what a burden her dream is. *He* has no idea of the weight of his demands, nor of his negligence. He is not aware that his behavior is the price he makes her pay for her dream. This is how he manipulates her, making her try so hard to reach him. This is how it slowly becomes unbearable. For *her* as she waits for him and follows him. For *him*, who is silent and runs away.

All their actions betray what they hope to obtain from each other, and they are both deceived. They keep up the game anyway, be it maliciously, to see how far the other will go before giving up the dream. They go on out of helplessness, and when they have had enough of the maneuvers, when they have sufficiently trampled each other, they will break up in disgust. *She* will say that she has once more been taken for a ride. *He* will say he's once again fallen into the same trap. Both will suffer because it didn't work out. For centuries, partners have waltzed to the same broken tune, but isn't it true that only a major crisis could make us consider changing the music?

THE COUPLE HAS BECOME A BATTLEFIELD

A Teetering Patriarchy

The man and the woman in the previous scenario are like many contemporary couples. Yet the war they are waging began long before their time. It is largely rooted in the organized power of what is called patriarchy, that is, a society dominated by the laws of the father and masculine values.

As such, we may well say, as Oscar Wilde did, "that two people in love become as one . . . but which one?" In traditional couples, domestic peace was based more often than not on the woman sacrificing herself for the benefit of her partner. Men and women united to form a "male" couple, one that subscribed to the dictates of a patriarchy. The woman would surrender her individuality, her tastes, her ambitions, and her creativity, in order to raise her children. At the altar, she promised "to love, honor, and obey," taking her husband's name. From the day women began to reject this status quo, crisis was inevitable, because we have no historical model for a life-style allowing individuals to live together while remaining whole and autonomous.

Patriarchy is a system of concepts that shapes social and psychological identities of men and women. This ideology tells women that their role is one of subservience to men. It is based on the following prejudice: that what men produce and think is more important than what women do, think, and feel. The result is that whatever is deemed feminine, emotional, and domestic is devalued. The patriarchal structure found itself challenged when women began to affirm that they were full-scale human beings. It explains why the war between the sexes began and continues, both inside and outside the home. In a way, the conflict could be summarized in one very simple question: *Who is serving, and who is being served?*

Like the sociologist Edgar Morin, we could also say that "women are the secret agents of modernity," because the progressive fragility of patriarchal culture follows the stages of their march to autonomy. Although there have always been women claiming equal rights,[1] it is only recently that their status has begun to change significantly. The invention of the Pill, in liberating them from systematic pregnancies, is no doubt one of the first milestones in the loss of power of men over their mates. Traditional sexual roles were challenged as the door to pleasure and lust was opened for women. The second stage of patriarchal destabilization is linked to their explosive arrival on the job market in the 1960s. Women began to exist at the economic level, breaking away from their financial dependence. This led directly to the organized and active feminism of the 1970s, which claimed equality for women in all spheres of life.

Naturally, this debate also profoundly affected the area of love relationships. It turned the modern couple into a first-class battlefield, where the challenge to patriarchy is played out, simply because it throws the opposing masculine and feminine cultures together into the crucible of daily living. Consequently, the fate of patriarchy is being decided in the kitchens and bedrooms, where the bonds are more informal, rather than in the workplace or in the political arena.

Patriarchy Exists in Each of Us

It would be an illusion to believe that the dispute could be settled by separating the good from the bad. Because behind this story lies another one involving the majority of men, who, like women, are also oppressed by patriarchal pressures. Men have to imitate a hard, heroic male prototype, unable to communicate feelings, and are considerably alienated from a large part of themselves. So much so that many women believe that men are incapable of any feeling and that they have zero competence when it comes to family organization and child education. Inversely, men believe that women are unable to think.

To continue fostering such prejudices is equivalent to perpetuating the inequalities generated by patriarchy. Would it not be timely for men and for women to acknowledge their solidarity in the same historical drama? Would it not be timely to acknowledge that there are executioners and victims on both sides? Does it not imply that both sexes become more conscious of their respective positions? The fact that many women fall into the "toughness" game as they struggle to succeed in the male world confirms the power of this terrible patriarchal law, which remains the same for every man and woman: Cut yourself off from your emotions and feelings if you want to survive!

In fact, "the couple" risks remaining an impossible dream as long as such perspectives rule our society. Patriarchal masculinity is built on the amputation of hearts and bodies. It is based on repressing sensitivity and sensuality, and on blocking the spontaneous expression of feelings. The remedy it offers for all our ills is the power of abstract reasoning, which imposes its law on all the other human registers. It is our collective participation—men and women alike—in this collective myth that removes us further and further from life and any possibility for intimacy with people and the world around us.

Indeed, patriarchy represents much more than organized social and political power. It does not exist in an abstract manner, independently from us. It exists first and foremost within us all. For example, we manage our emotions and thoughts according to its dictates when we always give more importance to external duties than to emotional values, and when we allow reason to continually dominate our hearts. Patriarchy has caused us to be terribly divided, thus inflicting a deep wound in every man and woman. The only possible cure for our ills[2] is to develop real intimacy between men and women who see each other as equal and complementary partners.

Toward a New Intimacy

The history of intimacy between men and women is not voluminous. Marrying for love is a relatively recent practice and living together out of love is even more recent. Apart from the necessity to start a family, our grandparents and great-grandparents often married to survive economically, to improve their social status, or to preserve or enrich their ancestral heritage. In many instances, they stayed together to avoid an accusing finger from the church and their neighbors. For them, intimacy was not part of the list of marital duties, nor was it important to be intimate with their children.

In former generations, the roles of mother and father, man and woman, were defined in advance. But, a sickly dullness began to gnaw at this stale notion of existence, so that we are now questioning the image we have of ourselves and how we relate to others. The roles of mother and father are not as obvious. We are beginning to ask ourselves what is a man, what is a woman, what is heterosexuality, and what is homosexuality? An explosion was inevitable! The crisis we currently face is without precedent, offering us a unique opportunity for growth. No other civilization has ever had the leisure to consider these issues on a large scale, which makes our times as exciting as they are troubled. Journalist and author Ariane Émond responds to the pessimism threatening us in the face of our disastrous relationships. She affirms that men and women have never been in a better situation, since for the first time in history they have begun to relate to each other outside of their prescribed roles.[3]

Patriarchy has generated a construction of masculine and feminine identities in such a way that the creation of the harmonious couple has virtually become impossible today. Yet the new venture is a tempting and stimulating one. But one thing is certain. Now that individuals are claiming their own independence, the new challenge concerning intimacy will not be based on one person sacrificing oneself for the other, but on the following paradigm: to be united while continuing to be two whole individuals, to be two independent persons while being constantly united.

In the next chapter we are going to explore the underpinnings of this book. However, if you don't care for theory, please feel free to go directly to the chapters that interest you. Although there is a logical progression in the book, each chapter is fairly independent and can be read on its own, making it possible to trace your own path in your reading.

2

On Being Born a Man or a Woman

THE CONCEPT OF IDENTITY

The Essence of Being Human

How can we be both separate and united? This is the fundamental question, in regard not only to the couple but to the psychological life of the individual as well.

To answer this question—which is the core of this book—we need some theoretical benchmarks. In this chapter, we will therefore define the following basic concepts: the formation of ego and its complexes and the roots of self-esteem, sexual identity, and the animus/anima archetypes. First, we will discuss the essence of being human, which serves to sustain identity.

Initially, identity requires a dual action: getting close to others to obtain love, and keeping a distance to assert one's difference. In approaching others, we seek a sense of belonging. In seeking a distance, we seek to explore our individuality. How we integrate this dual action has a determining influence on our love life, because everything takes place between these two poles of fusion and separation.

At the onset of life, all is One for the child. A baby lives in total symbiosis with its environment, just as in the mother's womb. Birth is the first shock that stimulates a child's awareness as an individual. But this is only the first awakening, and nothing is crystallized yet. For several months, the infant will have the sensation of being united with its surroundings, without feeling any separateness. Its mother is part of itself, or better still, the infant vaguely perceives itself as being an extension of her breast.[1]

As soon as the small frustrations of infancy begin to appear, such as a delayed feeding or cries of distress left unanswered, the child becomes conscious that his individuality is separate from that of others. As soon as he encounters the first jostles of life, the child becomes conscious of its existence taking shape. Without this friction between himself and others, there would be no subjective life, that is, life conscious of itself. Note, however, that it is not the frustration per se that creates self-awareness, but the revelation it provokes when it informs the child of his existence.

Self-consciousness is therefore the product of a withdrawal into oneself, a sort of contraction, in reaction to the outer environment's impact on us. But this withdrawal is effected in order to allow the individual to unfold as an entity in the universe. Indeed, the individual's function is to transform his primary reactions into new creations that will in turn be projected into the universe. That is why it is possible for us to address the formidable creative capacity of human beings. The circuit of life is thus established: action, reaction, transformation, action. The child transforms its hunger into cries, the cries make the parents react, and they transform their humane reaction into the act of feeding the child.

The tension between self and the universe, between self and

others, determines the psychological life of the individual. This is the essence of being human. The individual must accept this tension, for it assures his personal balance in the midst of movement and change. Mostly, it allows the individual to find his identity because in some way we could say that human identity is born in the midst of chaos. At the beginning, human identity finds itself clustered with other identities from which it must gradually differentiate in order to take form. If this basic tension pressing all beings to emerge from the original magma to become themselves were not present, we would remain engulfed, without becoming conscious of our own independent existence. The bud would never flower.

The Formation of the Ego[1]

Awareness of individuality becomes more stable and the impression of continuity throughout time is created as the infant grows. Little by little, the child's ego is crystallized, and the child now recognizes the reflection in a mirror as himself. The child enjoys his own company, as did Narcissus, who fell in love with his reflection in a lake. This is the famous *mirror phase* developed by psychoanalyst Jacques Lacan. The ego from then on occupies the center of the field of consciousness, and its emergence allows the true psychological birth of the subject as a human being who is able to speak of his subjective experience and say *I* in reference to himself.

The fascination by one's own image is what psychoanalysis calls *narcissism.* The child is naturally narcissistic, that is, centered on himself, and this phase is absolutely necessary because it is the basis of self-esteem, which will be discussed in detail later.

The child will subsequently assert himself, allowing his personality to grow in a more and more conscious way. While bonded with the mother and the father and identifying with their values, he will gradually separate himself from their wishes and those of his family environment when he begins his schooling. This important change will help him not only to differentiate himself from his family, but will expose him to other values from which he will once more have to distance himself in order to develop. The same logic will apply later as the identity imposed by a skill or a profession threatens to submerge the adult and blunt the ego's originality, and so on and so forth at every new phase. In forming human relationships, the individual tries to adapt while attempting to remain himself.

It must be emphasized, however, that the ego would not be able to develop itself without others, or without love. Throughout our lives, our individuality needs others to recognize itself, to develop, and to identify and differentiate itself. It needs others to both assert differences and embrace similarities. Moreover, our relationships with others serve to stimulate emotions that we will transform and express in the open. Be they negative or positive, our contacts with others keep us alive and kindle our creativity. Others prove to be more than a commodity with which we must deal; they are a passage through which we reach our own selves.

On Becoming Oneself

It is nonetheless a fact that many people curb the growth of their personalities and repress their originality through fear of displeasing others. The temptation to linger in one phase and to stop growing no doubt is there for all of us, to the extent that some of us never break away from our families or from our professional images. While remaining the anonymous members of a clan, a couple, or a profession, we feel secure, but our innermost originality suffers and will inevitably claim its due in the form of a physical or psychosomatic illness.

Developing one's personality and becoming oneself are much

more than a psychological duty; they are a basic need that no one can repress without paying a high price. That need is so satisfying that it creates a feeling of having accomplished oneself, and leads to the intimate knowledge of having found one's place in the universe and a meaning to life. This inalienable right to become oneself, this genuine thrust of autonomy, constitutes what the Swiss psychoanalyst Carl Gustav Jung names the *process of individuation.*[2]

Jung believes that the process of individuation motivates human beings to become most basically themselves while being truly united with all of their environment. The process unfolds according to the following phases: In the first phase, the individual becomes gradually independent from his parents and from the complexes formed because of them; the second phase involves his increasing competence in relating to others; the third phase draws him into becoming more and more the person he feels he is; and the fourth finds him becoming more *whole,* or more personally centered, while being united with the process of life in all its aspects.[3]

During the last phases of the individuation process, the dilemma of fusion and separation is resolved and the ego is united with the deepest level of being, the self, and there is no division between the individual and others. The ego is then the most genuine, while being also simultaneously united with all that exists. Therein dwells the mystery of our identity. Personality, community, individuality, and universality are all at once the substance of our beings. The road leading there is a long one, however. The ability to remain oneself in the company of others and having faith that we are accompanied even if we are alone are the paradoxical markers of our journeys. The inevitable friction between individuality and universality is the very essence of creativity and the provider of vital human energy.

The Development of Complexes

Breaking free from parental complexes seems to be the most difficult task in the process of individuation, since they are the ones that often prevent human beings from asserting their individuality. They are also the cogs in the wheel of love relationships. It is therefore important to devote a few lines to the development of complexes in general and of parental complexes in particular.

Complexes[4] are the interiorization of the dynamics we experienced in our childhood relationships. These are usually forged in relation to the highly charged emotional events and establish a long-term niche within us. Complexes become real inner voices pushing us to repeat the same basic patterns, having the power to lock us in negative behavior tendencies.

However, complexes per se are not negative as implied by popular language when, for example, the inferiority complex is mentioned. They are the building blocks of our psyche, which in turn is composed of our mental and emotional reactions as a whole. It may be said that each complex has its own ambience and its own color, created by the emotional tone of the event that provoked it. The emotion will subsequently behave like a magnet drawing to itself the events, thoughts, and fantasies having the same emotional content. These components mingle with each other in the unconscious and organize themselves in associative chains. This is what made Freud say that on the basis of any mental representation, one is able to identify the complex that produced it. Moreover, he established his method of exploration of the depths of the psyche on this discovery and named it *free association*.

One way of understanding this is to concentrate on the word *disgust*. If you dwell on this word long enough, it conjures up in your mind objects and experiences that, as a child, you rejected. If I think of that word, images of rats and garbage pails enter my mind. I see the mice- and snake-infested house I once rented in the country. I recall childhood companions who ate worms, and so on. The same exercise can be used with the word *joy* or any other word.

You will thus become aware that certain words are more powerful than others because they are more emotionally provocative, as, for example, the words *tube* or *hole*. That is because they refer to experiences you do not care to think of, or that you censor. The tension felt is a sign of *resistance*, the term conventionally used in psychoanalysis describing the ego's dislike of such unpleasant (or pleasant) thoughts. It wants to keep its property nice and clean by blocking such thoughts or experiences and *repressing* them into the unconscious. Complexes have inherited a bad reputation because we do not want to deal with them. In fact, when the complexes are positive we do not even notice them, as they are simply part of the general balance of our lives. They play a role as intermediaries between the internal and the external.

Parental Complexes

The observations described above may also be applied when referring to the development of parental complexes. The paternal complex and the maternal complex are part of the most powerful complexes of our psyche. Much like the other complexes, they summarize our parental relationships, having their own emotional color depending on the good, adequate, or disastrous experiences we had. However, it is important to understand that such complexes belong to us only, being our memory of the relationship and not an objective statement concerning our parents themselves.

The maternal complex applies not only to mothers. It condenses our whole experience of the maternal world. In fact, a number of the events that comprise it may have been experienced with a grandmother, an aunt, or even a wet nurse, depending on the significance of their roles in our lives. The same principle is valid in the case of the paternal complex comprising the sum of our experiences with paternal figures.

For example, I treated a woman whose parents had placed her several times in foster homes during wartime for her safety. She came to me because she had a constant fear of being abandoned. Her inner voices judged her severely instead of supporting her, and she felt persecuted. The contents of her parental complexes were particularly negative, thereby making her believe that she was worthless and that in her case it was useless to try solving the problem. The fact was that her parents were quite adequate. But her experiences of being abandoned at an early age, when the development of a child depends so much on the watchful eye of the parents, were bound to leave a tenacious mark on her.

As in the case of all complexes, those that concern parents may be positive or negative. An uneventful childhood where the child felt loved and accepted will generate positive parental complexes. These complexes will support the assertion of the ego and give the individual the required confidence to go forward in life. Because they favor a generally well-balanced development, they will never be subjects for psychotherapy. Even if an individual has had negative experiences with the parental figures of his childhood, it is possible that the result will be partially reversed if he is lucky enough to be influenced by positive parental figures.

It is therefore important to remember that complexes are not inert entities, nor is the psyche a museum. It has the power of an ocean continually stirring up its contents. The fish are the complexes we encounter. Sometimes charming, often terrifying, their vitality is what makes personal development possible. They can be modified, and by dealing with them consciously they lose their disturbing autonomy.

The Ego Is Also a Complex

You will perhaps be surprised to learn that according to psychoanalysis and psychology, the ego is also a complex. The ego represents our conscious personality, the way in which we know ourselves. It is composed of a central emotion that is precisely the feeling we have of identity and duration through time. It has a certain supply of energy to be used with the backing of goodwill.

If the ego occupies a central place and defines conscious personality, the other complexes can be seen as subpersonalities with which the ego is more or less in touch. Each *alter ego* has its own memory and a certain measure of autonomy. This is very apparent in people who suffer from multiple personality disorder, or schizophrenia. As entire fragments of a relatively structured personality suddenly erupt into the field of consciousness, they take the place of the familiar ego. The person goes through a total personality change and does not say, for instance, "I feel like Julius Caesar this morning!" but "I am Julius Caesar" and believes it.

If the ego were not a complex in the same way as the other more unconscious elements of the personality, such reversals would not be possible. Moreover, if someone makes us angry to the point of being beside ourselves, that is, outside of our familiar ego, it will be obvious that one need not be a schizophrenic to discover in oneself a totally different personality with unbelievable energy!

For Jung the formation of the ego and its complexes reveals the innate structures of the psyche. He gave the name *archetypes*[5] to those impersonal structures that are common to all human beings. This means that the human psyche always tends to develop in the same way in all human beings and in all cultures. For example, the mother archetype drives the child to develop a maternal complex, as if he were programmed in advance to comprehend the maternal aspects of his environment. In short, the archetype is a predisposition that is activated, humanized, and personalized according to a concrete experience. However, the complex formed in reaction to real and personal life experiences activates only a part of the archetypal field. In the case of the mother archetype, for instance, the complex contains opposites that range from the terrible devouring mother to the kind and nurturing one. In fact, this is what makes the therapeutic process worthwhile, since it arouses the dormant component of the archetype.

We Project Parts of Ourselves onto Others

Complexes are generally unconscious and remain so because we *project* them externally. A *projection* is part of the defense mechanisms that the conscious ego uses to protect itself from certain affects that could be disturbing if they emerged from the unconscious. The ego gets rid of these frequently repressed *shadow*[6] figures by lending them to others, so to speak. It projects these figures in the way of a missile, so accurately that we end up blaming others for flaws in us that are plainly unconscious. The irritation is generally a sign that a part of oneself has been projected onto another person. That explains why it is always other people who are wrong and who bear all the faults of the world.

What becomes immediately obvious is the power of that mechanism as it operates in love relationships. It becomes even more powerful when it is activated by the intense frictions of daily living. What is also obvious is that the couple can become a potent environment for work on oneself on the condition that we agree to acknowledge that what bothers us in the partner could very well be part of something unknown in ourselves. By our gesture of *withdrawing the projections*, it is possible for us to understand that what we are experiencing on the outside is a manifestation of the inner dynamics orchestrated by the complexes. Accordingly, the process of individuation requires that we strive constantly to bring the active forces of the unconscious to consciousness.

LOVING ONESELF

Love of Self Is a Condition for Psychological Balance

Let us now explore one of the poles of our identity, love of self. The basic feature of our identity and the key to its development reside in the love we have for ourselves. Self-esteem is a determining factor in our love relationships. By being aware of our value, we can avoid falling into dependent relationships where it is the approving gaze of the partner that gives us the right to exist. In the overall context of our research, understanding the strong link between love of self and love of the other is of primary importance. People who love others to the point of losing their beings do not love themselves sufficiently. They have forgotten the second part of the Christian precept, which says; "Love they neighbor as thyself!"

A healthy identity is based on healthy self-esteem. The whole idea is about trusting ourselves and believing in our value! Love of self gives us the authority to be ourselves without waiting for the approval of others, to seek and experience without judgment what gives us pleasure. In brief, it grants us permission to exist, to breathe freely, and to take the space we need to develop while respecting that of others.

Unless we have this self-esteem, we cannot claim what we really need to develop in a positive way and make use of our talents. We tend to believe that we do not deserve the best of what life offers. Some people even believe that they do not deserve to exist or that their lives are not worthwhile.

To be able to stop waiting for others' approval in order to appreciate oneself and life is no doubt the most basic and revolutionary victory of our lives. Choosing to live, choosing to love, choosing to celebrate the joy of existing, and becoming fully responsible for one's own happiness are absolutely the most creative deeds that an individual can accomplish.

But that is far from easy. The majority among us are still submerged by our pasts with their unresolved conflicts with fathers and mothers, by the inevitable clashes of love commitments, and by the negative voices within us. The fact is, that in order to be able to love, it is important to have experienced the feeling of being loved. The actions and eyes of our parents and other parental figures were the mirrors held before us so that we could learn the essential elements on which to build our self-esteem.[7]

During childhood, as we see the gleam of admiration, enthusiasm, and love in the eyes of our kin, we progressively integrate this positive mirror and learn to love ourselves. The integration contributes to the development of positive parental complexes that support us instead of denigrating us. The resulting self-esteem inspires us to trust ourselves, to be loyal to whatever aspects in us that are not appreciated by others, to stand up against adversity, and to turn life into a great adventure. The positive inner mirror becomes the basis of a healthy narcissism.

Many circumstances in life can trigger the development of a poor sense of self-esteem. These may have been, for instance, a sickly mother, an alcoholic father, or hospitalization at an early age. When what the mirror presented was negative, when no one watched over us, or if our parents found no pleasure in raising their children, a healthy self-esteem cannot develop. So instead of trusting our abilities, we are assaulted by constant doubting. All the trying experiences that made us feel rejected in our family environment will lead to the development of negative parental complexes that, instead of supporting us, whisper the list of our failings to us.

It is as if we had a naughty echo inside, saying as in the fairy tale: "Snow White is the fairest of them all!"[8] We begin to feel ashamed of being who we are and hate all the people whose lives seem easier than ours. They become rivals. We envy them and wish to destroy them, or worse still, we cling to them and imitate them in order to get the attention they seem to attract. We are caught in a sort of love bond that easily changes into hate if the person chosen as a model of perfection does not manifest his or her approval, or if he or she destroys our illusions by not recognizing our talents.

The narcissism in this case is unhealthy and contradicts appearances. In fact, here is an individual who suffers from a self-esteem so wounded that he gives the impression of being egocentric. But the simple fact is that the shaky self-esteem has an unrelenting need to be upgraded by positive comments and compliments. This explains why these individuals are constantly displaying what they are and what they do, just as the child wanting at all cost to be complimented on his drawing. If the individual is able to struggle against the negative images of himself suggested by merciless complexes, he will regain confidence and the behavior will disappear. But since the problem is deep-seated, this is often accomplished at the cost of a long therapeutic journey, which now brings us to a more detailed discussion of the roots of self-esteem.

From Almightiness to Self-Esteem

As mentioned before, the child is born into a world of total unity. For a long time, she will resist with all her might perceiving the reality of other beings because this would lessen her fantasy of being all powerful. Children are born monarchs and see themselves as the center of the universe. And it is very important that such be the case during the first months. All that devotion at the onset of life gives her a sense of being valuable and provides the building blocks for her self-esteem.

Little by little, however, she must accept not being the center of the universe. She realizes that her parents have interests that differ from her own and that the human beings around her do not necessarily exist for her sake. The million-dollar question is the following: How can parents give their child the possibility to move from her imaginary sense of almightiness to a more accurate perception of reality? How can they help her develop healthy self-esteem as well as confidence in her personal power? Indeed, the value we give ourselves is the result of a compromise between our need to be almighty and the limits imposed by reality. Then again, how can the sense of one's personal power be preserved even if it remains forever relative?

In theory, we are well acquainted with the following points. On the one hand, we know that parents are usually able to set limits to the child's sense of almightiness without blunting her assurance, by provoking small frustrations that she can accept without feeling rejected and discouraged. On the other hand, it is fitting for them to let go of their own almightiness as parents in order to make the child more and more self-confident. They should also let her gradually see their own weaknesses as human beings.

Unfortunately, life does not always correspond to our wishes. This is so true that if I were to evaluate the reasons for anyone resorting to psychotherapy, I would say without a doubt that lack of self-esteem is the principle motive. It is frightening to realize to what extent we are able to not love ourselves, as revealed by the most common scenarios leading to so-called narcissistic problems. The scenarios quite resemble the cases discussed in the following paragraphs.

People who have experienced intense or even traumatic frustrations at a very early age due to adverse circumstances or to parents who did not know how to love will react by trying to impose their law at all cost and to prove that they are worthy. Their world is not one of love but one of power. Besides, it is astounding to realize to what extent frustrated love converts invariably into willfulness. On the couple terrain, for example, power games often begin to surface as romantic love wanes. And it seems, the same terrible law applies to domestic dictators as well as to tyrants who crush their countrymen. All of them bear a dreadful self-love wound.

Psychoanalyst Alfred Adler based the totality of his social theory regarding the power instinct of individuals on what is called *organ inferiority*.[9] Whether real or imaginary, organ inferiority stimulates a need for self-assertion that knows few limits. For example, Napoleon compensated for his short stature by a devouring ambition that made him want to conquer the entire world. In each instance, the wounded almightiness acts out and seeks to take revenge. Think of the case of the man who is convinced that his penis is too small and who compensates by purchasing a powerful racing car, thus satisfying his urge to display his frustrated power in broad daylight.

The other possible reaction to the traumas of childhood is to collapse instead of strutting about. When the people around us did not appreciate or accept parts of us, when humiliating jokes emphasized our apparent defects such as a physical deformity or an intellectual flaw, it becomes difficult to love those parts. We ourselves keep on depreciating our real or imaginary handicaps and constantly fear being rejected because of them. This is how an inferiority complex is formed. It is the definite sign of a lack of self-esteem.

As we do not always compensate a feeling of inferiority by exaggerated self-assertion, the collapse may result from unbearable shame. Withdrawal will be the next step as we decide that we deserve no better than this sad plight and that, in any case, life is a miserable deal with nothing to hope for. Such resignation leads to a state of depression that could end in self-destruction, because we hate who we are.

This frequently happens when parents persist in being authoritarian, asserting through their actions and attitudes that they are always right. Their child will be convinced that he has no value and will attempt to prove his worth through excessive performances, or adopt the opposite position of taking refuge in mediocrity and defeat. This allows him to maintain his status as a perpetual child seeking models of perfection and clinging to people who seem powerful in his eyes. He denies his personal power and even gives it up to whoever has the sagacity to use it. This generates what is commonly called *dependence*. People become dependent on their love partners or their family environment as well as on the latest fashion worn by a famous star. This is their way of trying to heal the wound of the past and to avoid rejection. By playing this kind of game, they rapidly become conformists, joining groups where they dare not have opinions that would displease the majority. Belonging to a sect, to a street gang, or to a social club is valuable because it fits them with a custom-made identity; they dare not affirm their personal power, entrusting it instead to a collective authority.

When parents do not meet the challenge of using their authority and imposing limits, the child risks becoming tyrannical toward them and will adapt poorly to life. Unknowingly, the parents abandon their child to the mercy of catastrophic events that will inevitably disprove his superiority. He risks breaking down when confronted with his first failures, and becomes passive because he never learned how to resist obstacles. To protect his threatened almightiness, he may resort to futile daydreaming or drugs. Indeed, drugs have been used since early times to reinstate temporarily the frail sense of inner bliss that life inevitably disturbs.

It becomes obvious that the passage from the fantasies of almightiness to a balanced self-esteem is a delicate one. Life provides a variety of events that can prompt a person to hide, either behind the mirage of superiority or behind shame. In fact, the line between almightiness and depression is quite thin. However, as the individual uses his talents and dares to be himself, as he receives approval and love, a sense of security takes over. This can be achieved by connecting with the source of life that is love, and which does not contain the vengeful gaze of Snow White's step-mother. It means watering the flower we all have inside so that it will blossom.

One-Eye, Two-Eyes, Three-Eyes

The following Grimm fairy tale will help us to better understand the psychic dynamics that come between the ego and the com-plexes. In the story "One-Eye, Two-Eyes, Three-Eyes,"[10] the hero-ine has no father and is harassed by a cruel mother. The central problem is all about the lack of self-esteem, as discussed previously. It is about the crucial dilemma of human beings whose growth was not stimulated and whose conscious ego remains weak and poorly asserted.

The fable involves a devouring mother who lives with her three daughters, only one of whom is normal. The first has one eye, the second two, and the third three, and their names are One-eye, Two-eyes, and Three-eyes. The mother and sisters treat Two-eyes like a good-for-nothing chore girl. Besides keeping the house clean she must go to the fields every day to tend a little goat.

To interpret the story at a psychological level we need to imag-ine that this is a drama where all the characters impersonate what goes on inside the heroine Two-eyes, that is, everything that happens to her ego in full transformation. Two-eyes represents a woman who can never find enough strength to assert herself. Her jealous and envious complexes rob her of her power. In the story, the psychological complexes are personified by One-eye, Three-eyes, and the mother, who all mirror the interior habitat of Two-eyes. The two sisters represent Two-eyes' subpersonalities, the powers governing her conscious personality.

For example, when we have only one eye, our vision is reduced. At the psychological level, we could say that this displays a blinker vision, a unilateral attitude expressing unyielding opinions. As Two-eyes is under the spell of One-eye, she lacks perspective and sees only one side of the coin. She nourishes her rigid point of view by holding on to an excessive and obscure intensity, much like the Cyclops, who also had only one eye at the center of the forehead. She may even entertain malicious thoughts regarding those who oppose her.

The other sister, Three-eyes, represents the opposite attitude by being hypervigilant. Having three eyes, there is always one eye that does not sleep. She is constantly on her guard and consistently doubts herself. Because of negative parental complexes, her ego is undeveloped; she masks her weaknesses by clinging to categorical opinions. And she is fastidiously careful about her person— a defense against the impending judgments that may come from outside.

In fairy tales, a poor heroine symbolizes an ego that lacks the strength to assert itself. The weak ego is often portrayed as a little maid who is assigned exclusively to minor tasks, like Cinderella, who is still our best example of servility. In the case of Two-eyes, however, the weakened ego has an advantage: It has maintained a healthy contact with the instinctive world, as depicted by the meadow and her closeness to the little goat.

One day, as Two-eyes is in the meadow with the goat, she sits down and breaks out crying because she had been given only a small morsel of bread for her sustenance. A fairy appears and teaches her the magic formula that will give her the power to order a meal anytime, to eat her fill, and to make the meal vanish by using the last words of the same formula. The gist of the formula— "Bleat, my little goat, bleat, cover the table with something to eat"—is proof of the nurturing power of keeping in touch with instinct.

Now, as Two-eyes shrugs off the usual morsel of bread, her mother and sisters suspect that something is askew. One by one, the sisters accompany her to the meadow, and soon, Three-eyes, who never sleeps, discovers the stratagem. The mother then decides to kill the goat so that her daughter will no longer go to the meadow. The mother and her sisters eat the goat as Two-eyes watches from a distance. Here we see the cruel and demonic faces of the heroine's complexes blown to full capacity.

The power of negative complexes in people lacking self-esteem is such that they destroy what brings them comfort. As soon as they find something or someone that could be good for them, the complexes step in and harass them with doubts, destroying any hope that the help offered will work.

The good fairy appears once more to Two-eyes and tells her to claim the goat's entrails, the leavings that no one eats. She then orders her to plant them in the earth. From the germ grows a tree producing golden apples that are accessible only to the heroine. Thereafter, a handsome prince notices the apple tree, seeks out its owner, and offers her everything she desires. Two-eyes replies that all she wants is to go off with him to his kingdom. She becomes his wife, and later, being a good queen, she shelters her mother and her two sisters who have fallen into dire poverty, signifying that the complexes have lost their power and can no longer impede the ego's development.

The theme of the entrails planted in the earth also has psychological value. In the story, the solution for the ego is found in rejected objects that must be buried in order to produce and to be recognized for their value. This means that it is appropriate to stay in touch with our interior "refuse" if we are to complete the task of integrating the self. The "refuse" is the stuff rejected by a negative family context, by what was judged as unacceptable in us. The tree that grows from it gives golden apples, showing that fertility follows when we are in touch with nature and its cycles. Note also that in this tale, as in the story "The Handless Maiden" to be analyzed later, nature and its rhythms play a valuable role. By the same token, we can easily see the enormous damage caused by the split between patriarchal power and the natural environment.

In this case, the story's heroine has little to do for the transformation to occur, meaning that it is more important to *pay attention* to the natural process than to act. The good fairy representing the positive mother complex intervenes twice when the girl is crying: the first time when she is hungry; the second when her goat is killed. This suggests that by acknowledging our suffering and expressing it openly while abandoning ourselves to the soul's mystery, we initiate the creative process that heals the childhood wound. The cry for help coming from an ego that recognizes its own weakness is always a decisive factor in a situation of psychological grief. The suffering must be accepted if anything is to change.

This fairy tale has shown us how active negative complexes can be, and how they prevent the personality from growing. I must, however, make one last comment: It is rather interesting to see how, in stories portraying female heroines, transformation often occurs by merely being a witness of the predicament. In male-oriented fairy tales on the contrary, the heroes must ride up hill and down dale to attain the treasure. This implies that male psychology and female psychology are essentially different and brings us to the next discussion on sexual identity. For there is not only a love of myself, there is also a love of someone who is not myself!

IDENTITY AND SEXUAL DIFFERENCE

Sexual Identity Is a Psychological Construction

As one of the markers of psychological identity, sexual identity is expressed through closeness to others in love and sexuality. Whether we like it or not, every time we say *I*, it is a man or a woman speaking. All beings are born male or female. In humans, however, even if gender is determined genetically as in animals, sexual identity is not so rigidly determined. This allows more variety and creativity in our erotic expression. The dominant sexual orientation may even contradict the primary genetic determinism, as in homosexuality, where the individual desires a partner of his or her own sex. In other words, psychological sexual identity differs from biological sexual identity, and the effects of both are difficult to separate. When attempting to do so, we must keep in mind the strong influence of culture on the individual's life in general and especially on his basic nature.

Sexual identity can therefore be seen as a cultural construction based on the original data, that is, biological gender.[11] This vision has the great advantage of avoiding the prison of sterile debates that lead to the rejection of certain types of sexuality as being "unnatural." In my view, all types of human sexuality are at the least partly influenced by culture, and none is purely natural. Or, they are all natural if we accept the fact that nothing escapes nature.

Indeed, even in 1948, Kinsey[12] began to popularize an evaluation scale of sexual orientation based on six degrees instead of two. The research involved positioning pure homosexuals at one end of the spectrum and heterosexuals at the other. According to his study, only 10 percent of the population conformed to one or the other category. For example, the men in majority fluctuated between homosexuality and heterosexuality in various degrees.

The research also revealed that one-third of the men had had one complete homosexual experience with orgasm past the age of puberty. In short, everything is not so simple, as would imply locker-room and parlor conversations.

In spite of our moral and religious oppositions, or simply our own sexual orientation, it seems more psychologically realistic to consider sexual identity as something flexible. In a way, it can be seen as a construction combining instinctive, psychological, and even political and ideological elements. For example, a disappointing love relationship or long periods spent in the proximity of people of our own sex can very well lead a heterosexual to become a homosexual, or vice versa. In North African cultures, where men spend much of their lives together, a man may have intercourse with another man without believing himself to be a homosexual.

We are not aware to what extent our culture and our psychological wounds influence our way of looking at a penis, a vulva, breasts, and the way we make love. Our sexuality expresses our whole beings, including our psychological history. I will be very centered on my own pleasure if I am fragile in my self-esteem, or on the contrary, I will be more attentive to my partner if I am self-confident.

What Is the Role of the Same-Sex Parent Regarding the Child?

In the process of its development, our sexuality naturally assigns different roles to each parent according to gender. Generally, the parent having the same sex as ours will be the main influence in the construction of our sexual identity. The parent of the opposite sex will make us aware of sexual differences, so that through his or her eyes we get to know that we are male or female.[13]

The child naturally recognizes himself in the parent of the same sex, the one with whom he can identify and the model he will seek to imitate. The cornerstone of sexual identity for a boy is the contact he has with his father, and for a girl, her contact with her mother. One can immediately foresee the possible complications arising from such a psychological law.

If the parent of the same sex is absent, if he rejects the child, or does not reflect a positive attitude concerning his own sex, the small boy or girl will not be able to love the fact of being a man or a woman. When a child is not confirmed through his same-sex parent and when the lack is not compensated by another maternal or paternal presence, chances are that he will end up hating himself and being ashamed of himself and his gender. This absence of self-love finally leads to the problem of not knowing what is good for us in life.

In this respect, one must not adopt a reduced psychological view by demanding absolutely the presence of the natural father or mother for the child. Children need mothering and *fathering*;[14] they need men and women who treat them in a fatherly and motherly way if they are to shape their identity. Their need to be in contact with the feminine and the masculine must be satisfied. In my view, the true fathers and mothers of the child are not necessarily their genitors and genetrixes, but those who care for that child.

What Is the Role of the Opposite-Sex Parent Regarding the Child?

The parent of the opposite sex makes us aware of sexual realities and reveals our basic difference by the simple fact of his or her presence. That explains why most of the erotic fantasies and little love affairs originate from father-daughter and mother-son relationships. At three or four years of age, almost every little boy wants to marry his mother and every little girl wants to marry her father.

To grasp a more accurate idea of the influence attributable to each parent's gender, we only need to consider the different wounds men and women bear. In the case where the mother is present and the father is relatively absent, the boys often suffer from an identity problem, because they lack a masculine model. At the same time, their relationships to women have been facilitated by the presence of an attentive mother. A caricature of this situation would be a boy who is convinced that there will always be a woman for him in the world, while he remains fundamentally suspicious of men.

The reverse is true for girls. The wound left by the father is shaped by the emotional quality of the relationship. A girl is not certain that there will always be a man for her in the world, and therefore her quest to find one becomes a priority. Women often tolerate the most unacceptable situations with their partners, because of their deep-felt sense that it would be impossible to find anyone else with whom to share their lives. They can, however, count on their female friends if they are lucky to have had a close relationship with their mothers. If they haven't, friendships with women will also be difficult to establish, and they may even feel more at ease with men, despite the weak paternal presence.

The Ordeal of Sexual Differentiation

Sexual differentiation is a necessary ordeal because it serves to awaken the self. As discussed previously, the child lives in deep harmony with her surroundings. The experience is joyful or painful and unconscious for the most part. To bring the experience to consciousness, the child must differentiate herself from the world around her. One of the differences she will encounter because of its blatant evidence is the one existing between males and females. It is this experience of dissemblance that will allow her to subsequently return to her world of unity, but this time in a conscious manner.

Even as the child is fascinated by sexual differences, her first reaction is one of absolute resistance. Becoming aware of the existence of the two sexes constitutes an ordeal because it challenges the child's sense of almightiness. Learning that he or she will be forever only a man or only a woman makes the child realize that he or she is not complete, therefore imperfect. The task of entering into the world of interdependence and complementarity is not easy!

From this time on, children are intensely active, as the boy has to prove to himself that he is not a girl, and the girl, that she is not a boy. Asserting that their gender is stronger, more clever and special than the other, will allow the boy or girl to preserve some part of their illusion of almightiness, shaken as it is by the discovery of sexual differences. One way for the child to be reassured is to get closer to the same-sex parent, mostly by imitation. What better way to assert her resemblance to the same-sex parent and her difference from the opposite-sex parent than to adopt their specific domestic and social roles?

The question arises whether parents should maintain a strict division of these roles to help the child through the stage of differentiation. Absolutely not. However, the naturally different styles of mothers and fathers must be respected. For example, men do not change diapers the same way women do, and children are able to perceive these small differences. When the child reaches an age where he or she starts to differentiate, he or she will do everything to resemble the father or the mother, respectively. He or she will grasp the obvious differences between the genders in order to shape and embrace his or her own sexual identity.

When sexual differentiation is well established, it forms the basis for the future identification of gender similarities. The more an individual feels secure about her own gender, the less she will feel threatened when encountering differences. If a man trusts his virility, he can accept the idea of having so-called feminine qualities. Likewise, a woman who trusts her femininity will be able to accept her masculine qualities. When differentiation is not properly established, people risk going through life proving their difference by being overly masculine or overly feminine.

As a way of thanking me for a talk I presented, a university professor gave me a poem on his impending old age. The poem expressed his anticipation of the pleasure of wearing an earring without fearing to be judged as *gay*. The gesture was impossible for him at this stage of his career when his image was so important. It would betray his delicate feelings and cut him off from the male group that supported his status.

Consequently, when a man feels good about his masculinity, when he is appropriately recognized by the men he cares about, he can express his emotions without feeling threatened. Becoming even more flexible, he will even be able to exhibit the preferences and behavior identified by his own culture as feminine.

Sexual differences collide with our basic incompleteness. The confirmation that our lack cannot be remedied will spark our craving for completeness and launch us on the search for what is missing through romantic love. The fantasy of being all alone at the center of the universe will then be replaced by the fantasy of creating a whole universe with another person!

ANIMUS AND ANIMA

The Better Half

Is it really the narcissistic wound inflicted by the fact of our being forever only a man or only a woman that makes us want so much to be together in spite of differences and difficulties? Does the wish to be one in togetherness explain why the couple seems so natural? Is this why we look at every man and every woman while asking secretly: "Is this the man of my dreams? Is she the woman meant for me?" It would of course be childish to adopt such a reduced vision of life.

The simple truth is that *the man* and *the woman* on the sofa are not alone. The couple is unaware of the inner partners who are maneuvering their attractions and repulsions. They are the animus and the anima. This particular archetype begins to play its role at the onset of puberty, to help us take leave of our parents and to be psychologically independent. It is perceptible by the fact that each human being carries inside a more or less clear image of the ideal partner. It is this image that produces our fantasies and dreams, making us seek love in the hope of forming a couple. The unconscious has the innate capacity to create such an image, and as mentioned before, Jung gave the name *archetype* to this universal inclination. He gave the name *anima* to the fantasy image of the feminine in men, and the name *animus* to the fantasy image of the masculine in women.[15]

The Swiss psychoanalyst Carl Jung reached these conclusions by observing the dreams of several men and women. He noted that the men frequently had dreams about unknown and mysterious women, who often inspired them with respect. Women frequently had fascinating dreams about groups of men. Jung concluded that our sexual counterpart, the part that was repressed because of our confirmed gender, continues to live within as an image of the opposite sex.

Our so-called *better half* is really the one we have inside. It is our inner personality, but since we are not familiar with it, we seek it externally. We long for the soul-sister or soul-brother with all our hearts. No wonder our loves are so full of expectations and misunderstandings. We want our partners to absolutely fit the ideal image within.

The animus and anima appear to have the function of throwing us into the arms of love. However, their real goal is to be recognized as our inner features. Our failures in love eventually make us realize that our partners will never personify the qualities we lack and hope to find in a companion. By demanding that they change, we are asking our partners to faithfully personify our animus or anima. This is, of course, impossible.

In reality, the animus and anima invite us just as much to the external sentimental journey as to the inner creative journey. When, in the first part of life, we are learning about love and founding a family, the role of the animus and the anima is to detach us from the security of our family and to create our own. As we get older, they invite us to return within and to understand the deeper aspects of our unconscious as it longs to be expressed in ways other than through the couple, work, or children.

What Do the Animus and the Anima Look Like?

The same-sex parent has a strong influence on our behavior as men and women. However, our inner picture of a man and a woman is marked by the personality of the opposite-sex parent. The simple reason is that our parents are the first men and women we have known intimately. That is why we fall in love with someone whose character traits evoke those of our mother or of our father.

It is true that the animus and anima represent the archetype of life that calls us to develop independently of our parents. It is also true that these images that inspire the desire to love can remain imprisoned by parental complexes. When strong and negative, they inhibit the young man's or the young woman's craving for autonomy, a theme frequently described in fairy tales. For instance, the heroine is imprisoned in her father's castle tower, and the knight who frees her could either be her awakening animus or the symbol of his own drive to break away from parental security.

When the drive toward autonomy is blocked because of parental complexes inhibiting the ego's natural development, the animus and anima reverse their activities. The woman's capacity to take initiatives is changed into wishful thinking, and if the situation persists, the imprisoned animus becomes nervous or bitter.

In the woman, the animus represents her capacity to take initiatives, while the anima in the man represents his capacity to love. If a man does not make use of his emotions, his anima claims its due by being turbulent and impulsive. It seeks attention through irrational moods that catch him unwary. He may then sink into depression or despair, without the means to resist.

When the animus and anima are imprisoned in parental complexes, they are inevitably projected onto people who resemble the parents. This seems to be a trick of nature to force us to settle the problem, so that our creative powers can be liberated and used for our development.

In reality, there are few human beings whose animus and anima are totally free from parental complexes. The majority are at the stage where their creativity is still a prisoner of either the paternal complex or the maternal complex. As long as this is the case, people continue to get involved with partners with whom they reenact parts of their childhood scenarios. This will happen as long as the scenario is not transcended. In this sense, life is perfect, since it keeps on serving us the same dish until we become conscious of what we are eating.

The Collective Aspect of the Archetype

In a broader sense, the animus and the anima are not marked only by the personal father or the personal mother. The ways in which we are a man or a woman since the beginning of time also play a role in the formation of these inner personalities. A layer of our unconscious is endowed with a collective feature that serves as the basis for the personal unconscious. That collective feature reveals itself through the specific attributes of the men and women of our culture, and of the human species in general. For example, no one needs to teach us how to be upset or to fall in love, yet to do so, we often follow the predetermined models. The collective unconscious also inspires the way we conceive and represent the opposite sex.

Generally, the positive attributes symbolized by the *animus* are courage, initiative, stability, action, the word, and spirituality in its larger sense. The animus is represented as the man of courage and action, the artist, the charismatic leader or the spiritual master. These are the qualities that women often seek in men. The *anima* represents sentiments, impulsiveness, intuition, the capacity for personal love, the sense of nature, and the relation with the unconscious.[16] Culturally, the anima appears as the mysterious, evanescent woman; the earthy, sensual woman; the refined poet; and the spiritual guide or the priestess. These are the types of women sought by men.

Jung noted that in a man strongly identified with his rational mind and who does not respect his needs in the area of relationships, the anima will express itself in the form of uncontrollable and irrational moods that invade him unexpectedly. This real *possession* by impetuous moods, as if he were *possessed* by a spirit, will occur in a man's life as long as he is not consciously in touch with his inner femininity. This will also cause him to fall head over heels in love, and with the person in whom he unwarily recognizes parts of himself.

In other words, since he does not pay attention to his unconscious feelings, he does not suspect the power they exert on his conscious life. A caricatured female holds him in her grip. We see examples of this pervasive anima in the man who has the flu, yet complains as if he were going to die, or in the man who meets someone new and immediately falls madly in love. He will be all the more vulnerable to these influences if he does not pay attention to his emotional needs and his interior life. The unconscious makes him play these scenarios to make him aware of his feelings.

The same principle applies to the woman who identifies with traditional femininity. She stubbornly clings to opinions that are rationally undefendable. She has no proof to support her statements, but she *knows*, and that is enough. Her animus is attacking in a way comparable to the anima's attack on the man. She will not be able to shake off this gentleman who thinks he knows everything, until she gives him a chance to express himself more clearly and when she dares to question her opinions realistically and objectively.

It is also interesting to note that in dreams the animus often appears as several men: groups of judges, professors, children, and so on. However, in men's dreams, the anima appears as only one mysterious woman. Jung thus reached the conclusion that in real life men seek *the* woman through all the women and that women seek *all* the men through one man. This explains why women are more faithful than men in general and also why women are afraid of *several* men in anonymous groups, but feel at ease with one man. The opposite is true for men. They fear intimacy with *one* woman and are at ease with women in general.

Woman in Man, Man in Woman

To avoid any confusion on the subject of the animus and the anima, I would like to clarify certain terms. When I disuss *the feminine* in general, I mean the feminine values present in men as well as in women. The same is true for the term *the masculine*, as it refers to the masculine values present in the woman as well as in the man. When discussing feminine receptivity in men, I personally prefer the term *anima*, and to discuss masculine energy in women,

I prefer the term *animus*, simply because Jung's theory has given rise to considerable abuse. In fact, *the feminine* and *the masculine* we behold when discussing the animus or the anima always have a typed and conventional aspect. Yet the concept deserves to be more sophisticated. For Jung, these inner forms are in fact psychic images that develop to compensate the external conscious attitude. The following example will help us to understand.

In the Graal Legend, the hero Parsifal's lover is named Blancheflor. She represents the feminine being upon whom he has projected his anima. The name Blancheflor suggests that Parsifal's inner feminine traits are full of innocence, candor, and sensitivity. Yet Parsifal is actually a Gallic knight who is not in the least effeminate. He has courage and strength, and is greatly feared because of his violent behavior and brutality. Jung's research allowed him to ascertain the universality of this situation. Hitler had visions of the Virgin Mary, and macho men are often fond of sweet little girls.

Because this conception is more suitable as applied to psychic reality, it helps to avoid stereotyping and to understand how the image of a cutting if not brutal soul hides within a soft-spoken boy. He surprises no one by choosing a very affirmative woman as his partner. The same applies in the case of an austere girl who becomes the lover of a bashful boy. He represents the image of her soul, those qualities she must integrate if she is to know her intimate self.

This also explains how our attachments and the resulting complications are the result of our projecting such intimate aspects of ourselves externally. We seek the partners who will adjust to our unconscious soul, but when they no longer reflect our inner image as a man or a woman, the dream disintegrates. This accounts for a good number of quarrels and breakups.

The law of compensation operating between the soul image and the external personality, what Jung called the *persona*,[17] summons us to be cautious when we speak of *the feminine in men* and *the masculine in women*. In fact, the masculine and the feminine will vary considerably from one culture to another and from one individual to another. We may of course speak of general tendencies such as those insinuating that men are less in touch with their emotions and that women's sense of action and goals is less keen. But we must be aware that there are numerous exceptions to those rules. A lot of women are not very skilled in expressing their true emotions in love relationships, and we know of men who are not good at taking initiatives. Nor is it accurate to say that our love relationships are only a way of seeking the opposite-sex parent. A man may very well choose a woman who resembles his father, and a woman may love a man who resembles her mother.

In brief, we might say that the anima is the energy in men that inspires the need to love and to be loved, to care for others and be appreciated. It is the power of loving and giving, of infinite compassion, and of tolerance beyond reason. If this capacity is perverted, it becomes dependence, submission, servility, slavery, and masochism. If it is rejected, it becomes coldness, rejection, rigidity. All this will prompt a man to unconsciously seek partners who personify one or the other of these aspects to discover who he really is.

The animus is the energy that seeks to be accomplished by transforming matter through willpower. It is the impetus for action and movement. In its perverted form, it becomes frenetically manic, authoritarian, dictatorial, and sadistic. If rejected, it becomes passive, sloppy, and self-destructive. Women also seek partners who personify unconscious parts of themselves to discover who they really are.

The animus and the anima, integrated within each soul, constitute the wonderful and unfathomable human miracle. They generate all kinds of experiences of love, from the most sordid to the most sublime.

FAMILY TRIANGLE OR INFERNAL TRIANGLE?

The Family Portrait

In our discussion on sexual identity, we separated the role of the same-sex parent from that of the opposite-sex parent. We also discussed the possible injuries caused by parental complexes when such complexes are negative. Before going more deeply into parent-children relationships, we need to relativize the parental influences and show that they are rarely the only causes of children's mishaps. The theoretical section will end on this note.

Let us begin with the statement that the child does not fit exactly into the father-daughter or the mother-son axis. He exists above all in a father-mother-child triangle and participates with all his being in the marital relationship. This is very important, because being accepted as the third party means being accepted as another real person. The triangle has thus already become a minisociety.

The child lives in symbiosis with the parental couple to the extent of believing that he is responsible by his actions for his parents' separation, or for their harmonious relationship. The parental couple's unity is paramount for the child because for him it symbolizes the complementarity of the opposites that support the universe. That is why children of divorced parents have such long-lasting fantasies about reuniting their parents and are so happy when they succeed in doing so, whether the circumstance is joyful or sad, such as an anniversary or an accident.

Then again, even the triangle itself appears as an artificial division of what goes on in the family circle. The child does not see himself only in a simple triangle. He belongs to the family system and shares his position with brothers and sisters. Relatives such as a grandmother, a grandfather, or any other person occupying space on the family territory can equally be psychologically important for the child. In other words, the boundaries of the child's psychological reality are very permeable.

When we ask a child to draw a *family landscape* suggesting that he draw each person as an object and show how each one relates to the others, we will notice that the child's boundaries are unclear. Even if mothers and fathers are always in the center of the landscape, it becomes apparent that the father/mother idea does not always apply to the biological father or mother. The child very naturally gives the same importance to a substitute father or mother as to a biological parent.

This means that all the persons surrounding the child, close or not, are there in a fathering or mothering capacity, and they all play a role in the development of parental complexes. A warm-hearted grandfather may compensate for a cold father and thus rebalance the emotional energy of the paternal complex.

In reality, the child adapts quite well to a mixture of influences as long as he knows who is the person first responsible for him. Indeed, the tragedy of many of today's children is that they have no one they can count on. When the two parents are working and have no time to spend with their families, the children grow up in a sort of vacuum, and the positive parental images do not even have the chance to be activated. The children's masculine or feminine identities remain undefined, and the self-confidence and strength they need to face life are hindered.

The more we work with young children, the more we realize the importance of the roles played by nannies, guardians, or even neighbors in the family landscape. Certainly this is more valuable than a vacuum. Some children have only televisual models to learn about life, those stereotyped models of our culture that need to be humanized. But how is this possible when parents devote so little time to their children?

We realize how the family adventure can easily have catastrophic effects on the child's developing identity. The family triangle can likewise become an infernal triangle. Childhood wounds almost always result in negative thoughts about one's capacities. Giving in to morosity, the child withdraws and the isolated ego prevents him from affirming himself externally.

The markers used to measure a healthy identity are self-confidence; the capacity to make choices; to obey one's wishes and yearnings; the capacity to be in touch with one's feelings and needs; and the capacity to create emotional bonds. People with fragile identities are filled with doubt. They live in a hostile world that judges and criticizes incessantly. They are generally alienated from what they feel and feel guilty about their needs. They believe they do not have the right to express themselves. A healthy childhood is one that provides the child with the support he needs to explore the surrounding world, and to assert his feelings and needs.

Everything in the human experience seems to strive toward the expression of talents and individual originality. The happiest people seem to be those who have access to a mode of affirmation that satisfies them, whether it is gardening, handiwork, or artistic expression. They express their true selves through sexuality, the couple, the family, or work. It is this power of outward expression that allows them to be in communion with both the human and the natural environments.

The joy of living seems to be the reward of those who satisfy their primary needs and express their basic identity. What we call love may very well be the product of this contentment. The human being who has conquered his inner constraints and who has the chance to freely express himself lives in a world of plenitude and gratitude instead of a world where everything is always missing. Famine can be all around, but something fundamental continues to feed him and to make him happy.

Parental duty therefore consists in supporting the child's experimentations and in encouraging the way he expresses his individuality. The child must feel secure in his surroundings. If, on the contrary, the system becomes overprotective or too rigid, his creativity will be impaired and he will be deprived of his most precious tool: his capacity for self-expression.

In this regard, it seems that the best parents are not necessarily those who try to be perfect models, but rather those who have preserved a creative passion for life. We seldom encounter people who have followed exactly their parents' or educators' advice. On the other hand, there are many individuals whose vitality was stimulated by the influence of a passionate person. In the final analysis, what really leaves its stamp on the child is the parents' attitude when facing life's trials. The hopeless mood of a parent is often communicated to the small boy or girl, so that in adulthood they will respond to life's disasters with an attitude of defeat. On the contrary, when parents confront their trials with unshakable optimism, chances are that their children will do the same and say: "It's not the end of the world! My parents survived, so will I. Tomorrow's another day."

The Child Is Not a Blank Page

It seems difficult to deny the individual character of each newborn child. The specificity is so obvious right at the beginning that parents never stop marveling about it. Thus, the child is not a blank page on which they will write their scenarios.

We know from experience that certain aspects in the individuality of a human being usually escape our analyses. We can affirm with certainty that the parents' presence and the quality of that presence help the child to develop a healthy identity. But it is not the only rule governing the complexity of human beings, because certain factors remain incomprehensible. A boy originating from a psychologically poor environment may very well react by developing an exemplary capacity for affirmation. A girl having enjoyed the best in kindness and attention from her family may very well be prone to depression.

Finally, no one knows why an adolescent chooses to commit suicide because of a first disappointment in love. Her parents were adequate, she was good in school, and she had no problems of self-affirmation. Even if we could impute her action to a negative environment that hindered her inner development and self-knowledge, can we truly blame the parents who did their best or did not know any better?

The following quote from *The Prophet* by the sage and poet Khalil Gibran will perhaps shed a comforting light on our discussion:

> Your children are not your children. They are the sons and daughters of Life's longing for itself. They come through you but not from you. And though they are with you, they belong not to you.[18]

Reading this poem, it seems appropriate to adopt the psychological approach that grants personal power to the child. The parental role is not altered for that much, but it is relieved of its burden of omnipotence, and while the parents watch over and stimulate the child's development, they are not responsible for her fate. This means that they will be attentive to her as a growing person. They will respect her needs for self-expression while also being aware that this human being is creating her own life, a life for which she is entirely responsible.

We may even ask ourselves if the tensions existing between parents and children are not there to bring all the players to know themselves better through joy as well as through pain. Seeing the facts from this angle, there are no negative experiences. Everything finally serves to know ourselves better and to find our way in the vastness of life.

Beholding this great variety of individual fates, Jung was able to conclude even in his time that some beings need to express themselves through very dark experiences, such as murder, for example, to come to recognize the depths of their unconscious. Such a perspective makes one shudder and commands a great deal of tolerance when judging others. Jung's disciple, Marie-Louise von Franz, saw criminals as negative saviors who carry for us the wounds and pain we hide within. If each one of us dared to acknowledge our share of the shadow, perhaps there would be less bloody conflicts on our planet. Indeed, our fascination for hardened criminals reveals how much we intimately share their nature, whether we like it or not.

In any case, when we see how negative experiences function to reveal the fundamental joy of existence, we come to accept individual major crises as wonderful opportunities for change. It is undeniable that a difficult childhood, years of alcoholism, or even an episode of violence can act as stimulants to help individuals discover a more satisfying life. But it would be cynical to think that parents could have been sadistic enough to wish such episodes on their children, and to also hold these parents responsible.

No one can avoid suffering. It can even be welcomed, since it confronts us with the essential questions of life. The fact that it spares no one makes it undoubtedly a basic element of life, a thorn driving humans to embrace a more balanced attitude. It awakens as much as it destroys, so that in this perspective, it would be petty to accuse the parents for their children's suffering or vice versa. Humans need suffering for their development, and the attempts of parents to avoid it at all cost for their children may sometimes be unhealthy.

Having discussed these identity markers, we may now consider father-daughter relationships. This will help us to better understand the scenarios of *the man* and *the woman* on their sofa.

3

Fathers and Daughters: Love in Silence

THE SILENT FATHER

Prisoners of Stereotypes

If we were to stigmatize the *sofa tactics* scenario, we could say that *she is a woman who loves too much*[1] while *he is the man who is afraid to love*.[2] While these are well-known characters on the popular psychology scene, they are not spontaneous phenomena. Each has its own story, and both are rooted in the unsteady triangle of the traditional family where the father is absent and where the mother tries to compensate by taking on several roles at the same time. In the following chapters we will therefore study the genesis of these prefabricated images by looking at father-daughter and mother-son relationships. In fact, it is the silence of the father that creates *the woman who loves too much* and it is maternal smothering that produces *the man who is afraid to love*.

Naturally, there is always the danger of succumbing to blames and judgments when we allow ourselves to delve into the relationships between parents and children as we are doing in this book. In fact, since we cannot change the past, such an exercise makes sense only if it leads to a better understanding of our present behaviors. The past in itself is not interesting. On the other hand, the past that is still active in our daily lives, as we are unknowingly motivated by it in our choices, is highly interesting. Here again, however, it will be useful only if the analysis helps us to understand the damaging scenarios of the past and free ourselves from their effects.

At the beginning of a workshop held in the Sahara Desert on father relationships, a woman participant asked me if it was really necessary to "empty her bag." My answer was another question: Would she ask such a question if she had before her an exhausted and thirsty person who had traveled miles in the desert on foot with a backpack full of heavy and useless objects? I suggested that she would certainly invite the traveler to discard on the spot some of the excess baggage, even if this meant losing some precious time. He would inevitably need to inventory the items, decide which ones were useless, and determine to abandon them. The last step, but not the least, would be to get used to walking with less weight on his back. Obviously, the greatest obstacle to our development is the fear of freedom and lightness.

As mentioned earlier, we will now review certain aspects of father-daughter and mother-son relationships. This is important, because in order to stop defining the couple on the basis of childhood wounds, the dynamics of the past must be recognized and clarified. Again, this clarification is not aimed at identifying the real culprits responsible for our mishaps or to blame this person or that one. Its true purpose is to help understand the wounds that linked us with these persons in the same drama, and to transcend the wounds. In fact, according to Freud, the past that is not brought into consciousness is repeated. Or, according to Jung, what remains unconscious *happens* from the outside like a fate that seems strange to us, when it simply reflects the state of our inner life.

To verify these theories, there is no terrain as explicit as the couple. We never cease to be surprised by the fact that people choose partners who resemble their father or their mother. It can even be said that the more intimate relationships become, the more they reflect childhood dynamics that were not sufficiently clarified. When the bonds between parents and children are not properly untangled, the old dramas make a comeback on the stage of emotional relationships, to the extent that it can be virtually impossible to form a couple.

Love in Silence

In my role as moderator in group sessions on the theme of relationships with the father, I am always moved and surprised by the great tenderness women have for their fathers in spite of the wall of silence surrounding their relationship. I am also a witness to their anger, and sometimes their indignation, at having been abused. But always in the background, there is that bittersweet pain caused by the love that was never expressed. Years spent in silence. Love behind bars. A heartache that a woman learns to soothe as time goes by. A love ache that she does not accept, but that inevitably becomes part of her life. An ache that makes it impossible to meet anyone on a deep level. An ache that she clings to because deep down she is still saying it could have been otherwise. And the love that could have been different is the one she seeks forever and almost desperately in other men.

The next chapter will explore how part of the uneasiness felt by *the woman* on the sofa is the result of a deficient relationship between a father and a daughter.

A Vacuum to Fill

According to Christiane Olivier,[3] the little girl is in a more difficult situation than the boy during the first years of life. Having neither of the sexual attributes of her parents, she cannot identify with her father or her mother. Her life begins in an "identity vacuum."

As it appears, the vacuum metaphor plays an important role in the lives of many women. They are happy when they feel full, unhappy when they feel empty. Full when they have love and attention, empty when they have none. At the physical level as well as at the psychological level, emptiness and overflowing are the poles around which their lives seem condemned to rotate. In their minds, women have either too many pounds, oversized breasts, undersized buttocks, or they are too skinny, too flat, too small, or too big. They simultaneously have too much of one thing and too little of another—too much behind and too little bosom, too much tummy and not enough behind. And one shortage serves to justify another: "Perhaps if I had more bosom, I would be more daring."

The feeling of emptiness is undoubtedly aggravated by the silence of the father. The young girl builds up the idea that her father does not talk to her because she is not attractive enough, not intelligent enough, and with time the emptiness fills up with all sorts of negative beliefs. In the end, the child feels guilty about her father's silence and starts to underrate herself: "I have no value. I am not interesting. I will never measure up to what he expects."

Idealizing the Father

We could almost say that from that moment on, the young girl starts to weave her love fate. On the one hand she underrates herself, and on the other, she idealizes men and fills the vacuum with the fantasy of the prince charming. "Some day, my prince will come . . ." could in many cases be translated into "some day, my father will come, some day he will talk to me, and finally I will become a woman." And the fantasy will of course transform her first encounters with men into predictable catastrophes. No man is able to replace such an ideal image. But women cling to this ideal and impose it on their men. They find it less difficult to fail their romances again and again than to confront the vacuum hiding behind the ideal.

For a young woman, the fact of having had an absent father exacerbates her dream of being chosen by a man whom she will satisfy and please. Yet, because of that absence the mythical aspect of the fantasy never finds a human outlet and the woman remains a prisoner of her romantic dream. She is either a ragamuffin waiting for her savior or a princess locked in her tower who pines for her knight in shining armor. At the psychic level, this prison of fantasies is expressed in dreams where the woman is either the victim of a vampire or is locked up by someone horrible like Bluebeard. Indeed, the snare of fantasies has the power to suck the blood of life. When this happens, the libido is dissolved in romantic daydreams instead of being channeled in a possible and realistic love. In this case, we can truly say that the power of the animus is imprisoned by a negative paternal complex.

When a young girl has been deprived of her father, her need for attention leaves her at the mercy of her fantasmagoria. I have known several young girls whose unique dream was to go to Hollywood so that a film producer would notice their talents and bring them to the summit of glory. Our culture stimulates these mythical fantasies by putting feminine beauty on a pedestal, as in the case of certain great models who need only to be beautiful to become internationally famous.

A Dark Destiny

It must be emphasized that the vacuum and the dark thoughts that come with it are not easy to control. For many years, I had a woman in analysis who had lived in a family of several girls. The mother expressed a kind of pathological jealousy not only because of the attention her husband gave their daughters, but also because of her fear of his being eventually attracted to any female neighbor. She made up extramarital stories on his behalf and went into tantrums at meals. In such a context, the poor man found himself somewhat castrated. He remained tacit at the end of the table, barely speaking or looking at his family, while the daughters competed for his attention.

I was not surprised to be told by my patient that she had married a man as silent as her father. When she began therapy, she had been living with her husband for some ten years. The couple had a little girl who did not get much attention from her father. They had not made love in three years. Her husband spent most of his evenings either outside the home or buried in a science-fiction book. In spite of her dissatisfaction, my client declared anxiously at the end of our first session: "I don't want a separation!"

She lacked the self-confidence she needed to end the relationship that locked her in to morosity. In reaction to her father's silence, a state of constant doubting had taken hold of her. A voice whispered incessantly: "You will never find another one!" All her creativity was used up in imagining the darkest and most terrible scenarios if ever they came to divorce. Her daughter was of course the center of the stories she made up. She imagined her already an adolescent, having to see a psychotherapist because her parents were separated. This went on until she began to understand that her daughter would certainly prefer the example of a courageous mother who had risked the separation, instead of the example of a resigned woman.

The father's silence had provoked in this woman the development of a complex that had finally consumed her self-confidence.

The voice that continually traced a dark and inevitable fate was that of a negative animus, a prisoner of the paternal complex. It was only after the separation that she was able to reclaim her creativity and hush the dark voice. It took her a great deal of courage to finally reassert the control of her destiny, because symbolically her hands had been cut off by a deficient father-daughter relationship.

THE WOUNDED WOMAN

The Handless Maiden

The following tale is from the Grimm brothers collection, entitled "The Handless Maiden,"[4] where the heroine's hands are cut off by her own father. The story will be the basis of our discussion on the psychological mutilation inflicted by paternal indifference.

> A miller who had fallen on hard times agrees to sell to the Devil whatever stands behind his mill. An old apple tree is all there is, and the miller has no use for it. In exchange for it, Satan promises him all the riches he chooses. The miller happily goes home with his good fortune but is immediately horrified to learn that his daughter was sweeping the yard behind the mill at the moment of the transaction. Fearing to lose his life, he resigns himself and gives his daughter to the Devil. He asks her to get ready so that the Devil can come and fetch her in three years.
>
> When the time is up, the Devil comes to claim his booty, but the maiden has just washed herself and is so pure and holy that he cannot take her. He asks her father to forbid his daughter to purify herself by water. He comes for a second time with no more success, for this time the maiden has wept fountains of innocent tears on her

hands. He orders the father to cut off her hands or else he will take him instead of his child. The father obeys out of cowardice, but the innocent maiden weeps again so terribly all over her wrists that the Devil can no longer claim her. He loses all ownership over her. The father is relieved and promises his daughter all the luxury she desires until the end of her days. But she is so disgusted by his attitude that she decides to leave home in spite of her handicap and to find shelter in exile,

She soon finds herself in a country where a good king treats her with compassion and love. He marries her and has a pair of silver hands made for her. Alas, he must soon thereafter go to war, leaving his pregnant wife behind. The Devil, who has not accepted his defeat, takes advantage of the situation. He persecutes her by causing her to be repudiated and exiled with her child in the absence of her husband. She hides in the forest, protected by an angel. During this retreat, her real hands grow back, thanks to her devotion. When the king returns from war, he goes off to search for her and finds her. They can now resume their union and live happily ever after in the peace of love.

I do not elaborate further on the story because the beginning is what I wish to emphasize. Psychoanalyst Marie-Louise von Franz interprets this tale on two levels. The first is about the fate of the feminine and of women in a patriarchal culture. The second is about the psychological processes operating in the miller and in the maiden.

Let us begin with male psychology as represented by the miller. Marie-Louise von Franz makes us notice first of all the unconsciousness of this father who inadvertantly sells his daughter in order to obtain wealth.[5] She compares his attitude to that of modern fathers who, too busy with their careers, neglect the emotional aspects of their bond with their partners and their children. Metaphorically, it is as if they *sold their daughter to the Devil*, that is, as if they tried to get rid of their anima. In other words, this man has betrayed his own unconscious in order to succeed in his professional and social life. He put aside his capacity to relate, and fled from the inner conflict associated with expressing his personal sensitivity. That is why his daughter is the victim of the shadow within him, an unfeeling and greedy entity.

With finesse, Marie-Louise von Franz also emphasizes how in the fairy tale, the maiden is linked with the old apple tree, how womanhood is linked with nature. By getting rid of the old tree he has no use for, the miller symbolically splits from nature. By the same token, he splits from his inner femininity as represented by the maiden. The result is that while he is able to have impersonal and abstract relationships, he cannot commit himself to real and individual relationships.

On a wider scale, the analyst notes that in fairy tales it is always the heroines who have their hands cut off and never the heroes, because it is feminine creativity that has been repressed by patriarchy. The essential nature of feminine creativity is to produce by allowing germination and growth, while masculine creativity is realized by action and activation. Feminine creativity means to carry and allow growth to reach its term by doing everything at the right time according to nature's rhythm. The motif of the maiden's mutilation implies that patriarchy does not value that type of creativity. Besides, several among us are implicated in this mutilation: We are familiar with the kind of production that responds to the will, but we have lost contact with creativity that comes from the gut, that produces life in the ripeness of time.

More specifically, fairy tales of this kind symbolize the loss of autonomy of women in the midst of the patriarchal society. In their mutilated condition, they can no longer *take in hand* their own destiny. In the past, tales such as this one were part of popular expression and served as a critique of patriarchal civilization. Just like dreams, fairy tales expressed through images the depths of the unconscious. Fathers could in this way be warned that they should not abandon their families to seek wealth. In the tale we are discussing, it is significant that the father of the maiden is a miller. Millers were the first to live off the transformation of what others produced, the first industrialists. This fairy tale already predicted the gap that industrialization would create between man and nature as well as between man and woman.

Let us now consider the maiden's psychology. The father's negligence and his cowardice certainly symbolize a negative paternal complex victimizing the ego. But what does *sold to the Devil* mean? Psychologically speaking, it means going into a state of *possession*, where we no longer belong to ourselves. A good many women fall into such conditions. They are *sold to the Devil* by their fathers' indifference. Their wounded creativity turns on them and their surroundings. They become incomprehensible in the eyes of their loved ones. They try to control at all cost by tantrums, whimpers, and caprices. They are overmeticulous, manipulative, and inflict guilt on others. The animus that cannot find its appropriate expression externally becomes truly diabolical because it is imprisoned inside. It stomps about in its prison and scares away all who try to approach.

As explained earlier, when the creative power is the prisoner of the negative paternal complex, it is as if the drive for autonomy had been turned against the individual, dragging the rest of the personality along with it. Women so affected have a permanent black cloud over their heads. Even happy events find them complaining about something or other. Their lives are a series of crises and suffering. Having missed their father's warmth, their way of obtaining attention from their surroundings is by being unhappy. They often seem to find self-satisfaction in this behavior. In reality, they suffer under the power of that dark animus that will not surrender until the life force resumes its normal course.

Marie-Louise von Franz gives even more meaning to the diabolical animus that tries to conquer the maiden, and adds:

> Whether her endeavours are in the intellectual field or whether she asserts herself as an autonomous individual, she risks being possessed by her own negative animus or by excessive wilfulness, becoming as cold, pitiless and brutal as was her father.[6]

According to the psychoanalyst, the girl who was not nurtured by fatherly affection, the girl who has remained emotionally wounded, risks being possessed by a destructive intellectualism lurking to overcome her. If she submits to this diabolical animus, she becomes ambitious and cold. She will imitate her father by reproducing his most intolerable behaviors. She will become efficient and calculating, and just as her father did, she will repress her own erotic capacity.

The maiden in our tale does not follow this course. In order to defend herself against such a fate, she has only one resource, that of letting her hands be cut off, that is, renouncing her creativity and her capacity to take initiatives. She faces life as an orphan, feeling psychologically handicapped. She accepts mutilation in order to escape the Devil, and faces exile in order to be out of her father's reach.

Symbolically, the hand is an important element in the evolution of the human species. Thanks to a dexterous hand, the human being has escaped many determinisms and become able to make the tools with which to transform matter. But the hands are also an extension of the heart. Mutilation symbolizes not only losing power over our environment but also losing touch with it. We can still see and hear but we can no longer walk *hand in hand* with our child or our partner. Accepting mutilation by the ego means holding back our capacity for action. Our lives become vegetative and we lose touch with our fellow men. It is as if we were strangers in our own world, as if we had renounced all efforts toward autonomy. Luckily, in this case, because it is voluntary, the sacrifice will allow the maiden to heal in the midst of nature and to see her capacity for action come back to life.

The Incestuous Father

In its presentation of a cruel paternal complex and a diabolical animus, this fairy tale could be used as an adequate description of the inner drama of a girl who becomes the victim of another kind of mutilation inflicted by the father: incest. Incest is one of those crimes that occurs in silence, a silence full of deadly lies. In his presentation at an international conference on bioenergetic analysis, psychologist Réjean Simard proposed the following thoughts concerning a case of incest he had followed for twelve years. He noted that "it is not so much in her sexual identity that the severely sexually abused person is the most affected, but in her personal being."[7] She finds it difficult to remain in touch with her own existence, and to be intimate with her loved ones. The difficulty involved in merely "existing" indicates that self-esteem has been completely smashed by the father's acts. The following example will make this clear. It presents an atrocious aspect of the tale "The Handless Maiden."

A recent book by Gabrielle Lavallée relates the drama she experienced as a member of the sect called l'Alliance de la Brebis (The

Alliance of the Lamb).[8] Roch Thériault, rebaptized Moïse, was the leader of this small group. He was awaiting the end of the world with his three wives, his children, and two other couples in Quebec.

Lavallée relates how this sadistic and insane man amputated her arm without anesthesia because one of her fingers risked infection. She tells of the intolerable pain she suffered and the visions she had. First, she saw the human being she venerated become the very incarnation of Satan. Then a kind of grace descended on her and saved her from the pain, as happened to many martyrs. The eyes of her executioner became those of God himself. She believed that divine justice had finally been accomplished because the amputated arm was the one used in sexual acts with her father, who had abused her as a child. She believed that she would at last be delivered from the guilt she suffered since then.

As with many incest victims, she felt responsible for her father's aggressions. Ever since adolescence she looked for a fatherly figure who, through his love, would make her able to forgive herself and restore her dignity. She believed she had found it in Moïse. Instead of helping her to improve her self-esteem, he mutilated her. Her intense guilt brought her to consider herself as an apt sacrificial victim that would purge her childhood sins.

When a girl is a victim of incest, the wound inflicted on her physical integrity may even compel her to give the body soiled by her father to "all the men." She does this while taking shelter in a very tiny area of herself that she keeps virgin, but that she will offer to a lover or a pimp. The majority of prostitutes are probably victims of incest.[9] Their developing personality is wounded. Because they were not respected, they cannot find the way to respect themselves. They usually hate their fathers and all the men who come close to them.

In a radio interview,[10] a prostitute said that she was now the mother of a four-year-old son. She was twenty-eight and had just given up prostitution. The social worker who accompanied her during the program made her notice that for a mother who admitted to hating her father and the "damned race of men," she took very good care of her child. The mother replied that for the moment it was all right, but that she dreaded the day when her son's sexuality would be aroused and that he also would become a man just like those she hated.

In lesser degrees, the same problems of disgust for men and weak self-esteem are encountered in the girl who, without having had an incestuous relationship, had a "sticky" father who manifestly desired her too much. Such behavior generally provokes disgust in a child. It may bring a girl to barricade herself so that she becomes cold and alienated from her body. In fact, she is the one who has to maintain the barrier against incest. Since the father does not do it, and since very often the mother does not intervene, it becomes her responsibility to defend herself by building an armor of rejection.

She may also become an exhibitionist as another means of defense. Indeed, to avoid being possessed by her father she decides to offer herself to the eyes of all. The star of an erotic European film told me that during her adolescence she had gone to fetch her father in a bar where he was drinking with his friends. Reacting to the beauty of the buxom young woman, one of the men made an obscene gesture. The father rose and, to protect her, put his arm across her breasts and declared, for the damnation of his daughter who had never heard him speak this way: "Hands off! These are mine!" From that day on, she mistrusted her father and decided to prove to him that she would never belong to him sexually.

Incestuous fathers are not always the ones we think. Studies show that fathers who commit incest are those who did not have affectionate contacts with their daughter until she reached puberty.

Then again, there are stepfathers who, in reconstituted families, abuse young girls who are not blood relations.[11] In reality, affectionate contacts begun at an early age between a girl and her father are the best guarantee against incest. Who would wish to damage through unconsciousness and negligence the plant that one nurtured for such a long time?

The Incest Wish

Because it is naturally repulsive to humans, and in order to avoid disasters linked with consanguinity, incest has become one of the most universal taboos.[12] Another reason is that the males of primitive hordes did not want to quarrel among themselves on account of the women who had belonged to the father. Millenniums of interdiction have resulted in giving this act an immense power of attraction. Its energetic potential is released in the form of extreme fantasies. Since it cannot find an opening in concrete reality, the repressed emotion nourishes the imagination. The same kind of attraction can be applied to murder, which is another universal taboo. This explains our fascination for famous criminal trials and dark novels.

The desire to sleep with one's daughter or one's son, or the desire to sleep with one's mother or with one's father, is revealed in analysis as soon as the individual submits to in-depth questioning. The desire is often exacerbated by the sexual dissatisfaction of the parent or simply by the patient's own sexual deprivation. Most of the time it is satisfied at the imaginary level and is transformed into the fantasy of making love with an older or a younger person. Pornographic magazines for men exploit this gap by presenting young models in schoolgirl outfits or older women with large breasts.

Since it is essential that the interdiction be maintained for social and moral as well as for psychological reasons, one way of satisfying the incestuous desire is to adopt an averted form of liv-ing with an older or a younger partner, a form that avoids predicted judgments on the taboo. In the Middle Ages, for example, suppos-edly traditional marriages between young girls and older men legiti-mized the displacement of the incestuous desire.

The breakdown of established social codes facilitates these unions between older men and younger women as well as between mature women and younger men. The phenomenon also operates between homosexual partners. These loves allow the exploration of sentiments that were denied for a long time. Even if it is not a question of incest as such, the lovers find themselves in a metaphor of the incestuous situation that can reinforce the emotional inten-sity of such bonds.[13] I also believe that the breakdown of families and the abandonment at an early age of children by the father or the mother make it necessary to recapture the love that was defi-cient in childhood relationships. We try to heal a weak self-esteem by seeking recognition from a person who reminds us of the absent parent. It may be beneficial for a young man or a young woman to frequent someone with more experience and kindness. They thus find a transitionary parental figure that sustains their autonomy, but the endeavor is nonetheless risky.

Emotional Incest

From the subject of incest arises the question: What should be the correct distance between a father and his daughter? Incest is not necessarily sexual but is often played out at the emotional level. In this case, the father invades the emotional life of his daughter because he is incapable of letting her live her life. A young woman in her early twenties told me about the experience she had of such a situation.

She first explained that her father had left the family to pursue an artistic career. He drank a lot, even to the point of being an alcoholic. With great zest, she went on to say that when she reached adolescence her father suddenly woke up and became aware that she existed. He resumed contact with her, fully repentant. But instead of finding at last the affection she had been missing, she witnessed a strange reversal of roles. Her father simply took on the position of a son before her, putting his fate in her hands as if she were his mother. She revolted against this way of behaving. The responsibility was more difficult to accept than the burden of the vacuum that had preceded his return.

She revolted, but did so silently. The father was incapable of living in solitude and made his daughter guilty of his misery. He used blackmail, telling her: "You abandon me in my burrow, you leave me all alone." When I asked her why she submitted to such blackmail, she answered simply: "I don't want the burden of his death on my conscience. I want to hear him say, 'You're not responsible for me.'" The father was not able to maintain the right distance from his daughter, and she was no more able to define her own territory. The father's unconsciousness and the daughter's guilt made up the main ingredients of that emotional incest.

The young woman was living in a situation common to many "parentified" children, that is, those who have forcibly become the parents of their own parent. They are not able to separate from them because they are trapped in guilt. Most of their emotional relationships are formed with extremely dependent people exactly like their parents. So the young woman in question edited her boyfriend's university papers and could not bring herself to leave him until she was sure that he was sufficiently autonomous to survive any separation. This relationship was another way of dealing with the problem with her father on different grounds.

The Prudish Father

To the incestuous father can be opposed the prudish father. Extreme prudishness is in fact motivated by the incest wish. The incestuous father acts out his desire, while the prudish father inhibits the act. Most of the time, the father hopes by his control to protect his daughter from his eventual desires, indeed, against his own spontaneous physiological reactions. But this control and especially the silence surrounding it can also have negative effects. Such effects prevent many fathers from having affectionate contacts with their daughters, who usually do not understand the father's restrained behavior.

In fact, in the great majority of cases, the father does not touch his adolescent daughter and does not speak to her, especially at the onset of puberty. He does not know how or cannot bring himself to say: "You are beautiful, and I want you to know I love you," without feeling deeply upset by the ambiguity of these words— particularly since he has the tendency to sexualize all marks of affection or tenderness toward women. For such a father, feelings are a world so strange and troubling that he tends to confuse tenderness and sex, human warmth and passionate love. By his silence, he is getting ready to inflict on this adolescent daughter her first and most important heartbreak.

A good number of women relate that their contacts with their father were altogether normal and warm until the moment when, at age thirteen or fourteen, their world was turned upside down. Writing for a feminist magazine, the poet Hélène Pedneault tells about her childhood spent with a father who took her fishing and hunting.[14] She was proud of this special relationship. She felt confident and loved. But one day, without warning, the same father forbade her to climb on his knees and kiss him. The writer describes the alarm she felt. She could not understand her father's attitude. By trying to protect her, he had just wounded the newly born Eros of his adolescent daughter.

If he was afraid of his own reactions, the father had of course the right to forbid his daughter to climb on his knees. However, had he known that an explanation can transform a potential wound into its opposite, he would have adopted a different attitude. The

French therapist Dominique Hautreux asserts that many clashes could be avoided if the father simply took the trouble to say to his daughter: "You are beautiful and you are about to become a woman. You are becoming desirable in the eyes of a man and I am a man. I prefer that we respect a certain distance."[15] These words would confirm that she may enter fully into the world of desire since she is able to please a man. The words confirm the sexual difference she expects. We must never forget to what extent silence can become real violence. It can cripple the development of the young girl who is becoming a woman.

When the words are not said, when the prudish father does not explain his behavior, his daughter suffers. As she is in the process of becoming a woman, as her breasts are taking form, as her curves become apparent, as she is wonderfully proud because at last she can resemble her mother, a man, by his silence, is telling her that he finds her attributes dangerous. There are two possible reactions for the adolescent. Either she will manifest all her assets in order to seduce and attract attention, or on the contrary, she will try to flee from the sexual difference by wearing ample garments to hide her breasts and her buttocks.

A good number of men obviously confuse incestuous desire and what we could call *paternal Eros*. By this I mean a father's capacity to relate, to personalize love, a capacity for warmth and affection. It is not a question of sexuality, but a question of affection. I recall what the Zurich psychiatrist and psychoanalyst Adolf Guggenbühl professed in his classes, that a little flirting between a father and his daughter is welcome if the father knows how to set the limits.

When the father is not completely absorbed by his work, when his sensitivity is suitably developed so as to recognize the difference between Eros and incestuous desire, he has no problem forming a warm and affectionate relationship with his daughter. When the child is still young, it is this Eros that will arouse her wish to marry her father. The little girl wishes to give back to her father some of his love and affection. Later, her first attempts to seduce will be applied to her father also. Having reached that stage, she knows her father is not the man of her life but she still needs him. She needs his opinions and his affection in order to claim her own desires and her own emotional existence.

One can easily understand that an adequately expressed paternal Eros is a determining factor in the development of a girl. It serves to develop a positive animus that supports self-confidence and the taking of initiatives. Fortunately, there seem to be more and more fathers who are aware of their role. They do, however, remain a minority. Seldom are those who are able to offer the gifts of a warm and enduring presence to their daughters. As previously discussed, the reign of the missing father still prevails. Whether he is physically absent, spiritually absent, or simply an abuser, the relationship he offers his daughter is injurious and she will subsequently react by adopting behaviors that deal with the wound, but have no true healing effect.

DAUGHTERS OF SILENCE

In her excellent book entitled *The Wounded Woman*,[16] the American psychoanalyst Linda Schierse Leonard brilliantly describes the different attitudes adopted by women as a reaction to the wound caused by the father. The attitudes find their expression in the many ways women seek a man's attention, as they expect him to fill the void left by the father-daughter relationship. Thus, according to classic psychological types, some women remain eternal adolescents, while others become amazons. We must not adopt a fixed view of these types. They can change, and we may even play at recognizing dominant or minor aspects of ourselves in both types. I invite you to follow Linda Schierse Leonard's thoughts on this.

The Eternal Adolescents

Daughters who were deprived of their fathers' presence when they needed him to support their psychological development either remain imprisoned in their need to please, or confine themselves in revolt. They withdraw into their inner world or, like boys, build themselves an armor. They either refuse to look pretty or try to look like the evanescent girls in magazines. They discard the real woman, the one who is born, who ages, loves, and dies. Their real personality is never expressed.

After the example of *Sleeping Beauty*, who makes passivity a virtue, or of *Cinderella*, who is content with a subordinate role while she dreams of prince charming, *eternal adolescents* abdicate their power to please men. Whether they are married women or femmes fatales, or whether they become perfect housekeepers or muses with tragic fates, they have in common the following point. They are eternal adolescents who betray themselves and build their identity on the image that others, men in particular, project on them.

The eternal adolescent expresses her refusal to mature by leaving to others the responsibility of mapping her life and fate. Taking initiatives and making decisions are extremely difficult. Instead of acting in her own interest, she prefers to adapt to whatever is presented by life, or the men in her life. And when the situation becomes too difficult, she takes refuge in a fantasy world.

Linda Schierse Leonard distinguishes four types of eternal adolescent. The most common is the *darling little doll*,[17] "the adorable little thing to look at," holding the arm of a successful man. She looks proud and confident, qualities that even provoke envy in other women, but she herself knows it only a facade. She has become a puppet in the man's hands, continuing to please in spite of her inner turmoils.

As she goes on in life, the *little darling* finds it more and more difficult to mask her resentment and her bitterness. She is unaware of the anger that induces her to condemn her partner, while she continues to be passive and dependent. Sometimes, she will master the situation by treating her husband with extreme sweetness and charm. Great American television series like *Dynasty* or *Dallas* are full of these alluring dolls, who fascinate us by their callous and unfeeling behavior.

Behaviors such as these generally reflect the distress of a woman who was neglected by her father. He appreciated his daughter only for her charm and beauty, while her talents and qualities left him indifferent. To leave the circle of dependence and acquire her own power, she will have to accept breaking her charming little girl image, and risk displeasing by asserting her ideas and talents.

The other types of eternal adolescents are much like the ones previously described. The *glass maiden* uses her frailness and her hypersensitivity as pretexts to hide in books or in her fantasy worlds, to the point of becoming a ghost of herself.[18]

The *seductress* lives in the world of the unexpected and in the cheer of the present moment. Her plans disappear from hour to hour. She wants to live instinctively, without any form of constraint. Energized by love affairs, she refuses all forms of responsibility and obligations, and much like her male counterpart, Don Juan, finds it terribly difficult to commit to a lasting relationship. Her ad-lib existence is the revolt of a woman who was dominated by her mother and neglected by her father. She has not yet found a sense of her value, and her revolt prevents her from "establishing a true relationship with the man she loves."[19]

Finally, the *misfit*[20] identifies with a father who was an object of shame, a father who revolted against society or was rejected by it. The mother accordingly took adequate charge of the family organization, but the little girl remained affected by her father's plight. As she often tends to have the same self-destructive nature as her father, her fate will resemble that of her father. She feels continually compelled to be critical and to assert her differences. She finds it difficult to change, and stubbornly refuses to do so. She refuses to take part in changing society and its ills. It is almost a state of inertia. It can drive her to drink, drugs, prostitution, or suicide. She is frequently depressed and behaves masochistically. She whines over her failed life and her aborted relationships. Her deep conviction is that she has no value, and so seeks a god who will be all for her.

In practice, I have noted that the misfits were, in many cases, the victims of their father's or their stepfather's sexual abuse. They consequently became unable to love or respect themselves. A few years ago, in a Télé-Québec documentary[21] on suicide in the young, an adolescent told the story of her best friend, Linda. The girl had been raped by her stepfather between the ages of twelve and fourteen, and he repeatedly told her that "the bottom of a garbage bag deserved more love and consideration than she did." She had become a prostitute who specialized in fantasies of domination. She whipped her clients, inundating them with insults and vulgarities. Two weeks before her suicide, she had called her mother to ask her forgiveness. The mother's answer was: "As a mother I can forgive you, but as a woman, never!" The mother did not understand her daughter's interior drama. Linda needed her mother's forgiveness in order to go on in life because, as seen in the case of Gabrielle Lavallée, the incest victim often feels guilty for the very act that made her a victim.

The eternal adolescent needs to please at all cost. Her survival strategy is to attract the eyes of men by every means. Her strategy may be summarized as such: to be seen, to be admired, to be coveted, and . . . to be had! Unless of course she is a desperate marginal who is no longer able to uphold this illusion.

In therapeutic encounters, I have known women who stooped

to men's desires by responding to their fantasy images of women. One of these once dreamed that she was in a room decorated extravagantly with necklaces and bracelets. Her unconscious was trying to give her a picture of her reality: She was adding more and more gems and jewels to the pile to confirm her value. In fact, whenever a man offered her a gift, she saw it as an authentic expression of his commitment to love eternal. She responded to all advances, committed herself, and invariably found herself let down. For a time she blamed her partners, then blamed herself for being always at their mercy. But as soon as the emptiness and despair caught up with her, she started yet another affair to stop suffering.

Often, the eternal adolescent comes to a male therapist, in the final hope of being looked upon in a special way. This reveals how much she missed being "seen" by her father, an important factor in the process of differentiating her from the mother and confirming her worth as an individual. Then there is the risk of her falling in love with the therapist. I used to judge dramatic the fact that a woman should discover love and understanding in the analyst's den. With time I have come to understand that for certain individuals, that is the only place where love may be born, where there is security and absence of judgment. If the therapist strictly maintains the incest barrier and avoids sexual acts, the therapeutic relationship holds the possibility of preparing the client for a future authentic love with someone. The therapist will have been a transitional father figure.

The Amazons

To survive the wound left by the father, the *amazons* proceed exactly in reverse to the eternal adolescents. Instead of saying: "I will charm him and when he sees me, I will know that I am worth something," the amazons think: "I will prove to him that I am worth something, and on his own territory." A woman who has lived in the clutches of a tyrannical father will use the same despotic authority to get ahead in the world. She will submit others to the same treatment her father used on her. That is how the amazons keep the paternal wound bleeding instead of trying to heal it. Is this not what the legendary Amazons did? In one gesture, they rejected men and amputated a breast. Symbolically, modern amazons also sever a breast. For example, adopting male clothing and male behavior are ways of cutting themselves off from their femininity.

Eternal adolescents suffer from passivity; amazons suffer from hyperactivity. The former seem incapable of acting in their own interest, and the latter are simply incapable of receptivity. While the eternal adolescents would like to turn life into a series of happy days where they would be free of all responsibilities, the amazons become women of duty and principle. Refusing to be seen as seductresses, the amazons reject male seduction, even going as far as despising men in general.

The psychoanalyst June Singer, in a book entitled *Androgyny*, describes the modern amazon.

> The amazon is a woman who has adopted the traits generally associated with the male temperament. She identifies with male power instead of integrating the masculine qualities that could reinforce her as a woman. She thus renounces her capacity to establish loving relationships, a capacity that is traditionally associated with the feminine. Consequently, the amazon who empowers herself while denying her capacity to bond emotionally with other humans, remains one-dimensional and becomes the victim of the very qualities she had wanted to possess.[22]

Among the amazons, the one that Linda Schierse Leonard calls the *superstar*[23] (in Quebec, she would be called *superwoman*) is the type of woman who tries to succeed in everything. A real work-horse, she also wants to be the perfect housekeeper and the ideal woman. She strives to succeed like her father or overcome his failures. At this pace, she rapidly becomes parched. Collapsing under the weight of responsibilities, the exhausted superstar loses all touch with her feelings, and soon, nothing within or without will affect her. After a certain time, even her successes and realizations no longer suffice to give meaning to her life. At this stage, as if fed up with everything, the superstar becomes cold and cynical. Yet a deep depression awaits her. Under this coldness and cynicism hides in fact the fear of being rejected. It is as if she were telling herself: "The best way not to be deceived is to not expect anything from anyone."[24]

According to Linda Schierse Leonard, it often happens that the superstar had a father who treated her like a boy, expecting perhaps that she fulfill his own ambitions. Instead of respecting her sexual difference, the father mapped a masculine life and fate for her.

The problem is that she asserts herself wholly from the *doing* perspective without respecting the idea of simply *being*. In general, *doing* and *producing* are natural masculine conditions, while *being for the pleasure of being* belongs more to the feminine world. Of course, men and women must integrate their complementary aspects, their anima or their animus, but this is possible only when they are anchored in their identity. Thus, the man who identifies totally with his accomplishments has to cultivate his capacity for being and receiving if he wants to become a complete individual. In the same way, a woman whose capacity for being and receiving is well developed must integrate the masculine force to become whole. If these characteristics are inverted in the still-young man, he may position himself totally in receptivity instead of accomplishment. He risks falling into passivity and regressing into a defective maturation. The same applies to the woman who builds herself a masculine armor by neglecting her capacity for being. Her maturation deviates and makes her suffer.

The second amazon type applies to the woman of duty and principle: the *dutiful daughter*,[25] whose sense of duty and of principle was imposed on her by a very rigid domestic and religious structure. Being unaware of the tyranny of such a model, she assimilated it. She feels profoundly guilty when she does not fulfill her obligations. This is at least the picture that many of these women present in therapy. They have lost contact with their vital spontaneity and their originality. The austere nuns of our childhood are a good representation of such prisoners of the paternal complex.

I knew a woman who had an authoritarian father whom she made into a god. Having had to care for him very early because of her mother's death, she had given herself the mission to save him from the claws of melancholy. Down deep, she was married to her father. For a long time she kept her girlish looks because she did not have access to her autonomy. She felt very small. Indeed, she was married to an ideal that diminished her.

The woman of duty and principle has given birth to another type of amazon whom we all know quite well, the *woman martyr*.[26] This woman has elevated commitment and self-sacrifice to the rank of a fine art, corresponding altogether to the image some of us have of our mothers. While totally devoted to her husband and her children, she also needs to serve a cause or a religion. She acts as if she had no right to think of herself. But all her repressed needs find a way to express themselves through twisted messages: sighs, moodiness, silences, and blames, which become a burden for her children and surroundings. According to Linda Schierse Leonard, "The martyr needs to get angry at her own self-denial and to recognize that the shadow side of her strong, virtuous self-denial is the 'waif,' the misfit who feels herself to be rejected and wants to be pitied."[27]

The culmination of the amazon character is the *warrior-queen*, who opposes with force and determination the irrationality of her father.[28] She sees him as a degenerate and takes arms against him. A quotation from the poet C. S. Lewis describing the revolt of the goddess Oural against her father—who had decided to kill Psyche, her beloved sister—defines appropriately the attitude of the warrior-queen: "The best thing we can do to defend ourselves against them (but it is not really a defense) is to stay awake, to work hard, without listening to music, without looking at the sky or the earth and (before and above all else) without loving."[29]

These terrible words express a radical hardening. They remind me of the creed of the extreme feminists, who consider that to make love with a man constitutes "cheap labor." Such rigidity is just as irrational as the attitude of the father who originated it. Whether it applies to a mad, irresponsible, or degenerate father, the reaction finally betrays the same madness and the same excess. It amounts to cultivating a severe and joyless power, where everything is a chore, a sort of "do or die" attitude where every step of life becomes a battle to win. There are no moments to enjoy. Receptivity is seen as passivity. This is how the interior woman is evacuated.

The Feminine Wishes to Blossom

Up until the present, women had been brought up to be seductresses. Once married, they had to become women of duty and principle to personify the spirit of responsibility and seriousness that every good family should have. The shadow of these seductresses who have renounced their power lives on in the controlling and castrating woman. She in turn aims to overcome the shadow, because the seductresses have abdicated their power.

On the other hand, the woman who has espoused the fate of the amazon has certainly gained self-control, but she considers dependence to be inappropriate. She sees the least gesture of service toward a man as a weakness. Though she may rightfully refuse the shadow of dependence that has been a curse for women up until now, her life still depends on other human beings.

Work on oneself will break up these rigid positions and will eventually allow the creative woman to come to life. She can then sometimes be a seductress, and sometimes an amazon, while staying in touch with her basic impulsions and with her need for self-assertion. Her dedication to others does not go as far as denying her personal needs. She knows her power sufficiently so that she no longer needs to prove it. She can take initiatives, and is also able to negotiate with her partner.

Before taking leave of Linda Schierse Leonard, I encourage men to read her book and by descending into the feminine psyche to better understand their companions' struggles. For us men, who enjoy unwarily the privileges of patriarchy, it is difficult to understand to what extent the feminine ego has been oppressed, insulted, depreciated, and the great suffering this causes the women who share our lives.

The feminine longs to be born also in us, the sons of the different types of women I have just described. By imagining that these women exist within us, each in their turn, we are able to discover little by little the image of our own femininity. Some men have a marginal anima, while a fragile and whimsical anima resides in others. As for the woman of duty and principle, it is not rare that she is encountered among a good number of mama's boys, who go as far as martyrdom in order not to displease their surroundings.

MOTHER-DAUGHTER

A Love-Hate Relationship

The purpose of this book is to provide an understanding of men-women relationships. I have thus limited my discussions to father-daughter and mother-son relationships. But as mentioned in the preceding section, the child lives in a triangular space comprising father-mother-child rather than, for example, the limited axes of father-daughter and mother-son relationships. I therefore take the freedom to slightly diverge by adding a few considerations on the mother-daughter relationship.

The daughter is confirmed in her sexual difference by her father's attention. His presence allows her to separate herself and differentiate herself from her mother, allowing her to gain her individuality as a woman. However, we realize in practice that when father-daughter relationships are not sustained, they often impose an undeserved charge on mother-daughter relationships, so that it is not rare in therapy to encounter women who maintain an extremely ambivalent relation with the maternal figure. We could say that these women love and hate their mother at the same time. This love-hate could be expressed in the following way: "I love my mother because she is the only one who gave me her attention, but I hate her because she demanded too much from me. She controlled my school marks as well as the length of my skirts and the color of my hair clips. She meddled in everything and still meddles in everything. I've had it with my mother!"

What is the meaning of such words? Let us first of all mention that it is usual for the same-sex parent to ask much of his child. The child will often be used to reflect the parent's thwarted wishes and ambitions. But this risks becoming an iron collar for the child. Since it is true that children need to be dreamed by their parents, as if we were weaving their fate, it must be added that if the strands of the fabric become too tight, the parents' dreams can become suffocating prisons.

The many limits imposed by patriarchy on women's freedom have created the ideal context for allowing the frustrated dreams of mothers to block the development of their daughters' individuality. Thus, the ambivalent attitude of the daughter is partly the result of the mother's unconscious wishes that her daughter be *all* for her.

In counterpart, the mother will attempt *to be all* for her daughter. She wishes to be simultaneously the ideal mother and a model of emancipated womanhood. The final result is that she takes too much space. She demands a great deal from herself and in return demands too much from her child. She will finally blame her daughter for not confiding enough in her, and for not being close enough. She would like to be her child's friend, forgetting that she is first of all her mother and that it is difficult for children to be totally themselves with their parents.

The problem is partly due to the education that trained women to devote themselves totally to others. They were taught to forget themselves and to sacrifice their personal needs. Such a centering on others, however, has its shadow counterpart, which mothers do not suspect because they are acting for the good of the child. Mothers are not aware of their controlling behavior. So they suffer when their family shows ingratitude. This fate can be reversed if mothers are ready to hear from their daughters their own version of family events. They will then understand how they became intrusive in spite of their good intentions.

A crucial time for mother-daughter relationships is the one when girls arrive at the difficult age of fourteen. A good number of mothers then realize with apprehension that a gap has come between them and their child. When girls begin to signify to their parents that their group of friends is more important than they are, mothers cannot get out of the way. They complain about being rejected; they become frustrated, and do not understand that they are being discharged from their duties as mothers. They should see the time of their daughter's puberty as a wonderful opportunity to turn inward and reconnect with their own forgotten womanhood. The trial of their daughter's adolescence will not end happily as long as mothers do not learn to let go and trust in what they have already given their children.

The Idealized Absentee

On many occasions, I have encountered women who hardly knew their father. In spite of this, they entertain with him an interior relationship that is more positive than the one they have with the mother who cared for them. The absent father was idealized and had become the central pillar of the daughter's psyche.

One analyst related that, as a child, she saw her father only rarely because of his job. During many years, for her father's arrival, she insisted that her mother let her wear the same patched-up dress. She went into a tantrum if her mother refused to let her wear it, even if it had already become too small for her. The reason was simple. Her mother had once told her that her father liked her in that dress. This was sacred for the little girl, and to obtain her father's approval she needed to put all the chances on her side. Later, as an adult, she had a typically ambivalent relationship with her mother. While she could hardly differentiate herself from the mother, she still idealized the father who demanded nothing of her.

It must be added that many young women are still under the influence of the message conveyed by their mother, to the fact that they should seek their own independence and not count on men. They have the impression that independence has to be gained *against men*, to honor the struggles of their predecessors. They secretly long for a man's love and wish to surrender in his arms, but their conditioning tells them that this is wrong. They are often in an unstable situation concerning the maternal ideal. They feel guilty toward their mother, looking for cracks in her behavior that would legitimize a softer inner rule.

As mentioned previously, there is a special bond of seduction between fathers and daughters that must be respected. In fact, if the father has an influence on the formation of the girl's animus, the girl tends to personify the father's anima to get closer to him. A special bond between one unconscious and the other is woven. The daughter cultivates this secret and mysterious complicity in the anima's garden. It gives her the chance to rest from the mother's demanding animus. The daughter *divines* her father, sometimes being the only one to reach his inner world. This may result in dramatic attachments that may oppose the girl to her mother.

Other mother-daughter complications may also arise when the daughter approves in her father what irritates her mother. A woman in her twenties told me that her mother reproached her father for being weak and sensitive. These aspects were precisely the ones the daughter liked in him, since they were part of her own personality. Another woman told me that she began to enjoy sports because her otherwise reserved father released his spontaneity when he watched televised hockey games. She became a hockey fan to share his emotional outbursts. I have also encountered women who cultivated one of their father's hidden talents as a way of staying close to him and honoring his spirit.

An unconscious rivalry sets in between the mother and her daughter when the latter believes she is more in touch with her father's feelings than her mother. I have seen the surfacing of this hidden competition, when the daughter becomes a young adult and chooses lovers who are the same age as her father. This is a way of showing that she is just as smart as her mother, and that she understands men better than she does. If ever the parents divorce, the daughter may use this kind of situation to show her mother that *she* should have been able to keep her husband and avoid all this pain. Such behaviors are sometimes used by daughters as unspoken reproaches against their mothers.

In such circumstances, the mother rapidly finds herself in an impossible situation for which I have much sympathy. Even if a warm mother-daughter relationship promoting a positive maternal complex gives the daughter much self-confidence, she will still find it difficult to break away from the love that smothers her. If, on the contrary, the mother-daughter relationship is not so healthy, the daughter who cannot lean on her father to compensate will feel rejected. She will cultivate a sense of not having the right to exist.[30]

I admire those mothers who have succeeded in squaring the circle. Their relationships with their daughters seem to be free of silent antagonisms, certainly because modern women can choose to accomplish themselves through avenues other than maternity. They have less unrealizable dreams to project on their daughters, and we see an increase in the number of mothers and daughters who can relate with complicity and mutual respect.

These considerations will be resumed in detail when we come to the subject of mother-son relationships. For the moment, our discussion may lead us to better understand what is going on between *the man and the woman* on the sofa.

The Man *and* the Woman *in the Living Room*

She has been so deprived of her father's affection that she needs to live under the gaze of a man to confirm her existence. Due to her father's negligence, she is left with an emptiness and a lack of self-confidence, enslaving her to a need to please and to be desired. Her deficiency frightens her partner, because he has no idea of how to fill the void. People who bear such emptiness spend their lives expecting others to confirm their existence. In love relationships, these deficiencies are expressed by a possessiveness that says: "Look at me! Have eyes only for me! Tell me that I exist, and that no one else does!"

She dreams of a situation in which her partner's affection will open the doors to real love. She tries by every means to divine him just as she had divined her father. She wants to make him happy so that he will respond by being romantic and that he will find *her* way to freedom. But he always panics at her first approaches. She remains frustrated, all alone, hearing the words of a triumphant negative animus who repeats: "I told you so! He's not the man for you!" She tries to gain time and hides her dissatisfaction in the hope that something will change.

That is how the *woman who loves too much* is generated. We will see how the *man who is afraid to love* is generated. But first, let us see how a woman can apply a healing balm on the open wound left by the father's negligence.

4

Healing the Father Wound

THE DRAMA OF THE GOOD GIRL

The wound inflicted by the father induces women to live in waiting for prince charming. I would like to suggest some attitudes that may heal the wound and help the woman to end this waiting. Aggressiveness and self-esteem will be discussed, but first, let us consider the drama of the *good girl*.

In a book entitled *The Drama of the Gifted Child*,[1] German psychologist Alice Miller explains extremely well how a problem of narcissism develops in the child who was not sufficiently valued by her parents. The child develops antennas that allow her to intercept the needs of the people around her, even before these needs are verbalized. She uses this hypersensitivity to get their approval and to increase her self-esteem. It is easy to understand how the child rapidly becomes enslaved by such an attitude. It ultimately makes her give up her power and betray every original aspect of her personality. All this because she fears to displease others. She may even develop a false personality, the complete opposite of her real ego.

This is what happens to the good girl who is dominated by her paternal complex. Her creativity cannot find an outlet. She is kind and pleasant, but she does not respect her own person.

Sleeping Beauty

I recall the case of a woman in her thirties who consulted me during my training in Zurich. She was a university professor and had decided to take a sabbatical leave. She had isolated herself in her apartment to reflect on a new professional orientation and to develop her artistic talents. However, the leave was beginning to be like a period of depression, so that she could not bring herself to work. She decided to seek help. She was tall, attractive, and remarkably intelligent. But something prevented her from speaking. She would sometimes spend the entire session in total silence. The room would often be filled with a sleepy atmosphere, so I tacitly named her "my Sleeping Beauty."

As time went on, the situation became increasingly uncomfortable. I was continually being halted by the thorn hedge surrounding Sleeping Beauty's haven. All my interventions seemed to miss the mark, and she was quick to make me aware of this with a hint of irony.

She related how, during her childhood, she had spent much time alone in her room, and even in the closet of her room. She needed her father's attention, and her way of getting it was by enacting caprices and pranks. His invariable response was : "Go to your room!" Even now that he was dead, she continued to react as in the past by isolating herself in her apartment. But now, the injunction came from a complex, the negative paternal complex.

The father, also an intellectual, had found it difficult to bond with his two daughters. He felt threatened by their proximity. Moreover, he had an ambiguous attitude toward sexuality in general. While he allowed himself to go about the house in his underwear, he forbade his daughters to be seen in their nightgowns. He also took to hitting the ceiling with a broomstick when he heard the couple living above making love. The least we can say is that such demonstrations are not very promising for the awakening of any girl's Eros.

My patient's love life confirmed this point. The few men she had known had dependency problems, such as alcoholism or drug addiction. Her weak self-esteem made her chronically choose this kind of relationship. She believed men generally wanted her only for sex. She was waiting for the man who would discover her real worth and would relate to her in an affectionate way. Her creativity lay fallow. She was waiting. . . . Her sense of initiative, her decisiveness, whatever could allow her to face the world and to assert herself—all was in a state of inertia. She was waiting. . . . Yet she had enough intelligence to realize that there was nothing to wait for, and that it was up to her to unfold her wings. Then, as often happens in difficult situations, she had an enlightening dream.

She is in a lingerie boutique and is hesitating about choosing a bikini. The salesgirl shows her one. It is daring, sexy, and brightly colored. It fits her perfectly. Absolutely thrilled, she decides to buy it. She leaves the boutique and comes down the stairs of the store. She looks back and sees her father at the top of the stairs. She realizes he is the owner of the boutique. He pulls out a wheelbarrow full of fresh cement and pours it down the stairs. The dream ends as her feet are caught in the cement.

The dream adeptly reveals how the negative paternal complex was operating in this woman. A real conflict existed within her. There was a battle between her spontaneity and her need to express her talents and the complex that forbade her to be anything other than a serious intellectual.

The woman's dreams and her joy of living were locked up in the boutique owned by her father. She had the capacity to feel what was good for her, but whenever she wished to express it outwardly, the negative complex barred the way. She thus found herself paralyzed as if her feet were caught in cement, unable to move forward or backward.

This also affected her sensuality. She would have liked very much to wear her bikini to provoke men and arouse their lust. This would have confirmed her identity as a woman. But her interior father forbade her to display her attractiveness, the same way her real father had forbade her to go about in her nightgown when she was a child. Down deep, she was still obeying her father's injunction, "Go to your room!"

But what was she doing in that room as a child, and now, locked in her apartment? To understand, we have to look at what was going on in the realm of the animus. This life energy was also "in its room" because the paternal complex was unable to express itself outwardly. The animus had become a sort of "dream cocoon." The psychoanalyst Marie-Lousie von Franz affirms that this is another form of the negative animus. It becomes a cocoon full of wishes and of judgments defining the world *the way it ought to be*. It removes the woman from reality and deprives her of living an active life.[2]

So there she was in her apartment, dreaming! Dreaming that she was a great musician, yet she played no instrument. I attempted now and then to stimulate her with an interpretation, but to no avail. Everything slid past her. There was something missing in the process: It was aggressiveness. Where was her anger toward her father and her fate? This nice girl's anger seemed nonexistent. Her shadow was hiding, but where?

I then recalled certain events she had mentioned on the theme of seduction. She had told me how she generally perceived men's desires for her as expressions of their contempt. So as we explored this subject together, we discovered that she judged men as being mostly hostile toward women. She was afraid to approach them, especially those who were at her intellectual level. She feared that they might, by their judgments, destroy what little self-esteem she had. So she systematically chose losers.

This also explained her almost total lack of aggressiveness. The anger of the girl who had been ignored by her father was too deep and threatening for her ego, so she projected it on to men. This was the only way to survive in such a context. What she sensed as male contempt toward her was in fact the contempt she had for her father and the men who desired her. So it was a case of absolute denial of aggressiveness. To avoid facing the "bad girl" within, she cleaved to the good girl.

The woman badly needed this aggressive energy to rise out of her depression and to reinstate her creativity. Yet she was not able to own the anger, because her self-esteem was too weak. It is not easy to integrate the shadow and to live for several months with a mad woman inside. She had come into analysis to obtain the required support, because integrating the shadow meant betraying her father, and this was too difficult for her. Indeed, the man who had given her so little affection could not possibly be the object of her anger.

I saw before me the drama of a woman confined to gentleness in a prison of bitter depression. She tried with all her strength to escape from the negative paternal complex and to break free from the false personality she had developed to survive. She had by now bravely stopped exercising the profession that isolated her in the father's intellectual conformity. She could now pursue her creative skills. But to continue on her journey, she still needed to recuperate her aggressive energy. She had to burst her dream balloon and put an end to the power of the paternal complex. She had to face her dangerous shadow, if ever she would someday enjoy her capacity of self-expression and her autonomy.

I never knew the end of the story. Having completed my studies, I informed my patients that I would leave Switzerland in the current year. My Sleeping Beauty decided to end the therapy well before my departure. No doubt she preferred to abandon me before I abandoned her. I admit having been surprised, yet I accepted deep down that her decision was perhaps one of the first utterings of her power of affirmation. She had dared to displease a father figure to protect her emotions.

Legitimate Anger

Our discussion continues on the subject of feminine anger and its transformation. In my view, there is no healing process that does not involve anger. When a woman realizes that her life has been an imposture, she must first feel angry against those who abused her. Then, she has to understand that through her lack of self-respect, she keeps on doing to herself what others did to her. It is not enough that she be moved by her tragedy; she must also cry out and strike.

Therefore, as I have observed in my workshops on "The Relationship to the Father," women who have been deprived of the father have in common the problem of being unable to express verbal aggressiveness. In fact, they are ashamed of it. This is because when they were very young they had to resign themselves to hide in the shadow of the hostile feelings they had toward the father who had neglected, belittled, or abused them. Hiding was the only way they had to please him and to avoid losing the little affection available. As women, they still cannot risk to express the anger. It would be too dangerous for their ego to face the shadow that has accumulated so much resentment through the years. They know instinctively that the cauldron would explode if they dared lift the cover to look inside. Yet they will eventually have to do this if they wish to heal the wound inflicted by the father's negligence.

Expressing rage and anger against others without judgment, and preferably in a safe environment, is an essential phase. This can be done in group therapy, for instance, and even if it is only a phase, it is indispensable. By hitting, screaming, and dancing, women find an outlet for this immense source of energy. They are able to liberate offensive toxins, so to speak, and thus purify their psychological system.

The idea is to fully feel the rage in all its savagery, and to pour it into a symbolic container instead of a person. Another way is to draw or write. We must also remember to keep the door open to the emotion and to connect with it now and then. By doing so, we access the unconscious and develop our receptivity to the information it wishes to give. Whatever symbolic pattern we adopt, alone or in a group, the ego is involved and acts as a witness to the experience. And afterward, we must be faithful to the impulse in our everyday lives, not by acting in the heat of anger—which is sometimes inevitable when we have never been in touch with this part of ourselves—but by drawing from the anger a new assurance and a fighting spirit.

Anger that has been worked out is demystified. It simply becomes an alarm signal in the personality's instrument panel, indicating that a basic need has been denied. It is generally associated with the need for self-expression and self-expansion. All creativity that was neglected through fear of being rejected or hurt will find a source of hope and energy in this opening. For the woman hiding in passive waiting, anger transformed into a fighting spirit will thus give her determination and fortitude. For the woman who habitually fights men on their territory, the channeled anger will promote an intimate and personal capacity of affirmation, so that she will no longer need to disperse her strength against them.

The real work consists in responding to the needs brought to light by the anger. The rage that persistently expresses itself through blames and reproaches aimed at the executioners of our past comes from our not having integrated it psychologically. If it is not transformed, it becomes a prison. The solution to the problem lies within us, so we must look further. This is the second phase in the transformation process: the understanding that it is lack of self-respect that makes us tolerate abuse and take shelter in victimization. It involves recognizing that we are doing to ourselves the same things we accuse our father or partner of having done or are doing. The passage is difficult. It constitutes the real encounter with the shadow. We will realize that we are just as negligent toward ourselves as our parents might have been toward us.

In practice, how does this happen? In an article where she relates her own process, the journalist Paule Lebrun gives a good example of integrating the shadow through anger. As a participant in a workshop, she began to react strongly to the presence of a disturbed woman who ravaged everything "with her sarcasm, her venom and her spite." She felt compassion for such desperate and raw suffering, but the following day, she herself woke up with a "knife between her teeth":

> I was in touch with my own venom, you know the kind that every woman carries within; the Snake, ksss, ksss, ksss, come my love so I will kiiiisss you; the woman who has not digested the psychic wound inflicted on women

since two millenniums; the incredible collective anger that was crushed, first in rage, then in resentment; the anger that disappeared under the building and that is waiting for its hour.[3]

She began to dance, hoping to get it out of her system, but to no avail: She was overcome by the energy, strength, and agility of this "nauseatingly sweet" snake:

> I could feel its hidden power, its primitive indifference, its dangerous capacity to destroy. Did you know that all the murders, all the possible ferocities are sleeping within you, ready to show their dangerous faces? That day, I knew it was all within me: the best as well as the worst. . . . My snake coils were strangling several men in horrendous murder scenes. An energy knot came apart under my eyes, dispersing itself, light as ashes. Once the first motion of terror was over, I voluptuously abandoned myself to the movement. What had appeared so horrible some seconds before, became an exquisite dance.[4]

Afterward, when she tried to reaccess this new energy, she recognized it as the witch in her, the *bitch*, the "bitter, vitriolic woman, capable of destroying with words." When a woman acknowledges such a power, she knows that never again will she confine herself to a victim's role. To consciously appropriate this power is the third phase in the process of transforming aggressiveness into combativity and inner strength. From now on, the reptile will serve as a protector of her intimate territory, and will support her self-affirmation. The woman will be the creator of her own life, and the paternal complex will no longer pull all the strings!

To be honest, we must accept that we embody the dark aspect

of humankind as well. Paradoxically, this acceptance usually brings with it a relaxation of the whole nervous system, because we no longer have to defend ourselves from being this or that. We are what we are, quite simply, and we see ourselves as part of nature, which in its wisdom, made all things both dark and luminous.

Whatever the case, between the first phase and the last, we must be patient and unyielding. We must achieve the right attitude, and persevere in trusting the frail inner power that was not supported by the father. Throughout life, we continue to find the strength to persevere within ourselves and in the progress made. The satisfaction of having a life that reflects more and more our reality takes the place of despair, morosity, and resentment. The mute, deep anger that could express itself only through indirect ways finds a healthier exit in creativity and self-affirmation.

When the anger is totally recognized and integrated, it becomes a strength that generates initiatives and decisions. Life then becomes much more pleasant and intense, more joyful and bright.

HEALING SELF-ESTEEM

The need that many women have to be continually the center of attention betrays the wound inflicted by a distant or negligent father. These women always have a *face-to-face* relationship with their partner. They do not know how to enjoy the world *side by side* with those they love. They constantly feel the need to be supported by the approving eyes of a man. Their psychological balance comes to depend on it. They recriminate against men, all the while yearning for a partner, and they are not aware that it is the burden of their expectations that makes him flee. It is not an invitation to love that the man senses, but a wounded self-esteem that he will forever be trying to heal, just to have a bit of peace.

As long as a woman is not conscious of the lack of self-esteem caused by an absent father, she imposes on the couple an impossible burden of expectations, risking the collapse of the whole relationship. We cannot ask another person to solve such a problem for us. Besides, having a partner with this competence will not benefit our psychological development. It is by accepting to *pay attention* to the father-inflicted wound that a woman may gradually understand its influence on her relationships. She thus frees herself from much of her attitude of waiting "for the knight in shining armor." This does not mean that the security and comfort that come with love are to be shunned. But the rightful value of these gifts will be enjoyed on the condition that we develop the autonomy required to live happily without them.

Following are a few general comments on healing a weak self-esteem. They will complete the previous discussion concerning the integration of the anger shadow.

Renouncing Misogyny

The *daughter of silence* is the heir of paternal silence. She will easily become a silent and submissive woman. It is hard for her to feel confident and secure within when a man does not pay attention to her. When she is not loved enough, she feels threatened and defensive. Even if she asserts herself more easily and dares to express her ambitions and hopes, a part of herself continues to be silent, devalued by centuries of patriarchy. By isolating herself, she becomes an easy prey for negative complexes. To transform a self-esteem that is dependent on male approval and to heal the corrupted area of the paternal relationship, certain attitudes may be developed.

The first attitude consists in recuperating one's share of darkness, instead of holding men responsible for one's personal unhappiness. Part of this darkness contains denied anger. But the most neglected part and the most difficult to encounter is about women's own misogyny toward the feminine.

A woman consultant in organizational development for male managerial personnel confided to me that for several years she had tried to make men forget that she was a woman. For her seminars, she wore men's clothing and did everything to repress her sexuality and sensuality. This went on until she realized that she was choking her feminine self.

She realized this while giving a training course in California. The sun, the ocean, her newly felt freedom—all aroused her repressed sensuality. In a flash, she saw what she had done to be accepted by men, how she had overdeveloped her masculine side to the detriment of her deepest femininity. She was continuing the work of depletion begun in her family, at school, and at work. Her models had always been women of power with very developed masculine qualities. To be successful, not only had she denied a part of herself just as men do, but she had denied the core of her feminine identity.

The Montreal psychologist Linda Lagacé has devoted much time and thought to this problem. For her university teaching, she developed questionnaires to help women understand how they continued to give men the power to evaluate them. One original aspect of her work involved the way women devalue everything feminine in themselves, thus perpetuating male misogyny. She claims that the more a woman becomes conscious of her own misogyny, the more she can resist male misogyny.[5]

As long as a woman places responsibility for the devaluation of the feminine uniquely on the outside, she accentuates her position as a victim. To change this, she must finally admit that she also reinforces the patriarchal stereotypes: If it's feminine, it's worth nothing; if it's masculine, it's valued. By recognizing her own contempt, she no longer waits for men to change, but acts personally to initiate changes.

Changing is based on being aware of the double bind imposed on the woman in a patriarchal society. She is expected to be gentle, compassionate, submissive, and pliant. But all the while, her actions are not valued in our society, where merit is based on strength and affirmation. If she denies her masculine side, she becomes *feminine*, but she feels inadequate because her value is not confirmed by her surroundings. If, on the contrary, she denies her feminine side, she presents an image of strength while her inner feminine remains crushed and she mistrusts the women around her. The result is that she cannot appreciate herself, the woman she has betrayed.

Inasmuch as a woman unconsciously devalues the feminine, she remains vulnerable to misogynist judgments, and sees gender differences as a lack. Her idea of equality will tend toward the similarization of the sexes. A woman proud of her femininity is able to tolerate that men are proud of their masculinity and differences. It is essential that women recover the beauty of the feminine in their depth. Their task is to personify this special quality of being, instead of waiting for male approval.

Many women have such a weak self-esteem that they do not want to be together. As soon as they find themselves in a group of only women, they feel as if they are in the midst of losers. Competition, jealousy, envy, and vengeance are apt to emerge. In fact, they experience the same problems of every minority group, problems associated with hating oneself and one's group.

Integrating the shadow thus makes it possible to get rid of accusing attitudes when relating to men. A less hostile attitude toward them is possible because we better understand the action of the stereotypes they perpetuate. By ceasing to belittle our genuine desires, we can express them more adequately and take our place in the relationship. When we do not take our place, we become victims and we wait for the other to change. When we take our place, we become responsible. We find self-love and sometimes, to our great surprise, the respect of men.

Giving an Expression to the Animus

The fact of becoming conscious of the misogynist shadow forces us to do some basic soul-searching. This is difficult for the *daughter of silence*, who was brought up to forget herself, to be centered only on others and on what has a known value: the masculine world. For her, romantic love is terribly important. By being accepted by someone with an official value, she believes she is worth something. This explains why successful men are so popular with women. The more the man's value is acclaimed, the more chances it has of bouncing off his companion. This is the way love relationships are infiltrated by the problem of a weak self-esteem. This is the way it kindles expectations that no partner can satisfy.

The projection of the animus forms the basis for romantic love, and so much the better if the relationship provides the security we need for our development. However, the relationship will not really serve self-knowledge unless we make the effort to bring our masculine side to consciousness. As long as this masculinity is carried outside of us by men, we cannot discover our own value. The effort of integrating our positive animus, that is, arousing and personifying what pleases us in the partner, will liberate us from the inordinate importance we give to love in our lives, and will increase our self-esteem.

The idea is to cultivate a symbolic attitude and to consider the bonds we build, as so many facets of ourselves seek to become conscious. The integration of the animus brings a contentment and a confirmation of our own power. Our self-esteem grows wings. And we must not fear that one day all our projections will be withdrawn and that we will lose interest in love. Even if this happens, where is the tragedy? On the contrary, real love may begin when we start to understand what is being played on both sides. We may then truly learn from our partner, as someone who can initiate us to an aspect of ourselves.

In this connection, girls who missed their father are often attracted to older men. The father may have left home when they were young, so that they felt abandoned. By attracting an older man, they reinstate the self-esteem that was wounded by rejection. In many cases, they become the ones to leave their lover, to reverse the childhood rejection. Of course, relating to an older man may support the development of a new aspect of the animus through love. However, if the love serves only to put us back in our position as a silent little girl, the love will be lived in vain. We have once more fallen into the patriarchal trap.

In the same way, when women become collectively important, they cultivate relationships with younger men. They find an inspiration for their inner masculinity, which in turn is better received by less conservative men who are not afraid to express their tenderness.

By striving to be conscious of animus projections, women will need to adopt the "outsmarting" behavior of the masculine world less. Instead of expecting men to personify the gallant knight of their dreams, they can cultivate masculine values. They are thus liberated from constant disappointments and passive waiting. The values associated with prince charming, such as courage, daring, steadfastness, and integrity, can be theirs, no matter where they are expressed. They no longer wait for men to change. They initiate their own changes, and by the same token, they let go of the attitudes connected with their frustration.

The animus must learn to show its face and express itself. It must learn to speak. That is why it must not remain at the literal phase of the love projection. Therapy and support groups for women that may also include men are excellent places to learn. They provide opportunities to confront the shadow we discussed earlier. While admitting our dreams and problems to ourselves, it is essential to find a place where we are sufficiently respected and secure to speak of them openly. Whether they are individual or collective, these forms of therapeutic assistance become an important phase in our development. We are encouraged to connect with our feelings, and, becoming conscious of our true desires, we can speed their realization.

I wish to end this discussion on the animus by adding that it often has unsuspected resources. It can accomplish the most complex tasks. It can manifest its talents in a less disturbing way than by dishing out unfounded opinions and judgments. But it needs to be educated and disciplined. It must be given a task worthy of its intelligence, one that requires persistence to accomplish it. It must be confronted with objective reality through studies or appropriate information, or through a project requiring a great deal of sagacity. It is no wonder that in fairy tales it is the heroines who find needles in haystacks!

Imagining the Beauty of the Feminine

To correct a deficient self-esteem, resorting to the imagination can be an enormous help. If negative fantasies make our lives miserable, why not use their counterparts and fight fire with fire. While relaxing in our bath, or while listening to our favorite music, all we need to do is imagine ourselves in a state of harmony. We are full of love for our bodies, our feelings, and our minds. We embody in time a strength that exists on its own, blossoming without outside approval. The idea is to penetrate as concretely as possible into the imagery, then let it permeate each of our cells. The images, feelings, and sensations of the innermost feminine are invited to emerge. When they do, we explore them and then either dialogue with them, or draw them. In brief, it is a way of dreaming ourselves, letting the dream move and influence us.

The power of the imagination is not well understood. Surely it represents a possible path to the positive feminine archetype residing in every woman. It is a way of nurturing the woman who is burgeoning and who longs to be born. This new soul must then be clothed according to its fancy. There are various intensive seminars that offer encounters with Amerindian or antiquity goddesses. They emphasize the in-depth actualization of the feminine as it is bonded with nature. The goddess cult becomes a path toward the awakening of this inner quality. However, we must not maintain a literal attitude, or it could become idolatry.

The objectives are therefore to learn to trust in our capacity to express the feminine without yielding to the injunctions of a misogynist society, and to count on a loving and reliable force to lean on. It means opening the way to new values as women undertake the task of honoring and reinstating the innermost feminine. It is history's legacy to the daughters of silence.

5

Mother and Son: The Impossible Couple

THE MOTHER-SON COUPLE

A Psychological Drama

Following our discussion on father-daughter relationships, we now come to the other important theme, mother-son relationships. We will return to the sofa scene, to understand why *he* is afraid to love. It will be seen that, contrary to all expectations, sons brought up in a close bond with their mother do not necessarily become men who are capable of closeness with women, but are usually afraid of them.

I understand that mothers do not have an easy task. I am aware that, as a man, I will never experience what it means to give birth through my own body after carrying a child for nine months, while knowing that I will later have to encourage his or her complete autonomy. Mothers face the enormous challenge of never knowing if they are doing too much or too little.

It is also obvious that the parent whose presence is the most constant often is the one who makes the most mistakes and the one to whom children will address the most blames. In today's society, this role is usually the woman's and its effects are even more pronounced when a woman enters the relationship with a child in a wounded condition. The mother who has been deprived of her father's affection needs to assert herself, and she many times aspires to find her worth through a husband and children, which is certainly legitimate.

I am aware of all this, but I am also aware of the suffering of those sons whose separation from their mother is not an easy accomplishment. They become men who spend their lives in a prison of guilt, unable to confront their mother, or their maternal complex. This is not a very promising start for a man looking for a fulfilling role as half of a couple.

My intention in this chapter and those following, is to unmask a psychological and historical drama. I do not intend to burden mothers and sons in the conclusions I draw here. I intend to explore the nature of their bond, in both its beneficial and harmful aspects. An honest discussion will perchance bring some solutions, and begin the clearing of a new path for them.

The comments in this chapter apply particularly to the sons who had, or have, an intense relationship with their mothers. Less attention will be given to the children who did not benefit from the presence of a mother, which is a greater misfortune than that of having had "too much" of it, so to speak. Consequently, those who, for whatever reasons—large family, rank among the siblings, foster home, and so on—had few contacts with their mother, will feel less concerned by my remarks.

On the other hand, when discussing intimacy between a mother and her child, I do not refer only to the kind and attentive mother. The fusion phenomena operates in diverse cases. One example is the bond between an alcoholic or anxiety-ridden mother and her son. Researchers have reported that 30 percent to 40 percent of mothers worry so much over their child's development that they react to his first smile by thinking: "My God, he doesn't know what's ahead of him!"[1] This early apprehension already marks the quality of the intimacy that can develop. The child will probably be breast-fed on maternal anxiety as well as milk.

It must also be said that mother-child relationships are undergoing an important mutation, particularly because of women's work outside the home. The quality of the intimacy between working mothers and their offspring is changing, so that an excess of closeness is probably not what affects most of today's children. Many of them are greatly deprived of the essential nurturing love that children need to feel welcome in the world. In former times, there were evidently fewer actual single-parent families, but the situation was symbolically the same, since the fathers were practically just as absent.[2]

Of course, the fact that I am a man, and consequently a son, is without doubt part of the reason why I have devoted more pages to writing about mother-son relationships than I have father-daughter relationships. However, daughters may find comfort in knowing that their fate is much like that of sons. Readers who find that I give mothers precedence over fathers are invited to consult my book *Absent Fathers, Lost Sons*.

Following are some questions I found useful for my research:

How is it that closeness between mother and child result in impeding the personality development of both concerned?

How does this closeness curb the son's natural drive toward autonomy and independence, and the woman's personal development once she becomes a mother?

How is it that a bond that is usually formed out of reciprocal love ends miserably in deceived expectations on the part of an isolated mother, and in a shameful rage in the child who spares no effort to keep his mother at a distance?

Is the mother-child relationship doomed to be a love story with a tragic ending?

On Becoming a Mother

The Father initiates us to the world of human law. The Mother, in a symbolic, mythical, and archetypal sense, initiates us to the world of Being. By giving us life, our personal mother embodies the Mother. The law of the Mother's world is qualified by acceptance, openness, devotion, and generosity. Many of us may recall the concern of a grandmother when we were ill. As described by Victor Hugo, motherly love is the miracle whereby each child gets his share, while everyone has it in totality.

Yet, war breaks out on this terrain also. The most devoted mothers typically find themselves in some kind of conflictual situation with a child. This is especially the case when, for instance, a mother has no one to satisfy her emotional needs, and allows a son to become her partner.

This drama is partly the result of the way our society has been organized by patriarchy. Since it did not recognize the full range of feminine expression, it valued women only in their roles of spouses or mothers. They were expected to sacrifice themselves for someone, usually a man or a child. Being a mother had become more important than being just a woman.

This situation has prevailed for quite some time. For example, in the Roman Empire, people had no scruples over getting rid of girls. During the Christian Middle Ages, thousands of women were burned at the stake for being different. Not so long ago, Chinese babies were killed if born female. In Japan, a doctor working in an abortion clinic claims that, due to the information provided by amniocentesis concerning gender, innumerable pregnancies were interrupted, mostly when the fetus was female. In that country, sons represent security for aging parents, so that mothers deem it worthwhile to educate male children. In a not so distant past, even our own culture valued the birth of a boy more than that of a girl. One mother once confided to me that a nurse had brought in her newly born daughter with these words: "I hope you're not too disappointed!"

In the social context that, only a few decades ago, gave all the authority to men, a woman knew quite well where her power could be exercised: in motherhood and child education. She was the queen of her home. But her reign was a rather solitary one, especially since she knew that her kingdom was ruled by a king, and that she was, in fact, his servant.

Nonetheless, becoming a mother raises the woman to a higher social status. Pregnant women instantly attract attention on the street and in supermarkets, and are the object of conniving comments. Indifferent to her life before, families often wake up to a newly pregnant woman's existence, forever inquiring about her health and the progression of her pregnancy. Even otherwise uneasy men express a childlike fascination at the sight of a round tummy. The exception is of course the new father, whose often high anxiety is naturally justified.

"When you're pregnant, no one can deny your existence. It's obvious that you exist, it's physical!" Such was the loudly delivered affirmation of a woman during a recent conference I spoke at. In a society where we must show our productivity to justify our existence, becoming a mother constitutes an irrefutable proof of a woman's worth, not to mention the child as a valuable staple. It makes us better understand why, in a context of gender inequalities, women invest in maternity to be recognized and to satisfy their thwarted hopes. Motherhood can be one way of taking revenge on the frustrations associated with the denial of feminine values. Maternity should be a natural overflow of life, but some wounded women use it to fill a void and to heal what they think is their flawed existence. If pursued in this manner, motherhood is bound to impose a terrible burden of expectations on the child. His program at birth is present: to satisfy the emotional needs of a woman who missed her father and now lacks the support of a partner.

At first, women feel valued by their maternity, but they gradually discover that they lose this value as persons. In many cases, women give birth without having been born themselves.

On Not Knowing Where One Begins and Where the Other Ends

When a child is born, it is not easy to discern the boundaries between mother and child. Mothers and sons enjoy a blessed bond, but it will have to be gradually dissolved if they are to develop as individuals. If the separation does not happen, the child's future psychological life will be affected.

In this respect, the mother-son relationship is a particularly delicate terrain, because, contrary to the daughter, the son will have to relate sexually to a person of the same sex as his mother's. Separation is vital for the son's capacity to make a psychological distinction between his potential partner and his mother. Otherwise, these territories will be confounded and he will force his mother's attributes on his partner. He will soon find himself in the posture of a child, defenseless before a confused woman who cannot deal with the power she has been given. Or, he will resort to physical violence, expressing a rage that has nothing to do with her.

Mothers find it difficult to understand the nature and consequences of their son's problems. Yet, if a woman were to imagine that she had been born from her father's belly, fed at his breast for several months, and cuddled and imbued with his scent, she might have an idea of what happens to her son. When a group of women were asked to imagine having an emotional and sexual relationship with a person of the same sex as the person who gave birth to them, several reacted by stating: "It may be that I would find the presence of a woman vital, that I would need to be drawn toward the feminine before being able to make love with a man."

This is precisely the boy's dilemma, when he has no one of his gender to pull him toward the masculine. The problem is even more crucial when he must separate from his mother, and there is no natural catalyst, that is, a father figure, to help to untie the knot. The father's presence is therefore vital, and the mother must grant him as much space as possible in the parenting arena. This is why it is so important that when the father has deserted or is deceased, there must still be a flow of masculine energy in the home.

Separating mother and son is such a psychological necessity that in certain populations, the separation phase may last as long as fifteen years. For example, in some tribes, the boy who, at puberty, has been weaned from the maternal realm will see his mother again only when he takes a wife. It was also noted that when the fusion had been a long and intense one, the initiation rites were even more cruel and violent. This is much the case in cultures where the child shares his parents' bed over a long period of time, and where the separation from his mother is more gradual.

> The child is allowed to feed from his mother's breast as much as he wishes, sometimes continuing until his third year. He lives in her arms, skin to skin, and sleeps with her until weaning time. Afterwards, boys and girls sleep

apart from their mother, but at 30 to 60 centimeters away from her. In time, the boys are incited by their parents to sleep a bit further from their mother, but not yet in the "male area" of the house. In spite of an increasing contact with their father, the boys continue to live with their brothers and sisters until the age of seven or ten. The New Guinea tribes, being aware of the dangers of boys becoming effeminate, have extensive and traumatic rites of passage, to untie the extreme mother-son bond.[3]

Primitive peoples have always understood the necessity of separating mother and son to prevent conflicts and prepare him for his future relationships. They also have understood that the ideal person to preside over the separation is a father figure, providing the right setting for the child to learn about limits and frustrations. By the same token, he gains a relationship with the Fathers.

The Trouble Is . . . the Father Is Not Around

The seed of the conflict between a mother and her son is in the *dysfunctional* father-mother-child triangle. This conflict can develop throughout the years, beginning with a marriage of love between mother and son, and has the possibility of ending in bitter divorce. The triangle is dysfunctional because the man works outside the home, and the responsibility of providing a physical and emotional presence falls almost entirely on the mother.

Some men find it difficult to commit themselves as fathers. When their companion has a child, they have to forsake their positions as little boys. They feel abandoned and estranged from the whole birth experience, since the baby gets most of the attention. They become unbalanced in their male narcissism. In fact, they lose both the balance and the means to maintain it: their companion's emotional support. Their partner's motherhood awakens the unresolved problems they had with their own mother. As fantasy meddles with reality, their companion becomes as threatening as their mother might have been when there was no father to undo the mother-son knot. This no doubt explains the fact that 7 percent of mothers are victims of violence during their pregnancy. Also, young women are assaulted four times more often than others, as their companions have not yet adequately differentiated the mother from the partner.[4]

The defective triangle is in the process of adjusting its balance. Indeed, fathers are reappearing on the historical scene. The nuclear family is not collapsing. We see it struggling to survive, to be created anew. However, is it really a suitable means of survival for the human species? No doubt that, in the years to come, we will see new family models, perhaps more collective, where children without natural parents may be mothered and fathered adequately.

THE MOTHER-SON MARRIAGE

What happens when the triangle is defective? The powerful bond uniting mother and son will not be dissolved, but will be reinforced by the natural attraction between the sexes. Mother and son will be symbolically married, because the father does not fulfill his natural role of fostering his son's psychological development.

This is even more so when the absent father is also an absent love partner. New mothers find themselves emotionally abandoned at the very time when they need more than ever to be supported in their femininity, when they need to be desired in spite of their body's transformations. This may be a determining factor in protecting their vitality as women and in preventing them from disappearing into the maternal role. Also, expectant and new parents should make an effort to continue to be sexually involved in spite of the challenge of a new addition to the family, to prevent the couple from losing themselves in their parental roles.

The mother-son symbiosis is mainly the result of the mother's emotional hunger. Deprived of her partner's affection, she uses her son as a replacement. As time goes by, her *little darling* becomes *her man*, as she sits him on her husband's throne. The counterpart of the absent father is the loving and overattentive mother who, compelled by her sense of responsibility and her awareness of her child's needs, must fill two roles.

This symbolic marriage is a form of incest. It is not sexual, but emotional. The consequences for the son, given his weak self-esteem, will be comparable to those concerning father-child incest.

In Japan, mother-son incest with sexual intercourse is a more frequent occurrence than in the West. This seems in part due to the way their life is organized: Most women do not work outside the home after marriage, while the majority of men work six days a week and come home only to sleep. Furthermore, when a son marries, he still depends on his mother to make decisions concerning his marital life.

The Devoured Son

To summarize the love drama between mothers and sons, I will paraphrase one of Shakespeare's famous maxims: To eat or to be eaten, that is the question! Indeed, passionate love is often expressed in familiar terms such as "I love her so much, I could eat her right up!" The following dream sheds light on this symbolic reality. It belongs to a forty-year-old man who was a participant in a workshop on mother-son relationships.

> I am in my apartment. It has become a huge aquarium containing two fish, a small and a large one. The large fish is fiercely biting the small one. I see the small one's bones as it continues to swim and fight.

In other words, the man is still fighting with the maternal complex that is eating him "to the bone." He suffers from an identity wound caused by the absence of his father when he needed him to separate from his mother. Moreover, the father had asked his children to take care of her, so that their symbolic union with her became more intense. For the son, it meant being deprived of the masculine model he needed to differentiate himself from the feminine. He had to defend himself all alone against the mother, to succeed in affirming his masculine identity. As for the mother, she had no one to remind her that she was a woman.

Situations like this one prevent the resolution of the Oedipus complex, which would allow the son to give up his fantasy of being his mother's partner. It means leaving this role to his father and to seek other women. If, however, the father is absent, mother and son will become prisoners of each other, sometimes for the rest of their lives. The Brazilian poet Clarisse Lispector writes, "Our lifelong duty is to avoid being devoured!" Mothers and sons seem to forget this.[5]

The Devoured Mother!

The dream I related earlier is not only a symbol of the experience of a son being devoured by his mother. The little fish being eaten by the big one also corresponds to the woman's individuality being devoured by the maternal archetype. The mother is devoured by the Mother. There are thus two victims of the defective father-mother-child triangle. And besides the mother and son, the father may even be the third victim. He is exiled from his own family, and he is also alienated from his feelings because of the influence of patriarchy.

What are the advantages in being submerged by the maternal archetype? First of all, becoming a parent is a basic ordeal for personal identity. It is a real initiation that involves dying to one way of being and being born into another. It presents a danger, as the ego is fascinated by the new archetypal energy and risks to disappear into it, for a certain time at least. It is difficult to repress something that comes from the gut, a revelation that permeates the whole being with a new energy.

Women who become mothers discover new talents, new emotions, new preoccupations. They experience ways of being they never dreamed of, inner experiences that prepare them for the child's arrival. These states are a natural aid in giving birth and should not be underestimated. Also, by sacrificing their personal identity, many women suddenly find a new worth, and life is more meaningful. They feel able to face life's problems. They no longer struggle with the petty sides of their ego and the problems they had previous to the pregnancy. They become the Mother. The emptiness is gone. They feel fulfilled. They are in a state of grace.

There is no way to escape the power and fascination generated by the maternal archetype. It would even be detrimental to not succumb to it. Then again, Jonas had to enter the belly of the whale and then leave it to be transformed. Thus, if the Mother neglects her womanhood too long, her ego will suffer, since the Mother's role is somewhat collective. The ego must continue its conscious activities, using the archetype as a nurturing energy, not as a subtle trap. The *woman* must be asserted and must not be sacrificed to the task ahead, no matter how sacred. Ideally, it means recognizing this inner force as an ally.

How does a woman know when her personality is devoured by the maternal archetype? Is she well when her son is well, and is she ill when her son is ill? If so, she is submerged by her role, at least partly. When the woman's inner reactions are controlled by the son's moods, it is a signal that the archetype is automatically turning the woman into the Mother. Two fusions are now operating, one between the woman and the maternal archetype, the other between the mother and her son.

For example, one mother told me that every time her son had a problem at school, he would call her immediately. She would receive a phone call at work in the middle of the morning, to be told that he had once more failed his math exam. She would finish the day in a state of tension, worrying about her poor baby. He, without a care in the world, would come home after school, all relaxed; he had dumped his problem on his mother at ten o'clock that morning.

This sheds light on another risk associated with abandoning oneself without resistance to the maternal archetype. I refer to the fact that a mother often sees her child as a god. She ends up having a double responsibility. Besides boarding, feeding, washing, and clothing the son, she bows to the divine child who looks on, doing absolutely nothing. But beware! The little divinity will expect the same services from his future partner. This is how a mother unconsciously weaves the destiny of her future daughter-in-law.

All Marriages Have a Contract

The marriage contract established between a mother and her son is one of codependence. Codependence is a concept that explains the unconscious bonds linking a person with, for instance, an alcoholic partner. *Codependence* in this case means that each partner needs the dependence of the other to ensure some kind of psychological balance. This of course constrains instead of liberating. Each partner feels that it would be too dangerous to question this mutual dependence, because it assures a certain stability for their identity, even if it is sickly. Such contracts may be summarized as follows: "You are allowed to drink as long as it does not threaten our union; I am allowed to play the savior and martyr figure, as long as I don't stop you from drinking." In the mother-son couple, the boy will play at being irresponsible as long as he allows his mother to play her maternal game.

The marriage contract between mother and son could read as follows:

The son will remain dependent on the mother on the condition that she will never abandon him. She will care for him and always forgive him. In exchange for these small services, the son will grow but . . . without really growing. He is allowed to become a man, but only if he continues to be a little boy.

And the clause in small writing at the bottom of the contract, the one that is never read, and which is the most important, could be this one:

The parties will never separate from each other. By this clause, the son and the mother are discharged from any responsibility concerning the son's relationships with other women. A guarantee that he will find commitment to other women difficult is included.

Separation Is Prohibited

We will now discuss the theoretical aspects of the mother-son relationship, using the traditional formulation of psychoanalysis concerning the Oedipus complex.

An important element of the Freudian concept is that the son should give up his incestuous desire for his mother, under the threat of being castrated by his father. The threat is of course phantasmal and rarely expressed as such, but the son is afraid to lose his penis and so submits to paternal law. Even when the father is absent, the fear of castration still exists. It comes from other figures, personal (uncles, grandfathers) or institutional (church, state, school). To avoid punishment, the child accepts these laws. The acceptance promotes the development of his "super ego," the part of the psyche that enables human beings to formulate interdictions.

The classic formulation does not cover the whole of clinical reality. It ignores the fact that the mother's fusion wish has to be barred as well as the son's.[6] Her desire is expressed emotionally rather than sexually, defining the symbolic marriage discussed earlier. In the family, the *obligation to separate from the mother* under the threat of paternal castration is less the case than that of *prohibiting separation* from the maternal figure. The result is an absurd mother-son couple, a union having no possibility to be naturally consummated or to be psychologically dissolved.

In fact, motherly love forces the son to maintain the incest barrier. It makes him forever afraid of feminine desire, a fear he will have to confront in his future relationships with women. The son's anxiety facing maternal expectations partly explains men's traditional ambivalence concerning love commitments. They fear that they will once more be at the mercy of a woman without being able to set their own limits. This will be the case as long as a man has not resolved the Oedipus complex.

If a man has almost always lived without the real or symbolic presence of a father, his main dilemma will be enacted with his mother, since the father-mother-child triangle is dysfunctional. Responsibility for the separation from his mother, as well as the difficulties and the ensuing guilt, falls on the son. He gets no help, either from his father, or even from the illusory authority of patriarchal institutions since they have in many cases lost their credibility.

Ideally, the father's presence is needed to bar the child's direct access to his mother. It is also needed to limit her fusion with her offspring, so as to preserve her femininity. An evening in a tête à tête encounter with her companion, or a weekend without the children, would be beneficial for the mother who is possessed by the maternal archetype. It would loosen the bond. It would be like hearing her partner say: "Remember that you're a woman before being a mother. I'm the man in your life; your son is not! Besides, you're not alone with this child; he has a life outside of you. You can't be everything for him. Let him live his own experiences."[7] We said earlier that the father initiates the child to the social world; he fulfills this role by being present when the time comes for the child to separate from the family.

The boy desires his mother. He also wants to break away from her, as the process of individuation pushes him to go on developing, hopefully with the help of his father. The incestuous bond is important during the first years, because it is a natural part of the family bond. But as he grows older, the child will have to face other realities inside the home as well as outside.

Jung suggested that the child's fear of castration may very well be a natural element in easing the separation from his mother.[8] The fear develops more in relation to the almighty maternal figure than in relation to the father or paternal authority. That is why the mother will sometimes appear in the child's psyche under the guise of an ugly witch. The unconscious is prompted to produce these images because fusion represents a danger for the child's development. Something in the child knows that his mother must not be the center of his life, and that he must oppose the seduction for the sake of his growth.

When a woman's attraction to her son is under control either because the father is there, or because she has a satisfying partner, or because of any other factor, she helps the child to become an adult. His burden of guilt and his debt toward his mother will be lighter. He will not be compelled to reenact in his future relationships—because of his ambivalence—the drama of a prohibitive separation.

Otherwise, if either the mother's or the son's attraction to each other is not controlled, the child will develop a weak psychic structure. The ego will have a poor capacity for assertion, and will lack the interdictive authority to set limits. Refusing with a straight "no" will be just as difficult as committing himself by saying "yes." Above all, he will always be afraid of hurting others, since he never dared to confront his mother with the fact that he was not married to her.

I wonder if this situation could be the reason why men separate their sexuality from their emotions. In the case of emotional incest, there is no sexual intercourse. There is, nevertheless, the interdiction to belong to another woman in a love bond. A man's sexuality may thus become perfectly independent from his emotions. He will be able to make love with someone, but will not commit himself as long as his emotional nature belongs symbolically to his mother. He will even have to kill the love of those who come close, to avoid provoking the fury of his maternal dragon.

The second consequence of the unresolved Oedipus complex between mother and son appears in the autoeroticism of a good number of men. Pornography expresses and exploits this psychological situation. Men masturbate while viewing the bodies of women they cannot touch, like children looking out the window, dreaming of the day when they will be free. Men's autoeroticism, expressed in their often lifelong consumption of pornographic material, is certainly a symbol of the castration phobia.

Puberty, or the Open War

Even when the mother-son bond is entangled in an incestuous context, it works well at the beginning because both mother and child need love for their subsistence. But Freud noted that if the Oedipus complex is not resolved between the ages of three and five, it generally reappears at puberty after the *latency* period during which it seems to sleep. At puberty, the relationship risks being a power struggle between mother and son. Their wonderful love suddenly becomes a prison that hinders the development of each one's identity.

Puberty generally throws the impossible couple into tribulations that are by no means trivial. This is the "acne age," when there is a sudden escalation of the already existing tension between mother and son. As the son lacks self-assertion as well as masculine models to identify with, he will attempt to gain his identity as a man by defying his mother's authority. An open war breaks out. The desperate mother tries in every possible way to control her son, while he responds with increasing ingratitude. There are no limits to the possible and imaginable ways he can exasperate his mother. No wonder we call this the "ungrateful age." It marks the reign of ingratitude of sons toward their mothers.

In the son's unconscious, the fear of remaining imprisoned in the maternal world awakens the hero archetype and often that of the warrior. From a strict psychological viewpoint, it is an extremely healthy reaction that will prepare the boy for his future responsibilities, as his mother will not always be there to care for him. He will slam doors, play loud music, and adopt all kinds of macho styles, enough to horrify the most tolerant mother. "He was so gentle!" she claims. "How did he become so brutal overnight?" One mother recently told me that her son had nailed a six-and-a-half-foot poster in his room. It was the Terminator, the electronic brute created on-screen by Arnold Schwarzenegger. Every morning since then, he walked from his room, rolling his shoulders like a street brawler.

When faced with such behavior, it should be understood that the boy is not addressing the woman, but rather the Mother, the maternal function. Since initiation rites no longer exist to separate a mother from her son, he behaves, unknowingly, to make his mother get out of his way. This is the age when awkward speech and manners are another way of estranging his mother. Swearing, being dirty and smelly, telling vulgar jokes, and being delinquent— all are means of liberating him from the maternal yoke.[9] The behavior is in exact opposition to the manners taught by the mother, and has a specific value. It weans the son from maternal education.

If a woman understood the issue fast enough, she would suffer less and would facilitate her son's passage to adulthood. I have often told women on the edge of despair: "He wants less mother, give him less mother! The time has come for you to remember the woman in you. Let her live again. Be in touch with your wishes and your dreams. Rebuild your life."

Puberty Is a Second Birth

If I had to define the three most important times in the lives of human beings, my list would certainly include the fourteenth year along with birth and death. The end of puberty is so important for humans that it could be called the "second birth." It is the time when we are born into the social universe. Besides, in many ancestral tribes, one could marry at that age. For the boy as well the girl, the beginning of adolescence marks the awakening of a powerful natural drive toward autonomy. The period between fourteen and eighteen years has become the most difficult one for today's adolescents. At this age, they are equipped with the physiological elements that make them ready for life. They should be autonomous, but our culture denies their access to social responsibilities until they are eighteen and even older.

At the end of puberty, children no longer want their parents. They seek the company of peers instead. They discover love and social values. In fact, the most important communications between parents and children should occur before the child's fourteenth year. Afterward, children are no longer on the same wavelength as their parents; they intercept society's messages and are often rebellious toward their parents' morals. Consequently, the parental structure should begin to soften. Parents should begin to replace control with trust, interdictions with negotiations and understanding. Extreme severity or overprotection after this age will only shatter the child's life.

The importance of puberty escapes our understanding. Observers who trace the actual life curve of individuals note that today's period of adolescence is often prolonged until the age of thirty.[10] This is no doubt because we disregard nature. When parents and children are not separated at puberty, the weaning occurs later, sometimes during the middle-life crisis. Many parent-children conflicts would be avoided if parents were aware of this psychological reality.

The Antihero or the Aborted Birth

The awakening of the hero and the warrior in the adolescent is a manifestation of a healthy psyche. It indicates that the natural spontaneity has not been completely crushed by education and that the powerful drive toward autonomy can express itself. The contrary may, however, occur.

> A woman consulted me about her sixteen-year-old son whom the police brought home completely stoned on LSD, on two consecutive Saturday nights. Both times, he had tried to commit suicide by lying in the middle of the road. The mother was at pains to understand her son's behavior, since she had tried to make herself very small at home so he would have the maximum space. In spite of this the tension rose and rose between them. She reacted by being even more considerate and by hiding her own revolt.
>
> It so happened that the son was profoundly affected by this maternal behavior. Also, his anima was modeled on his mother's personality, and acted like a polite woman

who was afraid to claim her space. His fighting spirit was thwarted, so that he could not react to his depressive moods. His suicidal behavior was a reflection of reversed heroism. Instead of expressing his need to separate from his mother, all his aggressiveness was turned against himself. It was a matter of destroying his life instead of creating it. Crying in my office, the mother told me how such an attitude was beyond her comprehension. I offered the thought that perhaps LSD and suicide had precisely the role of creating a space where her comprehension could not enter. The mother had always been her son's confidante. Now he needed to get away from her benevolence and maternal influence. In my view, his suicide attempts masked an unconscious appeal to his father. She confirmed that there had hardly been any contacts between the son and the father since the couple's separation a few years before. I suggested that she should facilitate the meeting of the son and father if possible. When I saw the woman and her son a year later, the latter was living with his father and all was well. He had renewed a healthy and appropriate relationship with his mother and could now appreciate her comprehension without feeling threatened in his masculine identity.

I have witnessed the resolution of a good number of problem cases, thanks to the father's entrance on the scene. Even in healthy families, mothers tell how, from a certain age, their sons refuse to obey them. The father's presence is then required, because the son may listen to him more readily. During this period, adolescents are trying to prove their manhood. They need to test their strength by seeking disapproval as much as approval.

We no longer live as primitives; nevertheless, our predecessors understood that the weaning from the mother at puberty was an essential phase for the boy. They made this separation official with very elaborate rites that were just as important for the mother as for the son. The son was introduced to paternal figures that facilitated his entry into the adult world. The mother was included in ceremonies that expressed the pain of being separated from her son. She was able in this way to consent to the sacrifice, which was no small ordeal.

The mother who has devoted so many years of her life to the education of her children finds it difficult to disappear when puberty occurs. It will be important for her to have a companion or gratifying activities. If not, the sacrifice will be too painful and may never be complete. The mother will cling to her children. She will get more and more hurt, and the children will be more and more ungrateful. She will feel guilty for not having done enough. She will neglect her own well-being by trying to understand everything, but all her efforts are sterile. She must come to understand that her child's personal drive is the natural expression of the same force that launched her into motherhood. The adolescent is inspired by a revelation that drives him to separate even if he knows only partially what is happening.

The more the mother-son fusion is intense, the more bloody will be the war of separation. The more the human bond is symbiotic, the more it will arouse a passion that may result in violence. Family bonds are not an exception. The more the adolescent is confronted with a cowardly father who dares not confront his companion, the more accidents and casualties there will be. Unless of course the family, unbelieving, finds out that the son is living a kind of double life. At home, he is a good, polite boy; outside, he indulges in alcohol, drugs, and misdemeanors. The violence in this case is outwardly transposed. However, this is not to be overdramatized. It may help to know that 92 percent of adolescents of both sexes commit at least one delinquent act during this period. They need to test the limits of reality. We will surely not object to these statistics, particularly if we recall our own adolescence.[11]

The Right Boundaries

The best way to avoid war is to learn to set boundaries when the child is still young, so as to differentiate the mother's territory from that of the son. The right measure is difficult to find: If the mother sets too many limits, the child will rebel; if there are too few, he will not learn to manage his frustrations and will break down before them. When the hero archetype drives him to assert himself at puberty, the mother should gradually stop controlling. She will thus protect herself from her son's future ingratitude. Limits are necessary. They provide the child with a secure structure and a training ground for his behavior. Finally, mothers must be consistent in setting limits. Otherwise, the child will be confused.

A woman in her thirties has a twelve-year-old son. She has lived alone with him for several years, but now shares guardianship with the father. One day, she receives an invitation to an event in her family. Having no partner, she decides to bring her son. All during the week before, she goes about buying his first tie, his first suit, and little by little before her dazzled eyes, the lad becomes a seductive young prince. At the event, they spend the evening alone together, as the mother had decided to dance only with her son. The next morning, the little prince is expected to prepare his suitcase because his father is coming to fetch him. He is repeatedly told to hurry, but he doesn't budge. He is watching cartoons on TV. Finally, the exasperated mother gets angry and turns off the TV. The son gets up, takes her by the arm and tells her, with

murderous eyes: "I'll make you bleed!" The mother starts
to cry and seeks refuge in her bedroom.

What has happened? Simply this: After having been promoted
to the rank of lover, the son no longer wants to resume his place as
a child. Indeed, one cannot expect a twelve-year-old to understand
how he could dance with a woman one evening, and the next, be
forbidden to watch television. This incident was only a passing
one, but it illustrates quite adequately the problem of limits and
the importance to respect them.

When sons are overly mothered, they later find it hard to accept
life's ordeals when the mothers are no longer around. Their denial
of limits is often expressed by consuming drugs and alcohol. The
result: depressed and passive sons, unable to cope with life's frustrations. To make things worse, some mothers tend to exaggerate
when, feeling guilty, they accept to take charge of a now mature
son for the second time. They believe they did too little, when the
fact is that they did too much.

Such parents should be encouraged to practice what Alcoholics
Anonymous call *tough love*, that is, a type of relationship that sus-
pends their exaggerated concern for the son. It means letting
him face the ordeals of life by himself, even if he decides to regress
into helplessness. Of course, it is not easy to make parents understand this way of loving a child, especially if they see him rejected,
indigent, and miserable. If, however, they do not react, they risk
becoming themselves the victims of a human being who has
decided to destroy himself anyway.

Mothers are particularly vulnerable on this point. Having experienced a powerful attachment, some cannot distance themselves
sufficiently from their son to let him live his sad fate. They try to
mediate, and they lose their serenity. A seventy-year-old woman
told me during a workshop on mother-son relationships how much

she suffered to see her fifty-year-old son drown himself in alcohol. In spite of her frustration, she could not bring herself to break away. Her son drank, but she was intoxicating herself in the worst fashion by swallowing the dismal drama.

This is not an uncommon tragedy among mothers. I would like to tell the mothers who share this current problem that the time of responsibilities is in the past. As soon as the son's adolescence is under way, parents are no longer responsible for him. He must look after himself and choose what he wants out of life, no matter what kind of childhood he had. To protect their sons from the trials of life, mothers have the tendency to want to live in their son's place; but no one can live in place of another.

The best prevention against having two victims is for the mother to remember her femininity, and for us all to remember that we are personally responsible for our existence. It means to relish life and to have activities that chase away the dark spirits. It means to gain a sense of our individual destiny, to be aware that we are the first to be accountable for our personal lives. Ordeals can be learning opportunities to master interior states and obsessional thoughts. The tragedies that prematurely turn so many mothers' hair to white perhaps have a purpose: to remind them that their first duty is to let go of the Mother, to reclaim their womanhood and their capacity to love.

6

The Price of Emotional Incest

THE DOWRY AND THE DEBT

Basic Needs

We have just seen how the emotional frustration of the young woman who becomes a mother may lead her into a symbolic marriage with her son. Even if it is not sexual, the fusion can easily become emotionally incestuous. When certain boundaries disappear, and the child has to satisfy his mother's emotional needs, his frail psychic makeup is endangered. If the mother-child fusion is maintained beyond the first years, it will continue to affect the child's life. As an adult, his love relationships will be full of problems. There will also be important consequences for the woman whose motherhood was a priority.

To better grasp the consequences of the profound drama of mother-son relationships, I spent some time in researching an appropriate instrument of reflection. I found it through the psychoanalyst J. D. Lichtenberg, who, for the past forty years, has been intensely involved in observing infants. He studied the basic needs of infants, needs that are manifest at birth, needs that are innate and preprogrammed, so to speak.[1] He built a type of nomenclature, defining the basic human needs that have to be met to maintain a certain level of well-being. By examining which of these basic needs are inhibited or entirely repressed in mother-son relationships, we are able to form a quite accurate opinion concerning the price both persons have to pay for the fusion.

Lichtenberg classified the needs according to five distinct categories:

1. *Physiological needs.* If the infant is hungry or thirsty, if he is warm or cold, he expresses it spontaneously with cries or screams. No one needs to teach him these behaviors.

2. *Emotional needs and needs to belong.* The child needs to belong to a milieu, to a community that provides affection and comfort. He needs to be touched and fondled. He needs human as much as material warmth.

3. *The needs for autonomy and affirmation.* Here again, no one has to teach the child how to yell if he wants something, or how to quickly free himself to explore his physical environment. This is innate in the infant; it remains a constant all through life.

4. *The need to say no,* or the capacity to express his disagreement or his frustration. The researcher noted, for instance, that infants turned their heads away spontaneously from the breast when they are no longer hungry, or when food did not interest them. The notion of refusal is therefore present in us from the

earliest age; it is a component of our basic needs for expression.

5. *Sexual and sensual needs.* Just by observing a baby for a few minutes, we can see to what extent his senses are awake. After eating his fill, he screams with delight. He also expresses pleasure or displeasure when he senses his body's functions, such as bowel movements. Very soon his sexual needs will be expressed spontaneously, and their repression in our culture will be all the more fierce.

Of the five basic needs, we will consider the sexual and sensual needs, the need for autonomy, and the need to express a refusal. I would like particularly to help mothers understand that when they deny their own basic needs for their children's sake, the latter will often pay the price. Mothers are not usually able to behave otherwise, but the unconscious sets limits to blind devotion. In fact, the dowry brought by the woman to the mother-son wedding and the sacrifices she makes become the son's indebtedness. The debt will impose sacrifices on him also.

I Did Everything to Please Her . . . I Was Desperate to Please Her!
Let us begin with the needs for autonomy and affirmation. A fifty-year-old man relates the following:

> When I was young, I did everything to avoid hurting my mother; to please her, I wanted to be the best. I ran all her errands. I had good marks at school. My adolescence crisis did not happen at home; it happened later. For twenty years, I drank and chased women. I was married and divorced twice, leaving four children behind.

At fifty, I am waking up. I have just come out of my adolescence.

If we ever met this man's aging mother, chances are that she would not confirm this story. With a trembling voice, she would insist: "I don't understand what he's saying. I gave him all the space; I never took my own!" They are both trying to say in their own ways that they stopped breathing to please the other, to remove all restraints. To avoid displeasing the other, both sacrificed their needs for autonomy and affirmation.

As discussed in a previous section, personal identity gravitates around two poles: One is the need for closeness, and the other is the need for affirmation. In other words, we need to get close to be loved, and we need to distance ourselves to develop our consciousness. Individuality takes form thanks to the tension between these two simultaneously opposite and complementary poles. We choose one to the detriment of the other when, for example, we neglect our individuality in a relationship, or when we hide in a harsh individualism that shuts everyone out. This will result in all kinds of psychological complications. Indeed, we need others for our existence, and the group needs our individuality to maintain its vitality.

This applies especially to the mother-son relationship. The child absolutely needs his mother to develop, but he must leave this childhood condition to become a man. In the same manner, a woman must consent to certain sacrifices at the individual level to become a mother. But she must emerge from the maternal role to recover her womanhood and continue developing.

Unfortunately, expressing our needs for autonomy is often poorly received by families and society. The majority of people would rather not have this need, since it requires a good measure of aggressiveness to express it. The fear of hurting others interferes immediately, and this generates much guilt. And so, to avoid confrontations, mothers and sons prefer to give up each other's territories.

However, the real nature of mother-son encounters is evaded by this type of behavior. In fact, two people can convene only through conflicts and the resolution of conflicts, an essential condition to kindle life. If, for the sake of peace, we systematically repress all the innermost needs that risk causing friction, we walk straight into the realm of indifference and denial. No one wants to see the elephant in the living room.

For the woman who has totally identified with her maternal role, the repression of her needs for personal affirmation will lead to the following result: Her sons' and daughters' needs for autonomy will automatically be a threat. Even if the mother consciously wishes to let them live their lives, she will never allow her children to leave her. She would have the impression of being worthless, since she has already lost the sense of her identity as a woman, and it would be an even greater loss if she also stopped being a full-time mother.

I am aware that the maternal role requires that mothers set aside their needs for independence during a certain number of years, at least until their children reach adolescence. However, setting aside does not mean *renouncing* all expressions of autonomy, and depriving oneself of personal pleasures. The woman must remain in touch with her own self, independently of her children. It means having the courage to take this self seriously. She must ask herself what she would do if she were alone, with no children to look after, and try to find a satisfactory compromise. The exercise is not easy, but it will protect her from the sad fate of those mothers who forgot themselves for too long. Besides, if we have cut off our own wings of self-expression, chances are that the wings of those who depend on us will also be broken.

In analysis, I have noted that patients always spoke with emotion and sympathy of a mother who took the time to paint or to write, in harmony with her housekeeping duties. On the other hand, there may be harmful results if needs are satisfied in excess, for example, when the children are neglected because of personal pursuits.

What Sons Inflict on Mothers

The son who is trained to neglect his needs for independence because of the mother's insecurity is just as enslaved in the emotional fusion as is the mother. Both are threatened by the other's wish to be autonomous. A single mother who was living with three children in their twenties, one of whom had come back to live at home after a marriage failure, once whispered to me: "You know, children grow on you!" A good many women have stories about clinging adolescents, children who refuse to let her have a new partner because they would lose their direct access to the maternal breast. Fearing the loss of their acquired privileges, they do everything to annoy the man, and act as petty landowners who are losing a slave.

Modern psychology has much to say about the traumas inflicted on children by their parents, especially mothers, but little is said about the traumas inflicted on parents by their children. Mothers often find themselves being devoured by jealous and possessive sons. One of them told me that when a new man came into her life, her son suddenly became very hostile. He would check the time of her outings, and the next morning would ask at what time she had come in. A real tyrant, he even counted the calories in her food, warning her that she ate too much!

Another woman, who had recently remarried after living alone with her son, told me jokingly how her adolescent son was forever measuring himself with her companion. Every evening, during rounds of Ping-Pong, he would repeat his reckoning statement: "The loser leaves the house!" A sure sign that the Oedipus complex was being resolved ten years later than theorized. The newly formed triangle, with a father figure to block the son's automatic access to his mother, was helping both son and mother to liberate themselves from a relationship that was denying their respective needs for personal development. The woman was allowed to express her womanhood in the eyes of a man, instead of being only a mother in the eyes of the child.

I Love-Hate You!

"I lovhate you, so there! I lovhate you!" This is how one adolescent expressed his rage against the domination of his mother. "I lovhate you!" a cry from the heart, a cry holding all the ambivalence that is difficult to express between a mother and her son—as if neither mothers nor sons are allowed to feel any kind of hostility, as if loving were an obligation for both, as if it were natural. But is it not natural to want to take a holiday once in a while?

During the late 1950s, in Quebec, a song entitled "Ne fais jamais pleurer ta mère" (Never make your mother cry) was on everyone's lips. "Love her always," so the song continued. However well intended, the words meant that the child was forbidden to express any disagreement toward his mother, to say no to her interference in his life. Paradoxically, the message implies at the same time that saying "I love you" is forbidden as well. Love and hate are like hot and cold water; they both run from the same faucet. When one pole is neglected, access to the other is also blocked. Men have long carried this emotional rigidity without knowing its origin. When in a couple, they are often unable to say I love you, or to speak openly about what bothers them concerning their partner.

Most men, as they are so terribly aware of their mother's enormous sacrifice on their behalf, cannot bring themselves to tell her why they break away. Her sacrifice cannot be contested, and the very idea of confronting their mother turns them into unworthy sons. "It is simply not done! A son has no right to say such things to the woman who gave him life!" are the words that lock the debate in a sack of guilt. The result is twofold: We lose the possibility of relating honestly, as well as the precious opportunity to express all the love and gratitude we feel.

Today, well-functioning families present a different picture, where women identify less with the maternal function. Children learn to talk to their mothers at an earlier age and are more spontaneous in expressing their disagreements. And since the first years of childhood are determinant, the sons accumulate less obligations. They grow up with less guilt and ambivalent feelings toward their mother.

Of course, "Ne fais jamais pleurer ta mère" had its unsung counterpart: "Never make your son cry!" In my workshops for mothers, I was surprised to learn that the majority of them were not allowed to be anything but the *kind mother*. Fearing judgment, they dared not even mention the *bad mother*, the one who has had enough, who makes mistakes, who strikes, who is depressed. Yet, even if all the women were familiar with this naughty witch, it was taboo to bring her forth. They believed they had no right to claim these quite legitimate feelings.

Good mothers are afraid of leaving their family to take a rest. They feel obliged to enjoy being a mother. They should always be available and good-humored. They treat themselves like superwomen and have no compassion for their personal weaknesses.

In such a context, how can hidden aggressiveness be expressed, when a woman is so afraid to disturb? Well, it will come out in the form of illnesses, accidents, wounds, nervous tics, and episodes of depression. These manifestations all reveal her neglected needs for independence. Diseases or accidents provide the questionable advantage of legitimizing a rest without risking to lose the esteem of family and friends. This would not be the case if she dared to assert her needs while still healthy. By examining the context in which the parent or the child suffered a mishap, we usually find the event related to repressed moods and wishes.

In the course of his analysis, a man told me how his mother had badly cut herself with a poultry knife. I asked him to imagine himself in his mother's shoes at the time of the accident. The exercise made him see how his mother was enraged, exhausted, and totally crushed by her family duties. Having an accident was her only way of saying: "I've had enough!"

However, many adolescents find it difficult to express their frustrations when faced with intolerant parents. As they do not find the openness in their immediate surroundings, they seek other figures of authority such as teachers, or even the police. Repressed feelings lead them to commit small crimes, to have accidents, or to become ill. Whatever the crisis, it has its significance and should be seen as an opportunity to gain insights on the problem.

Holy Mother, Virgin, and Martyr

Sexuality is the third domain where the basic needs of mothers and sons are frustrated. As mentioned earlier, the opposite-sex parent confirms the child's sexual difference. For many sons, however, this difference is sometimes openly denigrated by the mother, if not totally ignored. Sons thus see their sexuality as shameful and dirty instead of as a source of pride and pleasure. Just as daughters need to hear their fathers say, "You're lovely, but you'll belong to another man," sons need to know that women will find them attractive.

It so happens that some mothers hate sex, especially if their sexual needs are not satisfied. Consequently, they will have sons who respect their mothers, but who will be quite licentious outside the home. Their uneducated sexuality finds an outlet in pornography, peep shows, nude performances, and so on, indicating their state of castration and their ineptitude for sound sexual activities. One man told me this story about his mother, who still treated him like a little boy even though he was thirty-five years old. He visited her one evening, took off his clothes in the kitchen, and stark naked, proclaimed: "Look, Mother, I'm a man!"

The psychiatrist and ethnologist Boris Cyrulnik explains this type of explosive affect. He sees a considerable difference in the emotional development of boys and girls. Girls have fewer problems, since, when still little, they are not sexually attracted to their same-sex parent. Boys, when little, are totally smitten with their mother. As they get older, they must inhibit their sexual reactions. This explains the anxiety they develop when their sexual organ is stimulated. They must block this urge, and the fact that they learn to do so early in life is precisely what causes future explosions. The more a vital energy is repressed, the more it risks bursting out unexpectedly and violently.[2]

A Persian psychoanalyst confirmed this when she told me how the explosive force of the Islamic revolution is entirely associated with sexual repression. The same principle applies to revolutions within families: The more its members are intolerant toward sexuality, the more inhibitions and explosions will ensue. Behavior patterns will be, off and on, either repressive or totally unbridled, and both are repudiated by women. The whole situation calls for more tolerance, and certainly a better approach to sexual education within the family.

Boy Meets Man: Sperm Secretions

In *Absent Fathers, Lost Sons*, I wrote about the fact that while girls are initiated to womanhood at the onset of their menstrual cycle, there was no equivalent experience for boys. My conception has evolved since then, and I now write about a natural sign of manhood for boys: sperm secretion. My oversight is significant in that it mirrors the fact that society completely occults this male counterpart of menstruation—perhaps because ejaculation is a pleasant experience, while menstruation is often painful, and perhaps also because negative judgments have changed such a pleasurable event for the flesh into a painful struggle for the mind.

When I was young, *nocturnal pollution* was the term used for involuntary sperm emissions during sleep. Pollution! One might just as well say dirt, garbage, toxic waste! What an awful way to prepare a young man for his sexual life. In tribal initiation rites, sperm plays a very important role. Most rites include drinking the sperm of an elder to assimilate his strength. Referring to ancient Greece, the cradle of our civilization, Elisabeth Badinter notes the existence of what she calls *pedagogical homosexuality*. Young ephebes were made to practice fellatio on older men as another way of ingesting male virility.[3]

The influence of Christianity did little for the value of sperm, considering the secretions mostly as a product of masturbation. An obsessed clergy turned the practice into a mortal sin, no doubt because it offers immediate relief, while the religious morals of transcendence are based on effort and restraint.

The great Thomas Aquinas, who authorized the irrevocable condemnation of this solitary pleasure, proclaimed that wasting the precious seminal fluid was equivalent to homicide. He wrote that since sperm was the seed of the human race, it contains man in his totality.[4]

At any rate, Christianity is not the only religion to condemn solitary sex. Most religions consider it as a loss of vital energy. Even psychology once professed that masturbation beyond adolescence was a sign of infantilism. Consequently, even today, masturbation is taboo, and a rather perplexing issue for parents. No one has a definite comment or thought on it; we are left to either condemn the practice or be silent about it. In open families, there is an increasing tendency to celebrate the girl's first menstruation with small rituals. Relations such as a godmother, an aunt, or a friend will read a poem and offer gifts and flowers. Could there not be a similar celebration for boys when their sperm begins to flow? It is certainly an important passage from being a child to being a sexual adult.

> A father told me about his son who was jealous of the cake his sister received on the occasion of her first menstruation. Taken aback, the father told him that when he would begin to ejaculate, he also would be entitled to his favorite pastry. One morning, the boy emerged from his room, all smiles, and proudly told his father: "The cake, it's for tonight!" The promise was kept.

Few men are able to brag about childhood celebrations around their sexuality. I believe that in bypassing boys' first sperm secretion, we miss a great opportunity to inspire them with a sense of their future duties. Coming of age sexually involves pleasure and freedom, but also responsibilities. This is a major turning point in a boy's life. Deprived of an appropriate recognition of this event, he continues to live in shame, guilt, and irresponsibility. The fact that many adolescents still refuse to wear condoms in spite of the danger of catching AIDS makes us realize that much needs to be done in the area of sexuality. We must dare to be more open with adolescents so they will be more aware of the implications associated with the pleasures of sex.

Above all, sexuality should be celebrated for what it is, a powerful and beautiful reality, but this seldom happens. We have no idea to what extent our whole beings are sexual. Each cell in our organism is sexual and is itself born from the division of two sexual cells. Sexuality expresses the very pulse of life. It is life's most spiritual manifestation, since it is part of the same mystery that generates and organizes life. To maintain a strict division between spirituality and sexuality means to maintain a limited view of life. It is the refusal to accept that we are here in this world mainly to create and procreate.

"Those Damned Men"

The sexual inhibitions of boys will affect their life as adults. During a televised interview, one man who had agreed to talk about the difficulties in his love relationships was able to define the cause of his unhappiness. He had spent his life trying not to be one of *"those damned men,"* the one his father had become in the eyes of his mother. So he repressed his sexuality with his partner because he had to be the opposite of his father in a couple. At the same time, he strayed into all kinds of extramarital affairs.

It is not easy for an adolescent to hear his mother's loud complaints about men's sexual behavior, such as, "They are all pigs!" In Michel Tremblay's play *Les Belles-Soeurs*, the leading actress holds a monologue that summarizes adequately the situation. This is about her husband: "And every night . . . he goes to bed first and waits for me! He's always there, stuck to me like a bloodsucker! God-damn sex! . . . A woman's gotta spend her life with a pig just 'cause she said yes to him once."[5] There is no better way to describe the nauseating situation of a woman who is overwhelmed by the church, by society, and by a husband who thinks only of his pleasure. She ends up hating sexuality and all its expressions, because her whole life has become a symbol of domestic slavery. But she recuperates a sort of symbolic virginity by transcending *the deed*. This is a sound reflex, but it marks another step toward the denial of her womanhood. By doing this, she consecrates herself as a martyr deprived of joy and pleasure and sentences the son's sexuality to follow the same blind alleys.

Today, it may be said that sexuality has been liberated. However, the debate around it is yet to come. As long as sexuality is not celebrated as a vital force to be treated with respect, it will continue to be disorderly and will not find its place in our scale of values. It will continue to be an obsessive issue and a chaotic force in the lives of many. Sexuality is an archetypal divinity. It has the power to take over our bodies and spirits when we do not give it proper homage. When we hide the goddess in the sordid corners of our psyche instead of celebrating her, she becomes perverse and ugly.

In this regard, the ancient Greeks have much to teach us. They would never have sent a sexually obsessed individual to the temple of Apollo (the therapist's office) to teach him to control himself. On the contrary, they would have sent him to pray and make love with the sacred prostitutes in the temple of Aphrodite. Indeed, the Greeks considered the obsessed person to be the victim of a neglected, vengeful goddess. Imagine one of these ladies whispering tender words to the patient: "So, what's the problem? Isn't it pleasant to make love? Isn't it a beautiful thing? Go, and sin no more! And don't forget our holy patron in your prayers! Make love and masturbate while celebrating the goddess instead of fearing her judgment." As long as the individual does not learn to respect and welcome the enticing Aphrodite in his life, he will be obsessed by this power who urges us to celebrate her beauty. However, it is possible to make love and masturbate every day without having any respect for sexuality. Also, we can renounce sex completely while respecting its importance. Our neurotic society is in great need of pleasure. This is abundantly expressed in publicity where images of seductive and sexy bodies are displayed. This explosive array is another way of compensating for the austere Judeo-Christian morality that denies the body's importance. Aphrodite may thus reclaim her rights, but we are still faced with a full-scale problem.

The Triumph of Austerity

It is not only sexuality that has been repressed in our families. All forms of sensuality have also been devalued. The family atmosphere was one of austerity. Mothers were responsible for the family budget and almost every aspect of family life. They had to uphold a sense of reality and duty, and their children were strictly disciplined. There was no room for play, for physical pleasure, and even for the simple joy of existing. Repressing basic needs indeed has consequences; the most severe one is the triumph of austerity.

To make an ironical statement on his mother's austerity, a man in one of my groups was heard singing a little ditty. It was "A Lament on *No*," which he had composed as a boy, and had sung with his sisters. It was a creative way to escape from the tyranny of a mother who invariably opposed her children's fancies. Nevertheless, the man had not overcome this negative attitude. The *no* to pleasure still plagued his life. So many people have lived in this kind of negative family atmosphere where playing and laughter were not allowed; mealtime was a cheerless and boring affair. People raised in such a background continue to show few skills for happiness. Their lives are dull or tragic, because they have not been conditioned to experience true joy.

GUILT

The Man with the Fork

Saturday, 10 A.M., I am moderating a workshop entitled "The Relationship to the Mother." The group is exclusively for men and they are in a circle. Each one has brought an object that symbolizes the best for him the relationship he has had or still has with his mother. I have hardly invited the participants to present their object each in turn, when one of the men throws himself to the floor in the center of the circle and tries to stick a fork into the ground, screaming: "I don't want any more, Mother! I'm not hungry, Mother! Can't you see that, Mother? I don't want any more!"

Benoît is thirty-five. He gestures and cries, trying to exorcise years of frustration. When finally appeased, he presents us with an example of a typical dialogue between his mother and himself when he visits her:

"You'd like to eat a little something, wouldn't you, my love?"

"I just ate, Mother, I'm not hungry, thanks."

"Come now, I made your favorite dish. Are you sure you don't want to eat a little?"

"Thanks, Mother, but it's true, I'm not hungry!"

"A small piece of cake then!"

"No, Mother!"

"I spent all morning baking this cake just for you; you must taste it! You can't do this to me! Come now, just a tiny portion."

Thereupon, she serves him the cake and he, enraged, ends up eating his mother's food because he cannot hurt her feelings.

In the workshop where this episode took place, those who spoke afterward found it increasingly difficult to speak out. As they tried to express themselves, the images of their respective mothers popped up with characteristics more and more idealized. A dark

cloud of guilt progressively covered the group. One of the participants who was dining with his mother that evening even left earlier. He feared some kind of accident might have happened to his
mother while he talked about her. Talking about their relationship
with their mother was nothing less than treason for these men.
Some kind of magical thinking gave them the impression that they
were actually killing her when they attacked the maternal complex. The latter seemed to have such archaic aspects that I finally
called it the maternal dragon. Using guilt as its major weapon, it
was maintaining its grip on the ego of each of the men.

As our workshop went on, I could not but realize how inade-
quately they were separated from their mother. They were not
entitled to their own lives. Psychologically speaking, the umbilical
cord had not been cut. The debt toward the woman who had sacrificed herself for their sake was too great. And later, after thirty,
forty, or even fifty years, when they were about to break away symbolically from the mother and to put the maternal complex at rest,
their inner selves were still sighing: "Forgive me, Mother, but it
isn't my fault!"

I wished to know more. So with the men, I began to explore the
childhood dynamics that were hidden under the guilt.

The Maternal Shadow

Most mythologies confer attributes of devotion and generosity,
and even self-sacrifice, to the mother. The various representations
of the *mater dolorosa* confirm this fact. But bizarre as it may seem,
the maternal figure also has its opposite aspect. It gives life, but it
also carries death. In India, for example, the goddess Kali, who pre-
sides at births, is also present when death occurs. It is said that she
even dances with joy in the blood of the dead. Each mother carries
this destructive aspect. She must be aware of this; otherwise, it
may turn against herself and her loved ones. In fact, a mother

risks becoming a witch when she denies that she has the power to give death.

When it is not consciously acknowledged, this maternal shadow takes many forms, the main ones being narcissism, perfectionism, overprotection, violence, and guilt projection. The development of these dynamics are in great part the result of the frustrated basic needs we discussed earlier. The dynamics will bond mother and son in a vicious circle of dependence and guilt, preventing the emergence of the woman and the man. But, needless to say, fathers can be just as narcissistic, perfectionist, violent, and guilt-projecting as mothers may be. And they inflict the same damage on children.

Children integrate the psychological wounds of the father or of the mother through parental complexes inside their psyche, so to speak. The complexes assault the ego every time it is not adjusted to parental injunctions. This is how all these wounds are transmitted from one generation to the other. Mothers who lacked a father arrive in the couple with a negative paternal complex; their creativity is crushed; they are disappointed with their partner; their animus is agitated; their aim in educating the child is to turn him into a god; they become overdemanding. The son develops a negative maternal complex in reaction to his mother's influence; he is afraid of women; he neglects his partner and his daughters. The daughters develop negative paternal complexes and marry men who cannot love, and so on. The dance never ends; the circle never closes.

The Narcissistic Wound

The first wound that is transmitted from parents to children through blames and reproaches is without any doubt the lack of self-esteem. The mother in our last example does not hear that her son is not hungry; she only hears that he does not love her. She cannot hear his refusal, because her identity is devoured by the maternal archetype, and is entirely based on her role as a mother. Her behavior is conditioned by her wounded self-esteem. Her narcissistic stability, that is, the value she affords her own person, finally depends on whether her son eats his dessert or not.

The degree of self-esteem of a mother is influenced by the wound inflicted by her father, and also by the fact that she lives in a patriarchal society that gives her little value. The endeavor of "raising an exceptional child" will give her a value and raise her self-esteem. In using her child as a mirror, she is at the mercy of his attitudes and behaviors to maintain her balance.

She becomes very demanding toward herself. Her unconscious wound and her love make her seek perfection on every level. But since this is impossible, she chooses one role, to which she devotes herself totally. This will be the safe place for her frail narcissism. If she is a good cook, she will not tolerate that her children criticize her meals. If she considers scholarly performance highly important, she will refuse failure. If cleanliness is her priority, she will persecute anyone who dares dirty the house. Her psychological stability forever depends on whether or not her choice role is offended.

Of course, one cannot blame a mother for expressing her love through caregiving; this role has sustained humanity forever and must absolutely be filled. However, the total investment of a woman's personality in this role leads to deviations of which she is the first victim. Her children will be the next victims, because she will expect that they respond to the same demands. Her personal value will be based on the fact that her children do well in school, speak correctly, are not rebellious, do not take drugs, or do not run away from home. Furthermore, she is likely to deny their shortcomings—even when the evidence is blatant—to avoid a loss of her narcissistic stability.

Invariably, the parental wound risks creating the same problem in the child. He will indeed develop a strong narcissistic character as he realizes that having a pleasant and sound existence depends on accomplishing a thousand foolish airs and graces. He does not love himself and will have problems loving anyone else. He will develop a false personality on the lines of what pleases his parents, while neglecting the other aspects of himself. He will then be accused of being self-centered, touchy, and incapable of empathy. All this is true inasmuch as his true self lacked positive reinforcement. Having lost touch with his innermost identity, he finds himself cut off from life and from the origins of love.

Suicidal at Eight Years Old

The man with the fork is a familiar example we can all relate to and is not all that dreadful; no one can boast of having a flawless self-esteem. But sometimes, the narcissistic wound of the mother is such that, to keep her esteem afloat, she will require no less than perfection from herself and from her children, claiming high performances in payment for her personal sacrifice. The integrity of her image depends so much on her children's achievements that she will deny indications from professors or other authorities that something is wrong. A blemish on her child puts her to shame.

Stephen has been admitted to a large hospital for children. He is eight years old. He no longer wants to live. A month ago, he had a tantrum in the school corridor. Crying and full of rage, he trampled his school bag, screaming that he wanted to kill himself. When taken to the principal's office, the latter realized that the child had lost all joy of existing.

Yet Stephen has top grades and is a model child. He comes from an equally model family. His parents seem to be a happy couple. They seem to give him adequate attention. Stephen learns easily and is talented in many other activities. Every evening after school, he trains in the gym and really loves it; on Saturday mornings, he has music lessons, and in the afternoon he takes lessons in diction. When he is not doing his homework, he practices the violin. When he is not practicing the violin, he exercises. Stephen's life is organized like that of an Olympic athlete.

During the past few months, however, he has had breathing problems. At Christmas, he refused to play his violin for his relatives. His mother saw this as a childish whim. Then he started to neglect his homework and to miss gym training. Then there was that night when he woke up with a start, having a powerful nightmare. He dreamt that he broke a leg during a competition; still dreaming, he cried for his mother, but as she approached him, she paid no attention to his pain and scolded him for his poor performance. Since then, he has nervous tics, is overanxious, and lacks enthusiasm. The mother responds sometimes with disbelief, sometimes with blackmail, or again with punishments and promises of gifts. She cannot accept the evidence that her son, so blessed by destiny, suffers from serious psychological problems.

The child is naturally open, spontaneous, and ready to help. He discovers his main reason for living through various mirrors, the most important being his mother's watchful eyes, and the attitudes of surrounding kin. These reflections are essential because without them, he cannot build his self-esteem and acquire a sense of his personal value. He needs to please. If his mother or other adults do not smile at him, he will search within for the cause and judge himself severely. Moreover, he will not learn to smile at himself. If he lives in disturbing and depressing surroundings, he will be disturbed and depressed. The mood around him becomes his own. Confronted with perfectionist parents, he will exaggerate his efforts to satisfy them and will become a perfectionist himself. Failing at a task may result in illness.

Hospitals count more and more children suffering from depression, at an age when the only preoccupation should be to play. Too much is expected of a child. He has an agenda that resembles that of a middle-aged adult. Then, when the demands are overwhelming, he has the impression that he himself is inadequate and at fault. He crumbles under the burden, and since he cannot name what is happening to him, his only reaction is to suffer a depression. The spirit of austerity has thus made another victim; the child is probably just as much a perfectionist as are his parents.

The naturally playful and creative child is sacrificed on the altar of perfectionism. He is offered courses and activities for the purpose of stimulating creativity, but the result is contrary; creativity is depleted. Certainly the child needs training and he also needs to channel his energy in challenging activities, but we must not forget that the spirit of play should come first. When the goal is to excel all the time, the child's vitality is broken.

Depression and suicide in children is one among other recent phenomena of our culture. The victims are crying out to us, pointing to society's alienation from life. The philosopher and geneticist Albert Jacquard refers to the baby-boomer children when he criticizes the generation that is sacrificed on the altar of excellence. As baby boomers realized all the possibilities of a thriving society, they made extreme demands on their children. They expected them to reflect their own dreams of perfection and their newly acquired almightiness as parents. Since they had been judged severely by their own parents, they were replacing the excessive authority they had known with demands for unequaled performances from their brood, the servants of their parental narcissism. Entire generations have thus lost the art and pleasure of living!

Overprotective Mother, Dependent Son

An athletic blue-eyed American shared the following during a workshop: As a young boy, he had lived several years with his grandparents on their farm. One day, as he came in from the fields, he sneezed. His mother's reaction was that hay and horsehairs were not good for him. The boy then developed real allergies to everything that was associated with farms, and could no longer visit his grandparents. He had to give up their healthy influence to stay at home with his mother.

The objects he chose to symbolize his relationship with her were hay, straw, and a few horsehairs, which he presented in a jar. This imaginative and charming man greatly resembled the symbol he presented, an uprooted plant enclosed in glass. When sharing open-air activities, we could feel his great vitality and immense pleasure. But this vitality was usually timid. When his turn came to present his symbol, he was visibly excited. The smells instantly invaded the room. He inhaled them forcefully and repeatedly. Then he said: "See, Mother, I don't sneeze anymore."

The mother of this energetic man was an anxious and overprotective woman. If he hadn't had the courage to look into his maternal complex during much of his life, he would still be an allergic, shy, and withdrawn individual. Smothering *overprotection* turns the mother's shadow onto her child. This gives him a negative maternal complex, and he becomes a dependent son. The pitfall lies in the mother's wish to protect her children from life's difficulties, *all* its difficulties, which is of course fallacious. Her good intentions smother the child. The overprotection prevents him from learning to draw upon his personal resources to negotiate with the inevitable frustrations of life.

The child's normal response to a stressful situation is to play. For example, if his parents lock him out for a certain time, he will have to deal with the anger, the anxiety, and the despair that come from being left alone. He will construct what has become known as *transitional space*, a cushion between the child and the world, between him and the impending sense of abandonment. He invents games in this space. He talks to his teddy bear as if it were Daddy and to his doll as if it were Mommy, and reshapes their company in his imagination. He thus defeats the sense of being rejected and of being confronted with heartless abandonment. But above all, he responds to the frustration *by his own means*.

Play is the process by which the child learns to manage difficult situations. It is the seed of his future independence. However, if such a process is to work, the frustrations must not be too extreme or destructive. Otherwise, the child cannot integrate them, and he ends up being inhibited instead of stimulated.

In the previous example, the child shifts from satisfying a need to have his parents actually present to a symbolic satisfaction of that need; he talks to his parents *as if* they were really there. This concept is essential, since the psyche is constructed according to such elements. It does not differentiate an actual sensation from an imaginary one. This explains why we can make ourselves sick with imaginary problems just as much as with real ones. Likewise, by visualizing creatively our well-being, it is possible to modify cellular processes and speed healing. The child who has not learned to shift from actual to symbolic satisfactions will always be at the mercy of his impulses and his immediate needs. He will not be able to delay his gratification. When the needs become urgent, he may abuse certain substances and even resort to violence to obtain them.

The overprotective mother who precedes the requests of her children to save them from suffering prevents them from learning to symbolically satisfy their needs. She unwarily keeps them in a state of dependence that may result in an incapacity to care for themselves and in a tardy development of their sense of initiative. Overprotection generates passivity, dependence, and anxiety in children, whereas appropriate protection encourages curiosity, self-affirmation, and combativity.

A psychoeducator who works in a daycare center for children with motor difficulties told me about the following episode:

A mother contacts her about her son who at four years old is still not able to button his coat and tie his shoelaces. The child is admitted for observation. The educator notes that he manages the above tasks quite rapidly. He has no difficulty whatsoever, and even helps the other children. Surprised, she makes an appointment with the mother to inquire about the home circumstances that prevent the child from performing normally. Afterward, she waits at the door with him as his mother is coming to fetch him. When she arrives, the child happily runs to her while rolling his scarf around his neck and buttoning his coat. The psychoeducator then hears his mother say: "Wait, wait, my love, Mommy'll do that for you!" This was evidently a case where the mother's protective behavior was provoking the very motor problem she feared her son had developed.

Overprotective mothers hinder their children by striving to save them from life's difficulties; their exaggerated fears prevent their children from dealing with problems they should normally cope with. The previous example shows us a fretting mother and a child who wants to please her by repressing his skills. He becomes a dead weight in her presence.

This smothering prevents the child from adapting to the world. His needs for autonomy have been denied, and he becomes a passive, dependent, and anxious adult because he was not encouraged to be curious and to explore. He is not skilled to react to his surroundings and to defend himself, to obtain what he needs, to use his frustration as a step to creativity. The parent has done too much for him, and this is unfortunate.

The epitome of the overprotective mother is encountered in the class of performing mothers who try to prove to themselves that they are good mothers. This is a way to negate their hostility, not toward their children, but toward the fact of having children. They are usually forced to have this attitude because, socially speaking, women are supposed to enjoy being mothers. Yet many women do not have this inclination. During a workshop I was giving in the United States with thirty-five mothers, a young woman broke out crying because she could not bring herself to love her child. This was the first time she could admit such a thing; it removed the terrible burden of seeing herself as a monster. She had forced herself to hide behind the image of an impeccable mother.

When a mother controls the child *for his own good*, she is betraying her repressed and unconscious rage. In the name of excellence, she demands cleanliness and goodliness from her son. If he does not rebel, he will become dependent and depressed. She turns him into a subdued son, an individual who forever asks permission to be himself and who excuses himself for what he feels through fear of disturbing others.

This adult will always bear a dead segment within. His shoulders will bear a child whose hopes will never be met and whose every dream will remain dormant. He risks doubting his true capacities and floundering in dependency problems. He remains the emotionally dependent child of his partners. He chooses dominating companions who take over his life as his mother did. Whether his dependency applies to alcohol, drugs, sex, or emotional bondage, he still has the profile of an adult who performs well, but who is passive toward his personal needs. Overprotection also hides a mother's extreme dependence on her child. He becomes the adored baby of a woman who fears her aloneness and her anxiety. He is bound and tied. She eats him alive to fill her emotional vacuum and to protect herself. The child is everything for this woman who has no life of her own.

In such a situation, maternal overprotection often results in its contrary: The child gradually becomes the parent. He is *parentified*, so to speak. The child becomes his mother's confidant, attentive to her matrimonial and existential dissatisfactions. But children are not fit to bear such burdens. Their enthusiasm and joy of living are inevitably destroyed. The most desperate men and women I have encountered as a therapist were almost invariably parentified sons and daughters.

In a few cases, I have witnessed that this *parentification* is the genesis of a man's violence toward his companion or, again, the reason for being incapable of an in-depth relationship with a woman. The mother's world has, so to speak, violated the integrity of the child's world, and the child hates women intensely. At the psychic level, this almost misogynist animosity serves as a wall to protect the man against the feminine world that has gone too far in challenging his autonomy.

Maternal Violence

The accumulation of repressed desires and frustrations hold us in their grip if we do not admit them into our psychic pantheon. The ego becomes submerged in an affect, leading it to perform blindly, and this is what constitutes violence against children. An American woman writer relates an experience she had while on vacation.

> At the last minute, her husband is held up by his work so that she finds herself alone with her three children. She had hoped for some time alone to rest and to write. She becomes aware of her mood changes from day to day; she responds in a more and more aggressive and impatient way to the demands of her children. One evening, as she can no longer contain her despair, she decides to give in to the violence within by practicing mental imagery. The fantasy she arouses petrifies her with horror. She sees herself as a demonic witch who hits her son's head against a wall and who relishes in seeing the blood flow. To her great surprise, the vision profoundly calms her. Her tension is gone. On the days after, she finds ways to organize her time and duties so as to be able to write. Her relationship with the children becomes once more creative and relaxed.[6]

This mother has found through visualization a creative solution to her distress. If she had not had the courage to face her violent impulses, it is very probable that she might have brutalized her children, personifying Kali-the-Destroyer in all her splendor. Yet in our society, the power of Kali-who-Brings-Death is totally occulted. Even if most mothers have a vague sense of her existence, they recognize this shadow only when they are actually furious. In such cases, they behave blindly, as in a state of drunkenness, possessed by destructive forces, partially conscious of what they are doing. Unless the emotion is released, the shameful rage will keep them in its grip.

The mother strikes her children but has no memory of her act. This loss of memory resembles the *blackout* of alcoholics during which they lose consciousness for a few minutes or several hours, while continuing to operate. The next day, they cannot recall what they did or said. This is a practical defense because it allows the shadow to remain unconscious; it is practical but terribly pernicious and destructive.

In our families, when verbal, psychological, and even physical violence breaks out, it is not the result only of male aggressiveness toward women and children. It is also generated by discouraged mothers who bear their plight in silence and who cannot admit their rage because they cannot bear to be seen as wicked. Yet by clinging to this attitude, they negate their shadow and worsen the situation. The aggressive impulse is transformed into violence in the unconscious. A witch emerges, and children are deeply afraid of her.

The Serpent's Power

In therapy, we often encounter adults who talk about the psychological and even physical violence inflicted on them by their mothers during childhood. I do not mean a spanking once in a while; I mean physical ill-treatment and punishment on a regular basis. Children so treated are broken in their spontaneity, and their relationships are doomed to be ambivalent. The bonds of trust they weave with others are fragile. They withdraw into themselves and choose solitary lives. Even if they are the sweetest boys in the world, their hearts are closed. They would very much like to have someone approach them, to be healed by warmth and welcoming, but this would melt the ice protecting their wound, and they would feel the pain once more. In spite of their needs for tenderness and compassion, they fiercely resist. And while hating those who offer their love, they also hope with all their might that they will persevere long enough to pierce their rigid armor.

Abused children are caught between two poles. They ferociously and fatally hate the punishing parent, and they are unable to express this hate for fear of losing parental love and attention. Yet this double-binding venom, left to sleep in some distant and forgotten part of themselves, will still find a way to awaken, in the form of violent fantasies, in self-destructive behaviors, in violent acts, or in psychosomatic diseases.

A man once told me about having spent his childhood devising the perfect crime. He was convinced that the crime should be committed gratuitously and without a motive. He imagined stray bullets flying about from where he fired unseen, hitting drivers randomly passing by the family home. The game allowed him to separate his passion from the actual crime, thus neutralizing the anger he felt for being punished by his mother. Since he needed her love and would have received more blows if he had expressed his hate openly, he resorted to fantasies, and directed them outside the home.

Alone in his room, he also played with a little rubber cobra that sprang up by means of an air pump. While his left hand operated the pump, his right hand had to withdraw as fast as possible to avoid being bitten. He had set up a drama that he could master, the scenario consisting of his mother's violent impulses and his own repressed desires to take revenge. The game had the advantage of changing his extremely painful experience into pleasure.

The abandoned children of Brazil, whose lives are constantly threatened, confront danger daily by inventing scenarios involving their eventual death. By this skillful technique, they have the impression of controlling a fate that escapes them completely.

The symbolic meaning of the snake game is even more important because we know that the child had a real phobia of snakes.

He became a meek, easygoing youth who expressed himself in low tones. He had depressive and suicidal moods; his combativity was totally undermined by a lurking violence. During his thirties he was diagnosed with a serious illness, and came to me on the advice of his doctor. In the course of his therapy he understood that he would recover his vitality and his creativity only if he recognized and connected with the violence that poisoned his existence. He suffered from the good boy illness: overadaptation, practiced with kindness but filled with a terrible fear of rejection. He had repressed his spontaneous reactions to the point of becoming a champion of endurance, able to survive unacceptable situations better than anyone.

This profound split from psychic and physical spontaneity is the central problem of the individual who was physically abused during childhood. He becomes resigned and untouchable. One part of his person is perfectly adapted to his environment while another continues to live solitary and submitted. He expects little from people. On the outside, he appears controlled and rational, but inside, there is a boiling passion. He cannot let out the steam for fear of the "timer-cooker exploding," as one workshop participant pertinently said. Such are the ideal circumstances for the outbreak of a psychosomatic illness.

The snake phobia developed by this child is greatly significant. We are familiar with mythology's Great Mothers, such as Egypt's Isis or the Hindu goddess Kali-the-Destroyer, usually represented with reptiles around their necks or arms. These creatures are not enemies, as seen in pictures of heroes struggling against monsters. They symbolize different aspects of the powers of mothers and of femininity. The same idea is conveyed in the Bible where Eve and the serpent collude. Some mythologists even believe that this animal is the principal symbol of femininity throughout the ages. The intrinsic nature of the reptile is twofold: It has the power to kill, and to bestow the secret of transformation because of its capacity to change skins. Snake venom has the power to heal or to kill.[7]

What We Fear Is a Feature of Our Own Selves

When a mother is possessed, unwarily, by the serpent's power, her child is full of fear. His fear of death permeates his every breath and inhibits him so much that his gestures are never complete. His fear of being repeatedly caught in the serpent's coils forbids all commitments. Fear and hate: What other feelings can a boy have when he is beaten by his mother? He hates. He later hates women with his adult heart, with all the heart of the wounded child. He becomes easily independent, but this is usually a false autonomy hiding a tremendous need for love and tenderness. He fears responding to love, because he expects his spontaneity to be greeted with snakebites; he will be bitten to death if he ever dares to be himself. He fears ultimate refusals, believing himself incapable of surviving. Women and the maternal complex both hold him down. And he will forever be their victim unless he recuperates for himself the power of the shadow, unless he recovers his capacity of affirmation.

If this work is not done, the son's rage will reproduce his mother's frustration on the terrain of the couple, where the man's repressed childhood rage will explode against women. So he

attacks his partner instead of working on the source of his belliger-
ence: the maternal complex.

For the mother as well as for the son, for women as well as for
men, the idea is to relinquish what we impose on others, the projection of our dark side. It means accepting that what we detest in
others is a feature of ourselves. That is the only way to recuperate
the energy enclosed in such complexes, the only way to protect
ourselves from acting violently, the only way to stop choosing partners who personify our worst demons, the ones we do not want to
exorcise.

The Weight of Sighs

As I have said previously, the dynamics associated with perfectionism, overprotection, and violence all have a common component: inculpation and the guilt it imposes on the child. When the
son is invaded by this guilt, it means that his negative maternal
complex is well installed and that it persecutes his ego. The guilt
creates a peculiar bond that compels the child to feel responsible
for his mother's well-being. He has no right to be happy when the
person who makes so many sacrifices for him is not happy about his
behavior.

The mother's continual sighing prevents the son from separating from her. It convinces him that his mother cannot exist without him and would never survive any of his tensions and eventual
attempts to separate. Any hopes to be independent are stifled by
guilt even before they are expressed. The feeling that he has no
right to break the sacred bond will follow him all through his life,
and will complicate his relationships.

In view of this psychological truth, we can easily imagine why
men feel so terrible when faced with any form of emotional separation or any form of commitment. They feel guilty, and just as
they felt responsible for their mother's happiness, they now feel

responsible for that of their partner. They dare not separate, so they drag out unhealthy situations through fear of hurting anyone. They must not lose their "mama's good boy" image. They cannot cope with the suffering they might cause by separating; the ensuing guilt would be impossible to live with.

Since they do not give themselves the right to be who they are, the guilt makes these men ashamed of their basic needs. They are caught in the same vicious circle as the mother who, fearing to openly express her needs, ends up manipulating her family to obtain what she wants. The companions of these men are soon worn out by such behavior, and leave them when the problem becomes obvious.

A good number of men simply decide not to commit themselves because they cannot face dealing with the emotional pain of love and the conflicts it engenders. I know of several who shrink away from their inner sighs and literally become hermits. Others choose to be totally artificial, forsaking their personal growth to cater to an image. They sometimes become public personalities who search for love on the artistic or political scene. In their fantasy world, they continue to strive being their mother's divine son. This double life is the only way for them to somewhat connect with their instincts without displeasing the complex, until the day they are exposed. And then comes the choice between being repenting ungrateful sons and accepting their humanity with all its tribulations.

Finally, to counter this castrating and ravaging complex, some men take refuge in the loftiness of dreams, of thought, or of spirituality. They seem to float above common reality, no doubt to avoid awakening the sleeping dragon.

Such is the picture of the "good boy," the one who would never hurt a fly but who is afraid to love. His anima is imprisoned by the negative maternal complex, just as the daughter's animus was imprisoned by the negative paternal complex. She had to face her complex. Similarly, the son will have to liberate his anima to find his way back to his heart, to reconnect with inspiration and creativity; he will have to recognize his shadow and confront his maternal dragon.

7

The Drama of the Good Boy

Santa Sangre, the Holy Blood

When Alejandro Jodorowsky produced the film *Santa Sangre*[1] some years ago, it seemed as if he wanted to illustrate what it means for a man to be imprisoned by the maternal complex and by guilt.

> The film is about a boy who lives with a circus. His father, a perfect patriarch, is the owner and director of the small band. The father is much attracted to the serpent-woman, the sexy contortionist in the circus. One day, his wife finds him making love to her, so she castrates him. To take revenge, the furious patriarch cuts off her arms, then commits suicide. The young boy sees all this and withdraws completely into himself. He is interned in a psychiatric hospital, and later when he has reached

adolescence, his mother brings him home. From that moment on, the son becomes the prisoner of his widowed and disabled mother, to the extent that his arms and hands become hers. He lives in the same clothing as his mother, feeds her, and knits and plays the piano in her stead.

One day, however, he escapes his maternal prison and lets himself be seduced by a woman who persuades him to create a new circus number with her. He is a knife-thrower as was his father. We then see an extremely erotic sequence where he hypnotizes his victim so she will not be afraid of his throws. The knives stick all around her with precision. The last one will be aimed between her open legs, symbolizing sexual penetration. But the hero's mother suddenly appears and his skills are destroyed. His hands begin to tremble. He hears his mother's shrieks, "Kill her! Kill her!" and plunges a knife into his loved one's belly. The adolescent's power has been totally undermined by maternal authority.

In a subsequent scene, we find him in a cemetery burying his victim. He is surrounded by various evanescent forms of women as they emerge from the surrounding tombs. The meaning is quite clear: He has killed one by one all of the women who have approached him. There follows a rather touching scene in which the man is sobbing over the body of his last victim and imploring the forgiveness of all his other lovers.

The hero finally kills his mother to protect the love he has for a woman he knew as a child and with whom he wishes to renew his life. In fact, she is the daughter of the serpent-woman. The film ends as the police arrest him for his mother's murder, while all his other crimes have remained unpunished.

At the symbolic level, the knife-throwing episode represents the arrival on the scene of the maternal complex, the power restraining the man who has not liberated himself from a possessive mother. At the most crucial moment, the maternal dragon intervenes to destroy his powers. In his love relationships, this man is compelled to kill, that is, to crush his partners, to betray and deceive them at the very moment they begin to trust him. Instead of seeking cooperation, he unwittingly submits to the injunctions of a jealous maternal complex, thus provoking power struggles and disharmony.

Psychologically, the theme of the cemetery scene likely represents the moment when the hero decides to get rid of his complex. The transformation is possible because he lets his heart be touched by the suffering he causes around him and by his own misery. As he becomes conscious of the drama, his capacity to love is awakened. His heart is opened by suffering. The other theme, a new love personified by a girl he knew during childhood, represents the liberation of his anima, the power that makes a man able to relate. True love is not possible unless this power has been liberated from the maternal complex.

The hero's arrest is also a theme that has a highly significant psychological value. As a man subdues his maternal complex, he ceases to shirk his responsibilities, by using others as cover-ups and by using the pretext of his difficult childhood. He is liberated, but is entirely responsible for his actions. He can no longer pretend to be the polite, gentle little boy. It is time for him to acknowledge his shadow, his power to cause suffering. He must also accept that he is culpable for his actions. He can no longer play the innocent. By killing his mother, he symbolically kills his childhood. That is the sacrifice to which he must consent to be a man.

Finally, we note in the film that Jodorowsky also makes use of the central motif of the fairy tale "The Handless Maiden." Perhaps the producer wished to follow up this tale by presenting the hero's mother with mutilated arms. The film thus prolongs the fable by showing what happens to a handless woman when she becomes a mother. She uses her children as extensions of herself. They must serve her wounded creativity and be totally devoted to her. They become the arms and hands that she has lost because of the ill-treatment of a patriarch. They have no right to be autonomous, and this is particularly true for the son. The negative maternal complex that he develops because of this bond makes it forever impossible for another woman to approach him. The woman who accepts the love he sincerely offers is playing with death.

Such is the cycle of human tragedy, as it is ceaselessly repeated. The holy blood of life never stops being shed. Men cut off the arms of women who then castrate sons who then cut off the arms of their partners in revenge—until love is strong enough to rouse a man to break away from his complex and to stop being mama's little boy.

The Dusty Heart of the Good Boy

The film *Santa Sangre* describes admirably the drama of the *good boy* imprisoned by a negative maternal complex. He is afraid of feminine power; he is afraid to love. The good boy is an individual who, while appearing open-minded, has an enormous resistance to commit himself to relationships. His heart is locked. To liberate his creativity and capacity to love, he will have to do as the film's hero: confront his maternal dragon and face his shadow.

The good boy suffers from the same malady as the *good girl*. He overadapts to the demands of his surroundings. Permeated by his mother's narcissistic wound, by her extreme demands and her blames, this man's heart is all locked up. He is the most charming boy in the world, but he experiences a huge inner solitude. This solitude is dominated by a severe maternal complex that forbids him from expressing his feelings spontaneously. His behavior is constrained. He does not enter the depths of his being, because that is where he hides the excessive suffering of the badly loved child.

To deal with this problem and to begin expressing his real needs involves changes that would be destabilizing. It would involve losing the esteem of the entourage on which he depends. Above all, this would entail a divorce from the mother and the betrayal of the symbolic mother-son bond. In fact, when parents and children are bonded by the same psychological problem, there is likely to be an unconscious pact forbidding either one to break away.

To change, the good boy must confront the guilt involved in leaving his dear mother and causing her pain. He must overcome the fear that she may not survive her son's change of attitude. But mostly, he must rekindle his inner fire and recover his vitality.

I will use the case of Henri as an illustration of these facts. After several months of therapy, Henri came to one of his sessions with a dream, which caused him great panic:

> I am washing my personal diary in the kitchen sink. As I become aware of what I am doing, I pull it out before it is too damaged and dry it diligently. I then set it to dry on the radiator of the living room, where a huge statue of the Buddha predominates. I notice that something is wrong in this room. First, it is covered with a thick coat of dust, as in a neglected attic. Then, as I look closer, I notice that burglars have invaded my home and that they have removed the living-room rug before putting all the furniture back in place. The violation makes me scream with horror. A cloud of particles shoots out of my lungs at the level of my heart, as if someone had squeezed all the dust from a full vacuum-cleaner bag.

The dream reveals to what extent the job of dusting his life was arduous for Henri. His surprised reaction to his laundering his diary and drying it afterward indicates his great ambivalence toward the therapeutic process. By drowning what he wrote, he could forget the difficulties of working on himself.

In real life, he had found refuge in an austere spirituality that served to keep his internal child at bay, the child who had sprightly reactions to events. He was frustrated by these moods and repressed with all his might, just like his mother had repressed his spontaneity when he was a child. That is why he put his journal to dry at the foot of the Buddha, hoping to be spared the confrontation with his emotions.

This spirituality only half satisfied him, since one task remained undone. He still had to clean the living room, and his heart asphyxiated by dust. He was horribly repelled by this idea, but it was too late. The rug had been pulled from under his feet by the burglars, and they had also taken the pains to put everything back in place after their misdeed. These childlike offenders are interesting symbols of the Greek trickster-god Hermes. As the patron of commerce and of thieves, Hermes is also the patron of psychological transformation, since the metal representing him is quicksilver, with its swift and unexpected alterations.

Henri associated the motif of the dust cloud coming from his lungs with the miners who were affected by asbestosis. Their lungs were literally clogged up by asbestos pollution. As he spoke of the cloud coming directly from his heart, he broke out in heavy sobs. He was facing the evidence that his choked heart was the result of his childhood. He had no right to love, to have a satisfying relationship. He inevitably chose women who had the same problem as his, and the ones who didn't, made him flee. In every attempt, his inner child hoped to find the love that would give him everything. He entertained the unconscious hope that a woman would deliver him from the curse of his mother. He waited for the welcoming woman who would understand him at last and give him the permission to fully express his passions and emotions. But he was forever disappointed.

The very idea of working on himself and of having to satisfy his needs disgusted him. His inner child deeply disgusted him, and he feared his violent outbursts, just as he had feared those of his mother. Everything in himself that reminded him of his mother was intolerable. He was horrified of having to recognize to what extent he was castrated from his personal power. He felt divided, fragmented, and vulnerable every time someone touched this psychic area. He compared therapy to an uncomfortable descent into a viper nest and had the impression that I was the one who forced such a journey on him. He sometimes openly expressed his hatred toward me and regularly spoke of stopping his analysis. His sessions were inevitably followed by nightmares and by headaches, due, according to him, to digestive problems. Yet he knew very well that they had nothing to do with what he ate.

Henri had no freedom. He had become a person who favors duty and principle above all else. Just like his mother. His life belonged to the most noble causes; he was a typical missionary, always ready to defend widows and orphans. His strength was entirely at the service of his saintliness, with none left to resist his obsessive sexual fantasies, which made him feel even more guilty. In striving to be a saint, he adopted an ascetic life-style and feared physical comfort. He told me that the living room appearing in his dream had in reality remained empty for some time, like a cold house without a heart.

The Gates of Hell

Healing is possible for the good boy, but it will not happen unless he goes through the torments of fiery emotions. It is not irrelevant that Christ had to descend to hell before resurrecting. Symbolically, this means that we simply cannot renew our lives without awakening the great life forces within, without the Devil adding his grain of salt. No one can avoid this ordeal if he wishes to recuperate his wounded creativity. No one can pass over this ordeal by simple intellectual understanding, nor pass under it by jumping passionately into a new creed. And neither could Henri bypass it by pretending to ignore his private suffering. He had no choice but to face the ordeal as he became engulfed in the violence he had been repressing ever since he was brutalized by others or by himself. He had to face it all with awareness, with courage, with a haunted and feverish heart. As the tension escalated, Henri gradually accepted to face the maternal complex that poisoned his existence. Besides, it was the only possibility for him to renew his relationship with his aging mother, who now needed his care and affection.

He continued the analysis in spite of his resistance. His dreams were full of frozen deer, of bright red convertibles on white snow, of subway tickets marking surprising destinations such as the *gates of hell*. From session to session, I encouraged him to allow his violent emotions to surface. And little by little, he dared to open up.

Behind the gates of hell, he discovered raw anger, a gaping wound. It was the anger of a flayed animal, an anger that nothing could alleviate. I supported his process and invited him to give in to his inner torment, at the risk of losing sleep, of ruining his notebooks, of proclaiming his insanity and locking himself up. He temporarily quit his appeasing meditations at the Buddha's feet. This man did not need to escape to the heavens. He needed to meet the living fire in the depths of his belly, the innermost fire, the basic element of any real transformation. The alchemists knew this, and so do the Buddhists. All the biographies on Yogis confirm the necessity of these feverish transitions. The whole being is on fire. And without this fire, meditation and ecstasy are a masquerade.

While up until now he had been satisfied with being the gentle, comprehensive, and compassionate victim who forgave everything, he became overnight a caged lion. He applied his energy toward keeping contact with the fire, without repressing it. He contained it, fed on it, and I beheld an obvious transformation. When he dared being the wild animal, his whole body was more present in the room. His strength was liberated (he never trained physically); he felt whole for one of the rare times of his life, enjoying it immensely. For several weeks, he was not plagued with his usual indecision; he replaced it with a courage and a determination I had never seen before.

He had resolved to change, affirming that he would do so even at the cost of his life. He was burning his past in the fire of inner passion. The force of the blacksmith bending hot iron was suddenly his, while he had always been only the reddened and hammered metal. He had never dared handling the hammer himself. He was breaking away from the good boy and, at the same time, from his maternal dragon. Although he still felt like a badly loved child, he could no longer hide from the fact that his real mother had nothing to do with his interior drama. He was now responsible for straightening out the situation and for transforming his rage into creativity.

At that point in therapy, Henri was sitting on an erupting volcano. Indeed, when primal forces are released, the basic conflicts resurface and the childhood dinosaurs make their inevitable appearance. The terrain was now ready for his encounter with his shadow.

The Sin Against Self

There comes a time in a person's life when the vital forces will no longer take part in the sin against oneself. We can very well relax, eat well, exercise, go out: Nothing works. The situation will not change unless we face the conflict that is rooted within. The perfect metaphor of this sin is the story of Cain, who kills his brother, Abel, and who is mercilessly hunted by the eye of God reproaching his crime. By killing Abel, Cain had killed the best of himself: sensitivity and spontaneity.

On the psychic level, Abel's murder by Cain symbolizes the condemnation of an individual to be nothing but the shadow of himself, and to live without joy. The price is high. No one can repress creativity without paying dearly. But it seems that fate has nothing to do with morality. It is left up to us—poor humans all more or less engulfed in this betrayal of the self, in the murder of Abel, in the sacrifice of the inner child—to muster compassion for our own cowardice. There is no room for the scornful: Christ's admonition "Whosoever has not sinned, let him throw the first stone" might very well be applied here.

In a subsequent exercise of active imagination, Henri created a dream about himself encountering his own sacrificed Abel. He recognized Abel as a timid and withdrawn young boy, living in a squalid room, making birds out of colored paper. At the beginning, the dialogue was more like a dangerous slalom. Sometimes the boy became a poisonous snake, and sometimes he had the appearance of a rioter who wanted to destroy the outside world. Or he became an avenging alley cat looking for trouble.

One day, the inevitable happened. The inner conflict erupted with all its force. All the hate and resentment felt by Abel toward Cain broke out. A fatal conflict was taking shape between the rival brothers. The gentle Abel rose from his depths and threatened to kill Henri if he did not find a new balance, if he did not respect his creativity. Otherwise there would be no existence possible other than the state of frozen despair familiar to those who realize that they have ruined their lives.

I have never, in therapy, assisted a scene as violent as the imaginary confrontation of these enemy brothers. In a state close to trance, Henri contorted and shook violently on the couch. The confrontation was full of screams and sobs, cynical comments, and bilateral accusations. There it was in broad daylight: the internal cleavage and the self-hate of a man who had, in order to survive and please his parents, sacrificed a part of himself that was absolutely essential. I was moved to tears by what I saw. . . . It seemed to be such a powerful manifestation of our human reality.

Following these explosions, the outcome I dreaded the most finally happened. The conflict was too raw, the enlightenment too blinding. When someone penetrates the heart in such a way and sees his whole life in a flash second, when he recognizes the conflicts that caused his lifelong torments, the therapist often observes an important withdrawal.

Henri associated Abel with the forbidden and morbid area within him, an area he now saw as a broken toy that he was unable to repair. He dizzied himself once more with duties and responsibilities to avoid facing his inner fire. In his free time, he masturbated frenetically and was bitterly ashamed. Wrongly no doubt, since his sexuality in fact expressed the irrepressible presence of something spontaneous within.

Henri's icy dreams reappeared as well. Just as our planet juxtaposes extremes without restraint in all its beginnings, he found himself in the tropical era one week and in the glacial era the next. But, he had touched the center. It was now a matter of time. I was confident that my patient would be able to make the necessary changes to renew his existence and mend the damages caused by the betrayal of his deepest self.

Subsequently, the task of integration went on at a comfortable cruising speed. As time went on, Henri was even able to laugh when he occasionally found himself caught by the good boy. He was able to give more and more expression to his tastes and emotions. His sexuality and his spirituality, dare I say, had lost their defensive and compulsive aspects and were more harmonized with the overall rhythm of his being. He could also relate better to his mother, because he was now able to resist his internal dragon.

Although Henri's love relationships remained problematic, he had a better understanding of his ambivalence and how it caused suffering to his partners. He no longer held those he became involved with responsible for his fate. Little by little, Henri's liberated creativity inspired him to hope for a deep and genuine love commitment, not out of a sense of duty, but because of a real wish to share his life with someone. He now had access to his intuition and his feelings. He began to trust more and more the feelings inspired by his anima.

The Psychological Dynamics of the Good Boy

Why do good boys continue to be good, when they know that they are paying such a high price for being so incapable of affirming themselves? Why do they go on paying for the goodness with bouts of alcoholism, psychosomatic illnesses, chronic fatigue, or inner torments? What makes them say yes when they want to say no? What prevents them from saying what they think, just to please their entourage? Why do they prefer the betrayal of their intimate convictions?

There is only one answer to all these questions. The good boy carries inside a devouring monster who pulls him into a hell of remorse, of doubting and of guilt, as soon as he dares expressing what he really thinks and dares to behave according to his feelings. To such a man it is a thousand times better to be gentle and compliant, at the risk of his health, than dare to cross the forbidden boundaries, to confront this monster who has the power to tear him to pieces and to slash away at what is left of his weak self-esteem.

Where does this inner monster come from? Who made these

tacit rules it abides by? The inner monster is the product of primary events experienced with intense emotions by the child, and which threaten to disintegrate his developing identity. To survive in this precarious environment, the child's ego learns a new set of rules. If the trauma of his childhood situation is too devastating, and if his feelings are overwhelmed by the threat to his identity, the rules of survival are even more solidly implanted. A violent parent, a frigid mother, early and ill-prepared abandonments, childhood illnesses— all are experiences that may contribute to the formation of an identity that relies on exaggerated gentleness. This is easy to understand: The child's only defense is gentleness, obedience, compliance, and complicity. He becomes the accomplice of the abusing parent in order to tame him and hold on to his love, the love he absolutely needs to perceive his own value.

"I won't do it again, Mommy! I won't do it again!" This is the too familiar cry of a child being struck for committing a petty offense. It is not only the child who is struck; his personality is also broken. He is forbidden to explore his body and the universe. He is told that curiosity is not allowed, that sensuality is taboo. Above all, he is told that the spontaneous expression of his feelings and ideas is not welcome. The end product is a performing child, the pride of his parents. Yet the product may also be an adult who never does what he likes in life for fear of displeasing, for fear of having to face the monster he carries inside.

The most charming, the most violent, the most tortured, and the most alienated men I have met in my profession are in majority the sons of mothers who were not able to greet their child's pain or distress. Some were even beaten so they would stop crying, because their upset mother was unable to cope with the situation. Today, these men continue to treat themselves with the same severity. They are still not able to greet the child within. They constantly brutalize the natural joy and spontaneity of that child, the child within who did not receive his proper share of tenderness. They respond to their inner needs by working harder, by indulging in more sex or more alcohol.

You Are Not Separated! You Are Not Free!

The social context makes it even more difficult for men to accept their sensitivity. Yet, there is no real virility without this in-depth acceptance. Otherwise, men copy the sensitivity of the feminine world. They do not attain the wonderful warmth, the sweet and earthy reliability of a strong and integrated masculinity. The integration is possible only if men have truly severed the umbilical cord. This is what the famous protagonist of the novel *Zorba the Greek* tells his disciple: that he cannot experience his spontaneity and joy of living because he is not separated! He is not free!

> You, my friend, you have a long cord, you come and go, you believe that you are free. But the cord, you don't cut it. And when we don't cut the cord. . . . But if you don't cut the cord, tell me, what does life taste like? A taste of camomile, of bland camomile! It isn't rhum that makes you see the world upside down![2]

It is always surprising for a therapist to see how unconscious areas keep on living. There is naivete in the belief that an individual can escape his affects by smothering them in work. On the contrary, this is a sure way to give them even more power, but the power is negative. Indeed, as they are not allowed to associate with consciousness and bring life, they use their power to bring death, to lead us to self-destruction.

The good boy carries a great void within, a void that no success can ever fill. His outward search for love and approval leads to more and more despair and depression. He will eventually do without vacations, making sure in advance that his time is all filled up. Afraid of castration, he continues to be gentle and kind as a way to keep peace, to hide his negative feelings toward women. But deep down, his anima still has the face of a devouring mother or a witch. Not having confronted his maternal dragon, he risks choosing a "controlling" woman, or perhaps an authoritarian woman, hoping secretly that she will oppose his mother and speed his separation.

Thereupon, we must realize that a man's anima is strongly marked by his mother's personality and that it will not unfold if the separation from the mother has not occurred. If a man does not separate and confront his fear of being rejected by the woman who gave him life, he will never be his complete self. He will never truly love. In other words, a man must dare to betray the symbolic marriage with his mother. He must risk hurting her and face the ensuing guilt and remorse. To gain his independence, he must sooner or later confront the maternal dragon.

The Anger of the Good Boy

What do we see behind the good boy's overadaptation, behind his guilt and his fear of commitment? Behind this surface there hides an anger against women that goes back to the first woman: his mother. Behind the good boy's pleasant facade, there is rage, an ingrained irritation caused by his mother's violation of his personal space. In reaction to this invasion, he developed an intimate and fierce opposition to either her caresses or her blows. No wonder he has become so secretive and mysterious: he has no means of defining his private space, of coping with the maternal dragon and the woman upon whom he projects this dragon.

He closed his heart forever in reaction to his mother's intrusions, which he perceived as a betrayal of her love for him. He vowed that no one would ever again abuse him this way. But, just like the good girl, he fears to look inside himself, to touch this anger that prevents him from loving and trusting women. But eventually, this anger will have to be borne. And fate never fails to spice it all up.

The anger will start boiling again when the good boy tries to have a relationship with a woman who is emotionally empty. As she finds him unable to satisfy her hunger for affection, her disappointment may prompt her to invade his space, and his personal world will once again be treated as if it had no worth. His letters will be read, his telephone messages intercepted, and he will be accused of not wanting to make commitments. The cauldron will explode.

Nevertheless, such a forced repetition of the dramas of the good boy and the good girl may hold unexpected opportunities. In any case, it may invite the good boy to pay attention to his basic needs, one of them being the need for personal space. He will realize how important it is to define his territory and to stop being compliant. By asserting himself, he avoids the misfortune of discharging his anger on his partner. He allows the anger to be transformed into positive power, even if it appears demonic at first. After all, it is impossible to make soup, planets, or human beings, without the transforming action of fire.

In connection with Henri's process, I began to appreciate the presence of infernal divinities in religious cosmogonies. For instance, devils are the precious guardians of the vital fire. Without their support and warmth, no process is possible, and good boys remain angels with broken wings. If, at the underground level, that internal fire is unnamed anger, at the ground level it is the fury of living; on the upper floors, it is the pure joy of existing.

To connect willingly with the rage thus leads to the rehabilitation of the world of emotions, especially the so-called negative emotions that play an important role in the general harmony of the self. They are the signal that a basic need has not been respected, and when fully admitted, they allow the individual to retrieve the sense of his wholeness. It is then possible for him to heal the gap between reason and passion. The disappearance of this gap leads to the genuine liberation of the anima. From the moment the individual no longer judges his capacity to feel and to love as a weakness, he has access to the emotions and intuitions that can guide his life. The anima finally plays her proper role.

Choosing the Worse of Two Evils

In summary, the psychology of the good boy is all about a weak self-esteem. So, to feel adequately good about himself and to stay afloat, the good boy seeks the recognition of the people around him: family members, colleagues, love partners. That is why he is kind, generous with his time, even-tempered, and a real galley slave. The day when the needed recognition is missing, the voice of inner reproaches cries out. The reproaches come from two sources. First, there is the interior mother who has become a tyrant, demanding more and more goodness and perfectionism. Second, this shadow's brother takes advantage of every empty moment to make the ego stumble and plunge into the morosity of a depression. This happens in complicity with the anima who is unable to use her talents on the love terrain. The interior mother clings to the status quo and to the respect of conventional values. And as the enemy brother designs to overthrow the existing order and to establish a new mode of existence, the conflict between these two characters plunges the ego into a state of ambivalence. This is what eventually breaks down the good boy's health and his resistance to disease.

If he listens to the gentle Abel, the individual soon finds himself in a state close to terror. That is because the maternal complex raises its voice and takes on the appearance of a hissing dragon, warning the ego that shame and dishonor will result if ever it asserts its creativity. To obey the dragon means to invite despair.

Besides, it must be noted that when an individual has had major lacks in his childhood because of family events or the personalities of his parents, the parental images he integrates often preserve their archaic or mythological forms: those of children's fairy tales. Normally, these characters are humanized as the person develops. However, since many people have a tardy development because of traumas or deficiencies, they still carry the archaic forces that enslave them for the rest of their lives.

The conflict is sheer torture. If, to obey the interior mother the ego clings to perfectionism, it avoids the flames of the maternal dragon and obtains a relative peace. But this peace is not satisfying in the long run, since it is raised on the tomb of a dead child; it has no stamina. And the child comes back each night to haunt the adult. He then tries to ignore the child by hiding under a kind of sugary comfort, by indulging in the best of foods and the best of sex. He puts up with it, so to speak. Deep down, only the ego sees through the imposture. But changes are for later. Finally, he may not be so unhappy; but neither is he so happy!

Like Henri, some individuals disdain comforts and use spirituality as an escape from both the mother and their wounded creativity. Yet they risk seeing life completely pass them by. They take refuge in a fear that transforms the shadow's brother into a demon equipped with all the vices and sensualities.

The fear of living and spirituality are not to be confounded. Authentic spirituality is a flower in the midst of life. It does not dread manure, nor the depth of the soil, nor the sun's heat. It needs to make love, dare I say. It cannot be developed counter to sexuality, counter to the life force itself. A spirituality that does not integrate sexuality in a broad and vital movement becomes tedious. It becomes the servant of the negative maternal complex that forbids living. It is based on an unconscious fear of life, thus losing all its value as a growth vehicle for the individual.

Creativity alone has the fire, the power to transform cowardice, obsessions, deficiencies, and wounds, on the condition of course that we have the courage to approach it. Otherwise, all the pain that an individual can suffer makes no sense and no one benefits from it. In this latter case life becomes a muddle of bitter reproaches against parents. The individual who has not dared to confront himself cannot benefit from a difficult childhood. He will never grasp the full value of all his problems, how they can serve his self-knowledge and be transcended. Without this transcendence, he will never get close to the ecstasy of living. The good boy can only resolve the neutralizing inner conflict by choosing the worst between two fires: the maternal dragon or the infernal fire. He must choose the infernal fire. The inevitable effects of this choice will be chaos, rage, fear, and guilt. But they are transitory. We cannot avoid getting scorched, and we may even lose our lives. To endure the torture, we must ask ourselves continually: Is life worth living when our soul is betrayed?

A full, exuberant, bustling, and spontaneous life is our most precious essence. What avails the good boy to be loved by everyone if he ends up losing all value in his own eyes? To respect life is our first duty, and as clumsy as we may be in doing so, it is still better than having a life based on controlling the lives of others because we have reached a state of psychic death. True beauty is based on the respect of creativity and is never dull. Psychic death is like a drought. It kills more surely than famine or war.

We cannot escape being carried off by the force of spring when the breakup occurs. It tolerates no procrastination and threatens to smash everything. We can only follow, happy and content. The ice finally breaks. One day or another, sooner or later, we must have the courage to confess our sin against life and listen to our inner voice. Otherwise, by allowing our sources of interior renewal to dry up, our sense of self will be lost and we will perish in the most absurd way.

8

Reflections on the Role of the Mother

THE MOTHER-SON DIVORCE

Why Is the Separation Between Mother and Son Important?

This chapter is not officially part of the trajectory of this work. However, since the previous chapters gave abundant considerations on mother-son relationships, I decided to present a few thoughts on the maternal role. I hope they will help in alleviating any anxiety my words may have caused.

During a workshop on mother-son relationships, a fifty-year-old man told of how he felt enormous pressure from his family, who wanted his parents to move to the apartment above him in the building he owned. He could not get used to this idea, and after searching why he hesitated, he said: "The fact is, I'm not afraid of having my parents live above me; I'm afraid that my father will die and that I'll be alone with my mother.

The very thought of her living on the floor right above obsesses me. I'm unable to say yes, but just as unable to say no!"

The story does not require a lengthy epilogue. This man does not wish to reproduce the living conditions of his childhood when he feared that the powerful domination of his mother would curb his access to manhood. At age fifty, he makes it clear to us that he is still not separated from his mother. He is still imprisoned by the maternal complex. How should he avoid such a drama?

The Mother-Son Divorce: A Sacrifice

During adolescence and at the onset of adulthood, the separation between the mother and her children is generally a silent issue. There is no special ritual, and usually no discussion. There are no expressions of love or of regrets. Mum is the word. Everything should be settled as if by magic. That, however, is not reality. The son continues to live in the mother and the mother in the son, in the form of specific dynamics that are either beneficial or unhealthy, and they are repeated because they are unconscious. Moreover, the impending separation involves real pain for both sides, since a bond is being sacrificed. By dodging it, our society simply condemns this man and this woman to remain in their old roles, instead of enduring the divorce and getting on with their lives.

When the relationship between two persons has been as intimate as mother and son, the partners are bonded for life and must undertake a conscious labor to avoid the development of harmful dynamics. Even if they have not lived together for many years, even if they never talk to each other, or exchange only on trivialities, the mother and the son are bonded in their unconscious. In fact, it is because of this bond that our childhood continues to live in us in the form of ideas, emotions, and behaviors that permeate each moment of our existence.

In my therapy sessions and seminars I insist on the importance of mothers to understand how difficult it is for the son to become a man, especially if the father is often absent. She must accept that her son cannot be her partner, or her friend, or her lover. She must face real mourning. She must learn to let her offspring go, and see where she stands in her life as a woman, without trying to compensate by becoming indispensable for her son.

The mourning is more difficult for mothers than it seems at first glance. In the workshops I directed for mothers and sons, I realized to what extent mothers found it difficult to separate the mother from the woman within. They accepted easily to recover their wishes and their dreams as women, but they still wanted their son to be the chosen witness of this development. To me, it seemed that they somehow wanted their son to give them the same attention as a lover would.

A charming woman in one of my workshops wished to send the love letters she had received from her husband and lovers to her thirty-year-old son. Her wish was that her son would "know" her before her death. She complained of his resistance to her advances as he invariably repeated, "You'll always be my mother!" He was just trying to maintain the emotional incest barrier. Yet, it is understandable that a mother should find it hard to accept the autonomy of the person whom she cared for and loved the most. This aspect of the maternal drama is difficult to admit and therefore often not adequately dealt with today.

Likewise, a mother's physical desire for her son is still a totally taboo subject in our society. Yet, many mothers with whom I have worked have disclosed this kind of desire or fantasy. The repressed desire arises when the son chooses his first companion and has his first sexual experience. I have heard several mothers admit that they would have honestly preferred not meeting their son's girl-friend. This unresolved problem of incest, even as a fantasy, is cer-tainly not isolated from the difficulties experienced between mothers and daughters-in-law. The only obvious solution still holds: The mother must reinstate her womanhood and attract a man other than her son.

In the absence of dialogue, the son very often finds no honor-able way to leave his mother, especially if he has replaced her hus-band. In general, his departure is either explosive or politely silent. The physical distance he spreads between his mother and himself is eloquent proof of the size of the problem that remains unresolved and of the anger that was not expressed.

To avoid such an outcome, the mother must prepare herself to let her son follow his path toward autonomy, as soon as he reaches his fourteenth year. She must understand that to conquer his maternal complex and find his place in the world, he must over-come his natural tendency to believe that life will always be easy and without problems. He must conquer his fear and fully confront life's difficulties. To do so, he must develop a strong character, and this is done only in adverse situations. That is why the mother must do herself violence, and when the time comes and the possi-bilities are appropriate, she must let him face alone the ordeals of life. Contrary to popular belief, men are not motivated by power, but by fear; the fear of physical blows, of defeat, of having to mea-sure up to someone stronger. Therefore, it is not by hiding under Mommy's apron that courage is learned.

In reality, a mother cannot initiate her son to the masculinity that is associated with the loss of innocence. In a fairy tale entitled *Iron John*,[1] the key to virility is hidden under the mother's pillow and the son cannot ask for it; he must steal it. This no doubt explains why sons hide many things from their mothers. They know that if they behaved otherwise, she would lose sleep over it.

They thus try to create a private space where their masculinity can be developed. Of course, this learning should ideally occur in the presence of the father. When this is not possible, and inasmuch as it does not entail serious excesses, the son's secrets must be respected.

A child has a life to live and a path to follow. This may be difficult, but the best a mother can do is to get out of the way as soon and as often as possible. She finds the detachment all the more difficult because she has the impression that she created this path with the best of her maternal endowments: her love, her capacity to guide, and her caring attention.

A mother can equally attenuate the risks of conflict between herself and her son by refusing to become the father's messenger. The latter must be allowed to initiate his own communications with the children. She must particularly not fear to send her son to him to deal with subjects belonging to his area of authority. She may be surprised at the results.

The overall attitude should therefore be to stop worrying and expecting the worst, to learn to detach oneself, to let go. In this respect, here is a story about a grandmother who allowed her grandson to haul his sleigh to the top of an icy hill all by himself. In spite of his numerous falls, the child refused her help, and she finally agreed to let him go on alone. She was rewarded by a smile of victory when he reached the top and proudly declared: "I did it, Grandma! I did it!" She confided to me that had she been his mother, she would not have let him do this; she would not have had the necessary detachment. But she would also have deprived herself of his triumphant smile. This suggests that mothers would benefit from playing grandmothers before their time.

When Children Become Encrusted

Today, economical recession, unemployment, and expensive education do not make it easy for children to separate from their parents. These are all factors that influence both sons and daughters to either prolong their stay with their parents or to return after leaving. In some cases, this suits the mother, as it allows her to postpone the inevitable sacrifice and the painful confrontation with her empty nest. In other cases, the mother whose domestic duties are supposed to be terminated and who looks forward to taking off her apron now sees her role unduly prolonged. The truth is that no psychological benefit can come from remaining either in maternal or in childhood positions. It hinders the autonomy of both mother and child.

Sons have a particular tendency to fall asleep in the comfort of a situation where a servant is at their disposal. A clean home awaits them; their clothes are washed; their meals are always ready. They take all this for granted without being aware that a person sacrifices her needs to provide these services. They adopt the belief of the preceding generation, that it is natural for a woman to serve, that this is her destiny.

There must then be a courageous confrontation with the family members, so that everyone will fittingly partake in the household tasks. When actual physical distances cannot be established, it becomes urgent to create psychological distances by changing the family's habits.

If the children refuse to cooperate with the new rules and share in the chores, the remaining option, undoubtedly cruel for a mother, is to show them the door. This is, of course, a taboo gesture that will entail guilt on the mother's part. But guilt, here as elsewhere, is the price to pay for erasing the yoke of history.

If the situation aggravates between the mother and her children to the extent that they no longer talk to her and use her only to get money, it is time to call it quits, to ignore them, and to start a new life. The more a mother clings to such a situation, the more she risks getting hurt. Besides, children eventually resume their relationship once they have gained enough independence. This, however, takes a few years. It often happens that sons in their thirties suddenly wake up and recognize their parents as human beings just like them.

A mother always has to struggle to remain in touch with her femininity. She must fight against the maternal archetype; she must fight against patriarchy, against the bigotry of society, against her own children when they tend to become encrusted, and sometimes against her own husband. In any case, children need to find fault with their mother, so why not provide them with the real arguments! The same applies to couples when they separate. Even if both partners wish for friendly negotiations, they generally need to quarrel before being able to break away. Aggressiveness thus appears to be a natural aid in the separation. That is why, among other things, mothers should not take their children's blames tragically when they leave home.

In the midst of all this, it is wise to remember that an adequate separation of psychological territories between mother and son is precisely the guarantee of better relationships in the future. A few years ago, in São Paulo, Brazil, I visited a couple, friends of mine who had built their house on the property of the man's parents. In fact, the two houses are so close that they have an adjoining corridor. This was justifiable, since properties in this city are highly priced. As I witnessed the arrangement, the psychoanalyst in me could not help seeing the corridor as a badly severed umbilical cord. I finally decided to talk to my friend about this. He burst out laughing:

> You North Americans are crazy, thinking that if we live close to our mother, the symbiosis continues, and if we live further away the problem is settled. Between my

parents and myself, the boundaries are well defined. Even if the homes are close, they would never allow themselves to comment on the way I organize my family, and they would never dare knock on my door without having telephoned first!

When the Children Are Gone

When a woman has invested her whole identity in motherhood, she suffers bitterly to see the nest emptied of her offspring. She finds herself discarded along with her declining vitality, at the very time when she needs more than ever the support of those she loved so much. Imprisoned in the maternal role, she lives through her children, following the events of their lives as if she were watching a televised drama. She has lost her individuality. Her life has been devoured by the archetype.

I believe our mothers should be greeted with compassion. We should also acknowledge the fate history has traced for them and reflect on it. The archetype that inspires the greatest self-sacrifice should be perceived as a land where one resides temporarily. So, even if it nurtured the mother with all its flavors, she must one day accept leaving it to pursue her development. It means that she has to accept the sadness, the despair, and the depression of a retired mother, to turn the page and renew her life as a woman.

With the children gone, it is time for the mother to evaluate the situation. Instead of criticizing or blaming herself, she should rather honor everything she did for her children. Whether it was too much or too little, she must respect and love her accomplishments. Recalling all her sacrifices as a mother will help her to remain positive and treat herself with indulgence. The best attitude still consists in seeing the past and present difficulties as so many ordeals that will have served to help her to know herself better.

Finally, to reinstate the woman, it is often just a matter of enjoying the small pleasures of life. Each woman has a child within who needs to be allowed to live and to play. Through the enjoyment of daily pleasures, the ones that cost nothing but that warm the heart, a woman can gradually reconnect with who she is. The era of sacrifices has passed. The time to think of the self has come, even if a whole culture had forbidden this for so many years.

The happiness of the re-created woman will no doubt be the catalyst in reactivating the bonds with her now adult offspring. This is the best possible path to reconciliations.

THE SINGLE MOTHER:
SQUARING THE CIRCLE

Absent Father, Lost Son . . . ?

In France, I was told several times that the title of my first book, *Absent Fathers, Lost Sons,* could arouse guilt in some people, and that it could even hurt the women who raise their sons all alone. It seems that by aiming to awaken the fathers to their responsibilities, I have also caused anxiety in mothers. The questions posed by these women and my sense of their factual concern prompted the following thoughts on their behalf. Basically, the concern could be expressed as follows: Is it true that a single mother can do nothing to foster her son's masculinity? Or, in a more positive approach: What can a mother do to help the development of her son's masculine identity?

Let us begin by saying that it is true that the mother who is alone to raise her children has several paradoxes to resolve. When she works outside the home, she tells herself that she cannot be a good mother in such conditions; when she stays home, she tells herself that she should be working so that her children will not be deprived and so that they will enjoy the same advantages as other children. If she tires herself out and does not take the means to recover, she risks becoming too permissive or not enough; she lets everyone do as they fancy or she imposes too many overly strict limits on everyone, including herself. Because she is so often frustrated in her feminine desires and ambitions, she risks becoming dependent on her children to satisfy her emotional needs, thus entailing all the consequences I spoke of earlier. Looking at this whole picture, it is not surprising that many single mothers have a great deal of anxiety when faced with the issue of their son's education. While giving much love and generosity, they are very sensitive to the small and big problems that never cease to occur. I believe that the following attitudes may help.

Taking a Break Now and Then

I said earlier that the son needed to have a strong character in order to grow and find his place in the world. Adversity is the only thing that can form a strong character. Therefore, the mother's absence—even for short periods—represents the first ordeal that confronts the son. It is the first rebuff, the first limit opposing his sense of almightiness. In the best of worlds, it is the father who, in sharing the important father-mother-son triangle, imposes on the child this apprenticeship in frustration. But the woman who lives alone with her children can reproduce almost the same conditions, at least as far as the son's frustration is concerned, by creating what the psychoanalyst Françoise Dolto calls a *symbolic third person*.

Having a symbolic third person means, on the whole, to have an activity or a reason that separates a mother from her child on a regular basis for long or short periods of time. It may be a job, a hobby, a love relationship, or a circle of friends, no matter. What is important is that the satisfaction she thus obtains allows her to accept the guilt associated with the separation. Of course, it is always a matter of balance, and it is clear that one can exaggerate here also. The principle nonetheless remains the same: Within the limits of common sense and inasmuch as it avoids all the harmful consequences of the mother-son fusion, what is inherently good for the mother is also good for the son.

In this respect, we must remember that for children, the worst thing besides having been deprived of parents is having had too much of them. Just as the son should never try to please his mother at all cost, it is extremely important for the mother to not be perfect in everything. "I must admit that I am happy when he goes off to his father," said one mother to me after a discussion on the relationship with her son. This admittance made her woman's heart dance again . . . and her son was no worse off for it—on the contrary!

Allowing the Son to Resemble His Father

We know that children need mothering and fathering. We create the masculine from the masculine and the feminine from the feminine. It is therefore important that children have enough interaction with significant persons of both sexes. However, it may happen that the shock of the separation impels a mother to prefer keeping her son away from his natural father or from other masculine influences he needs to develop his male identity. This is not beneficial and indicates the need for this woman to settle her problems with her ex-partner, if at all possible. She must also examine the life she had with her own father. Simply because, as long as she has not settled her problems with these men, she will tend to repress the child's inclinations and behaviors that remind her of those she loved and no longer loves. In other terms, she will find it difficult to allow her son to resemble his father or his grandfather, which is inevitable anyway. He has it in his genes, as we say.

This may have serious consequences for the child. For example, the child whose mother openly denigrates the father (and vice versa) will be caught in a conflict of loyalty. He will have one attitude toward one parent, and another with the other parent, a behavior that reveals how much he is divided, which is not very promising for his future. But if the child realizes that both his parents are able to cooperate in spite of their separation, that a form of love and friendship persists beyond the gap, he will be reassured. That is why we must encourage and help the struggling partners to settle their differences. When this is impossible, they must be warned about the danger in not respecting the child's love for the absent parent. His father may be an alcoholic or a criminal, and the child may still love him. And unless it involves moral or physical danger for the child, provision must be made for some kind of contact.

On Being Careful of How We Speak of the Father

The importance of paying attention to how we speak of the father, the importance of the qualities we grant him and the names we give him in his absence, is clearly shown in the studies on sons of widows.[2] It was noted that the sons who had hardly known their fathers and whose mothers did not remarry were better off than the children who had been abandoned by their fathers. The reason is simple: Widows tend to idealize the departed husband and to remember only the good times. "When your father was here . . . ," they begin, and then create in minute details a positive image of the father, which the child will make his own. He does not have a real father, but he feels supported and accompanied by an interior figure, one that confirms his legitimacy.

One of these fatherless sons who had been born in a small village told me that his father was always spoken well of, and that he never stopped being proud of him. The son, now divorced, has nevertheless no problems being a father to his two small daughters, who will always be a priority in his life.

The mutual esteem of the ex-partners is thus a primary condition for developing the positive feminine and masculine images from which the child builds his identity. This is because the two parents, even separated, continue to form a couple in the child's mind. His ideas of unity, cooperation, and complementarity are based on this couple, and will serve him throughout life. It is not the divorce that is so catastrophic for the child; it is how the parents cope with the separation. Mutual respect is the best guide for adopting appropriate behaviors.

Above All Else: The Child's Welfare

When both parents are able to collaborate, they will find it desirable to share guardianship according to the various forms that best meet the child's needs. When collaboration is impossible, it is better to grant guardianship to one of the two parents, to prevent the child from becoming a hostage in this love war. The psychoanalyst Françoise Dolto even recommended in these cases to leave the boys with the father and the girls with the mother; the proximity of the same-sex parent will thus assure the formation of sexual identity. It must be added that it will be much easier for the child if the rights of guardianship are flexible through the years and also if the separated parents do not live too far from each other.

When children can count on their parents' love, they are able to develop in the most intricate situations. I once knew of a ten-year-old girl who was separated from her father at the age of three; she had lived with her mother, who subsequently had another partner during five years. Afterward, living alone with her mother, she became, in my view, a model of sensitivity and creativity. She made friends easily, and without subservience. She had become superbly autonomous. The tribulations of moving from one home to the other, from one father to the other, did not seem to have perturbed her. What was her secret? It was the love of her natural father and the love of her stepfather. Both literally fought for her presence. She felt loved and wanted; she felt welcome everywhere she went. The collaboration between her mother and the ex-partners was exemplary. Everyone seemed to have adapted to the situation, and the child's welfare was their main priority. The girl was never made to feel rejected or responsible for her mother's separations. On the contrary, she knew she was loved, and this was the source of her self-confidence.

I Did It My Way . . .

Research sheds further light on the importance of the single mother's spirit of independence as an element of success for her children's education,[3] particularly in relation to her own childhood situation. The less she feels forced to do things the way her mother did, the more she and her children will benefit. She will have more freedom in following the models of education and interaction best suited to her situation, even if they have nothing to do with the models sanctioned by the cultural influences of her original milieu.

The mother must remain in touch with her own being, and do things her own way. She must not listen to whisperings around her, dictating a line of conduct for her children or her ex-partner. In other words, she must not subordinate the well-being of her children to family pride and morality.

Trusting One's Children

Instead of trying to fill in the gaps as soon as they appear, it is better to say honestly what is wrong and to let the children find the solutions to their own problems. Children are able to cope better when faced with obvious frustrations than when they are unexpressed, and frustration is a source of creativity. The following example summarizes this reality. It is the testimony of a seventy-year-old widow who had to raise her three sons on her own.

When my husband died, the oldest of my three sons was thirteen, and the youngest six. It was a terrible shock. Overnight, I had to go to work to put bread on the table. I was very conscious of the need created by the father's absence, so I took the following measures. To start with, I inventoried the men in my family and in my husband's who could be possible substitutes in each son's case. I didn't ask for a large scale presence, but a constant dosage through the years. That's how each child acquired a kind of tutor, someone with whom he could share an activity from time to time.

I told my children: "Your father's dead and you need a father, so you'll have to find the men who can play this role!" I put aside the fear of possible molesters, and began to encourage my sons to associate with teachers, trainers, or other older men. I did my best to support their male friendships and their membership in organized groups such as the Boy Scouts or the neighborhood softball team. All in all, I find that all this went rather well. Today, my three sons are each married and earn a good living.

This woman's genius is that she did not treat her children as dead weights by shouldering all the responsibilities. She was aware of the profound deficiency they would suffer, but she trusted their capacity to fill the void left by the absent father. She also overcame the understandable fear that something grievous would happen to them; this was another mark of her faith in her children and in her destiny. In other words, she did not want the family to withdraw onto itself because of her fears.

Among other things and in all circumstance, the right attitude must be sought. The mother must be sensitive to the suffering of the child by giving him the time to experience his frustration, by giving him the opportunity to fill his own needs creatively. Finally, she must remember the woman within and give herself the chance to satisfy her needs, the chance to stay alive in spite of maternal duties. As I mentioned earlier, children may not always follow their parents' advice, but they never forget the example of a courageous mother who remained young at heart and full of vitality.

RECONCILIATION

The period of reconciliation between a mother and her son often begins under the banner of reproaches. Reproaches a mother finds difficult to hear. She has identified with her maternal role for too long, and she needs to uphold the image of the good mother because that is all she has left. She cannot understand that the reproaches, far from being a sort of vendetta, are the beginnings of a reconciliation. The bad blood must flow once and for all before any real love and affection can reclaim their rights.

I accompanied in therapy a man in his forties whose main childhood memory was of having been beaten by his mother. One day, he confronted her with this. She asserted that she did not remember having ever lifted a hand to him. The son took it upon himself to recall the precise circumstances. At this point, the mother began to cry, accusing him of folly and malice, asserting that whatever she had done was for his own good. She then retreated into an impassable grief, interrupted by heart-felt sobs.

My patient grasped at this point that behind the mother figure, there was a woman in hiding, that her investment in the maternal role was so great that she had lost sight of who she was; her personal identity merged entirely with her family duties. She could not remember what had happened because this would have threatened her psychological balance. It was as if her identity had been extracted all at once. She was not hearing that she might have made mistakes in performing her maternal role; she was hearing that she was a bad person.

In the months following, the poor mother thought she would go crazy. She felt judged, that a tribunal was sitting inside her, obsessing her with the guilt of being a bad mother. So she cut herself off from her son and built a wall of silence between them. All this lasted until he assured her that his confrontation was not meant to hurt her but, on the contrary, to form a more authentic relationship. The argument reassured her, and the broken bonds were repaired.

During the following year, she became ill and had to be hospitalized. At her bedside, holding her little hand in his, the son felt great waves of tenderness and emotion. He wanted his mother to live. He was filled with joy, feeling so much love for the human being who had given him life. He knew at that moment that the dark times he had imposed on his family for so many years had not been useless. It was the first time in years that he was conscious of having a real emotion toward his mother; he was finally able to love. And his love was no longer imprisoned by the resentment he had felt until now. I wished to know whether he would have gone to his mother's bedside if there had been no confrontation. He answered yes, but that he would have done so out of his duty as a son, and not the way he finally did, out of love for the woman who gave him so much.

Stirred by this eloquent testimony, I cannot but encourage mothers and children to lift the veil of the past; it proves to be a forceful action toward enhancing what remains of their lives. It is not a matter of indulging in endless reproaches, but rather of creating a space where each can recount his version of the family story while being listened to and respected. Mother and child need not have the same view of the story. They must simply try to understand, without judging each other.

Many adults are reluctant to disturb their retired parents for fear of hurting them. I persistently entreat them to put themselves in the place of these parents who do not understand why their children have taken their distance and finally broken all ties. Would it not be better that each presented his truth, so that the relationship can be rekindled instead of letting it smolder in the ashes of indifference and superficial politeness? To a patient who feared that he would literally kill his parents by behaving this way, I heard one of my colleagues respond: "You won't kill them, you'll add ten years to their lives, and liberate them from the burden of the past."

How can we hope to settle world problems if we do not have the courage to talk to those who gave us life? How can we believe we can mend the social fabric if we never dare to address what has not been said, what could not possibly be said during childhood? Through my own experience of talking honestly to my parents, I realized how much this liberated me. I stopped being afraid of people older than myself and I now enjoy their company. I feel more deeply energetic, because I am no longer split from those preceding me. I know that, according to my capacities, I am simply going ahead on the journey begun thirty thousand years ago when the first humans arrived on earth. I rediscovered my parents and the sense of my personal history.

9

Love in Distress

When we love, there is no difference between biting and embracing.—Heinrich von Kleist

FROM SOFA TACTICS
TO BEDROOM BLOCKADES

The Reign of Repetitions

We are now at the culminating point of this work: man-woman relationships. As discussed in the first sections, the impasses of the present are largely explained by those of the past, since they are simply reenacted at the fore-scene of love relationships.

My belief is that we persistently repeat the same behaviors as long as we do not disengage the symbolic image imprisoning us behind all these repetitions. The lesson is always the same: It is by daring to confront the paternal or the maternal monster that we deserve the right to be ourselves.

The majority of individuals find it difficult to feel, to validate, and to express their real needs for fear of being judged or ridiculed. All sorts of internal complications prevent them from obtaining what is good for them, and this applies primarily to their choice of love partners. They must not be judged on these relationships, for who is to say which partner will best lead a man or a woman to self-knowledge and to the confrontation of what lurks in the unconscious? We will therefore examine the expanse of these repetitions on the couple terrain, while keeping in mind that they constitute opportunities of becoming aware of the unconscious dynamics at work.

Living in a Couple Is Not an Obligation

A word of warning is required. The couple ideal can become tyrannical, and we must take our distances from it, so as to be able to discuss it honestly without having the impression of committing a crime of lese majesty. To me, it seems impossible to discuss any love life if we do not first step backward in order to gain some perspective on the subject. While admitting the fundamental importance of the couple in a society, it must not be seen as an absolute. People who live alone are quite capable of living full and happy lives; they may cultivate selective heterosexual or homosexual relationships or remain sexually inactive altogether.

If we accept the idea according to which only heterosexual couples should form our society, that they should be sexually faithful and committed for life, we may as well never address the difficulties of the couple. The existential ordeals of couples make sense only if they lead each partner to a form of self-scrutiny that includes their sexuality and their life-style. The couple must not be made into an essential condition of life. This would be equivalent to considering those who do not adapt to this form as "abnormal." And they are not rare.

In reality, the couple is not everyone's cup of tea, but almost everyone tries to join the tea party, with more or less cheer. What do you expect; we no longer have convents and monasteries to justify celibacy! In view of this situation, we could find it advantageous to speak of the couple as a vocation, of celibacy as a vocation, of homosexuality and even "Don Juanism" as vocations. These could be callings for the soul to seek its most fitting expression through a different life-style. This would avoid our judging and condemning all these forms . . . and having to explain everything.

With this warning in mind, we may begin our discussion by paying a visit to *the man* and *the woman* who have just left the sofa battlefield and are now in the bedroom . . .

The Woman

Well! You can't say the evening was a success. After the afternoon dispute, you're still tense, and so is *he*. You're sad. You tell yourself that you must do something anyway, otherwise the way things are going . . . no, you'd rather not think about it. He's still in the bathroom when you enter the bedroom. You remember vaguely the words of a friend who suggested that in desperate situations, black lingerie and vodka are always great armaments. As for vodka, you won't go that far; but the lingerie is worth a try. Yes, the lace bra and the garters . . . that always keels him over.

The Man

You enter the room. She seems to be sleeping already. So much the better, because you really don't have the energy for anything, and certainly not those interminable pillow discussions she likes so much. She calls this intimacy. Well! As far as intimacy goes . . . ! You put out the light and lo, under the sheets, your hands can't believe what they feel. Ah! The little rascal is wearing her garters and her lace bra. Even if you pretend not feeling, your heart is beating faster than before. You even sense an erection coming. You get closer and hug her warm body. Your worries have already gone. She resists your embrace, finally grants you a kiss, and asks you to light a candle. She plays the untouchable virgin, and you have to admit it works every time. You love the fact that she is never quite won over, as if it were always the first time.

The Woman

You feel his hands on your body, and it reassures you. Your little stratagem works. You begin to relax little by little. It really wasn't so difficult, a pair of sexy garters and there you are. His hands wander over you and you feel like cuddling up to him. You feel him all over your back; he's getting excited. You rub yourself against him and you surrender languorously. The problem is that he's already concentrated on your sex and your breasts. He's already pinching the tips but you aren't yet aroused. You try to play anyway, hoping that you'll feel something, but nothing works. The more he gets excited, the more you pull back. After a certain time, you start getting really nervous. You feel more and more like an object, like a toy he uses only to give him pleasure.

The Man

All was going so well. It was so exciting. Of course she had to start being complicated: "Kiss me! Kiss me all over! My back, my legs, my shoulders; I need a little bit of tenderness. I need a little bit of romance."

Romance! The gross word has been said. She always finds you too unromantic; you are too hasty in doing the deed. Your male pride has just been given a flogging. The truth is that you have never understood her idea of romance. When you desire her passionately, it means "sex"; and when you don't want her, she says there's a problem in the relationship. The other day, after a somewhat drunken party with friends, you had tried to kiss her under the full moon, while going back to the car. For you, there could be nothing more romantic. You didn't want to make love on the street, you only felt like playing the teenager. And even here, you're told that you're obsessed and only want one thing. The next day, she excused herself by saying that she was preoccupied with her job. But you, you're more and more confused. Does being romantic mean that you should never have an erection when you kiss her? You're simply not built that way, and that, she must someday understand. Grumbling, you turn your back to her and snuff the candle.

The Woman

Another bedroom impasse! It's obvious. You tried to improve things, but they only got worse. You feel ridiculous in your lace bra and your garters, so you hurry to take them off. You do so noisily, making sure that he cannot help but notice. Is it so difficult to understand that you crave tenderness? Is it so hard to understand that you like being won over slowly, that you like being desired, and divined? It isn't that you don't like making love; it's the way it's done. Everything is in the manner. Sex for the sake of sex is not what you enjoy. But sex with caresses and tender words, wow! That's really something!

Ah, there he is again! Men really have no pride. Once aroused, they don't know how to stop. There he is touching your breasts again. Really, he'll never understand. And you can't lodge a complaint for sexual harassment against your own companion. You let him go ahead but you're totally disconnected. This body rubbing against you, this panting voice breathing automatically "My darling! My darling!" all seems more and more grotesque. If you don't stop him now, in five minutes you're going to feel like you're being raped.

You sit up all at once and turn on the light. You tell him in an unambiguous tone of voice: "I don't ever want you to call me darling again!"

The Man

Ah, this is too much! You answer in the same tone of voice, that not only will there be no more "my darlings" but that there will be no more real tenderness either. You've had enough of being the one who's always available. She never makes the first move in foreplay. She never proposes to make love. It's always you. But that's the end! From now on, she'll be the one to take the first step. She'll have to guess about you. If she believes it's so easy to always be rejected and to always start over again, she has a surprise coming! You're going to take a holiday from eroticism, from romance, from everything. And she can very well organize the trip.

While you're in the midst of these thoughts, you suddenly sense your father's voice within you. It makes you want to cry, this old couple scenario. The same tension, the same silence, the same problem. Your mother's fatigue, your father's unsatisfied desires, just like yours. Is it really possible? A sexual revolution later . . . yet the same old story. You shut up and turn out the light. You grope for her hand in the dark, but she turns away. She's all stiff now. Your words have probably hurt her. So you stay there with your eyes open in the dark, unable to say anything, waiting for the storm to blow over.

The Woman

You know he's there in the dark with his eyes open. You know he's trying to reach you, to be comforted. But you can't cope anymore, feeling so misunderstood. You feel you've given so much of yourself. You do everything to make his life pleasant. You're attentive to all his needs. Could he not possibly approach you with a little bit of tenderness? Is it asking too much?

You hear your mother: "Men are all p- - -!" You don't exactly think that, but almost. Will this go on forever? Will it be the same for you as for her, a long wait, and final resignation? That would be too stupid. You feel doomed. You tell yourself it's not that serious. Yet, what's going on between you two is so terribly heavy. You seem to never arrive at the rendezvous at the same time.

Run Away from Me, I'll Follow You!
Follow Me, I'll Run Away!

I know, I know . . . You thought it only happened to you! Sorry to disappoint you . . . It happens to everybody! It even happens among two men or two women. There is always the sexual element and the romantic element. And it looks so much like the Mom and Dad scenario.

I know, I know . . . There's also another scenario. He's so gentle and sweet; he cuddles up against you like a little boy on his mother's breast. He shares your caresses, but the erection doesn't come. It never comes. You think it's because your body has aged, but in reality, you could be a top model and nothing would change. The truth is that you frighten him, and he doesn't know exactly why.

I know, I know . . . There is also another scenario. Between you two, things are good sexually. The problem: Sex is the only thing that works. You take the initiative to caress. She takes the initiative to caress. You invent exciting little tricks; she proposes some also. She loves dressing for you, undressing for you. That is not where the shoe pinches. The matter is, every time you want to settle a problem, something blurs communications. If you dare remark on something, she feels immediately attacked. She feels guilty and withdraws. Or she accuses you and bombards you with blame. You are no longer facing a woman; you are facing a little girl. You try to explain the basics of communications between two people, how to be somewhat rational and logical, to be coherent with oneself; absolutely nothing changes. So, using your great wisdom, your diplomas, and all your psychological knowledge, you begin to accuse her of being the cause of all the ills on earth. And she tells you that this is no way for two responsible human beings to communicate.

The woman goes toward *the man*; he becomes irritated. She turns her back on him; he seeks her out. He keeps her at a distance, but when she threatens to leave, he retains her. Run away from me, I'll follow you! Follow me, I'll run away! The distance is forever the same between the two. They never meet.

The man and the woman do everything possible to maintain this distance, because at the unconscious level they are too mingled in each other. The web of projections and expectations they unwittingly spin around each other is what prevents true harmony. Their territories are confused, and there resides the reason for the war. Their conflict is based not only on "who is serving" and "who is being served," it is based on discerning "who is who."

We could be tempted to admit that this is so. For in order to break away from our historical heritage and to arrive at forming a couple wherein two identities may exist, each person must be differentiated, and conscious of oneself. The inherent frictions of relationships thus offer a great opportunity to achieve this consciousness.

Seen under the positive angle of a quest for differences that leads to true harmony, this war may thus be seen as a battle for love. It serves the equality and complementarity between *the woman* and *the man*. It is true, however, that it may also distance them for good if they do not succeed in containing the tensions existing between them.

Essentially, the frictions send them both back to what the other provokes in him or her. That is where self-knowledge begins, because our reactions do not belong to others, they belong to us. Whether negative or positive, the emotions, thoughts, and even the feelings our partners stimulate in us are disclosures of what we are, and they reveal what we still ignore about ourselves. This self-knowledge prepares the way to conscious communion in love, where each gives up his munitions and his powers to experience Unity.

It is therefore good for each of us to plunge into this world of repetitions that, if well understood, may lead to a better knowledge of self and of life.

THE FEAR OF COMMITMENT

Never Make Your . . . Partner . . . Cry!

The dysfunctional father-mother-son triangle drives the mother and the son into a symbolic marriage; a peril for the future man-woman couple. The son's first unions will plainly serve to demythi-cize the maternal image. Most of the complications would be avoided in this area if the father had claimed his role as the mother's partner and had given his son the attention he needed. This not being the case, the latter struggles with a maternal com-plex that devours him unawares and that he projects onto his com-panion. The projection automatically provokes the repetition of the past; he will begin to behave with her as if she were his mother.

In reality, few men have conquered their maternal dragon. Besides, we sense the vestiges of the negative maternal complex in the almost universal complaint of men: "I suffocate with my part-ner!" Hearing this, we get the impression that they suffer from the *noose syndrome.*

Better known as the fear of commitment, the noose syndrome rests on the sacrifice of the need of affirmation and autonomy, on the interdiction to express negative feelings, and the repression of sexuality, all having been experienced during childhood. The ele-ments of this tacit contract between mother and son are quite often transposed as such in the couple.

As I said earlier, a good number of men do not succeed in conquering their maternal complex, and remain imprisoned in guilt, inhibited in their power of affirmation. For these men, "Never make your mother cry!" becomes "Never make your partner cry!" The fear of saying no to the one we love has quite a perverting effect, because when an individual is unable to affirm his resistance, he is also unable to open up and say yes. When a man, like our *man*, has difficulties in claiming his space in the love relationship, when he continually steps aside presumably to please his companion and avoid causing her suffering, the latter ends up feeling extremely lonely.

Through fear of displeasing, he overadapts. He serves his partner as he served his mother. All this with the intention of making her happy and obtaining a smile. So much so that she sometimes goes into therapy to complain: "Oh! He's very nice, he takes out the garbage, he prepares meals. He cries from time to time. But I feel abandoned!" If she dared, she would add: "My impression is that he has no balls!"

Obviously, the strategy used by *the man* to avoid a conflict with *the woman* does not make her happy. To avoid all quarrels, he leaves the whole domestic and emotional territory to her. The ensuing loss of vitality is severely felt by the couple.

During a therapy session, a "good boy" voiced his thoughts on the difficulty of separating from his wife, as he kept a mistress for several years: "I believe I'll be able to leave my wife only if I'm sure she'll forgive me." He hoped she would absolve him in advance for the trauma she would suffer because of the divorce. He chose to remain in an ambiguous situation because he feared to hurt someone. The truth is, by pretexting to spare his companion, he was only protecting himself; he had to uphold his image. He did not want to be the culprit, the executioner, the one who brings misfortune. He had thus forced the couple to tolerate years of unsatisfactory marital life by fearing to confront his maternal dragon.

The man himself also suffers serious consequences by denying his needs of affirmation and autonomy. We frequently see "good boys" succumb to bouts of aggression when the repressed power of expression comes out in its negative and destructive form. Anger can break out at any moment, whether in reaction to incongruous remarks, or when he has had too much to drink during a party. Even if he never intended to be the executioner, the one who brings misfortune, he is compelled to get rid of his interior tensions. And when the situation becomes unbearable, he ruins the lives of all his loved ones.

Even if *the man* feels guilty, he does not understand the true reason of his anger. He does not understand that the unconscious is thereby seeking to break the status quo that is artificially upheld by the ego. He does not understand the psychic importance of this ill temper. He does hear the voice of his creative anima trying to pull him out of his morosity and to lead him to his true vitality. He only knows how to excuse himself for his excesses, only to start over again at the next opportunity. Nothing will be resolved until he makes contact with himself and ceases to judge his inner movements. The time has come to stop pleasing Mommy and start pleasing his soul in its search for a fuller expression.

Sometimes, *the man* is able to choke his fear of displeasing and his aggression by hiding in silence. If I asked him why he finds it so difficult to speak in his most intimate relationship, he may very well end up saying that he is ashamed of what he feels. He is ashamed of his aggression and his negative emotions. Defining his space in the couple is an arduous task, since he has no personal inner space. In fact, the other side of guilt is shame, shame about internal movements, shame about having personal needs.[1]

This is also explained by the fact that a man is educated to live externally to himself. The internal world is forbidden to him. In his view, to express emotions is to act like a woman. Moreover, by exposing his intimate feelings, the man fears that he is supplying his partner with munitions. He fears being controlled and losing whatever small space he occupies. He defends his identity by being silent.

If I also wanted to know why women's tears frighten him so much, he would tell me that when he was small and his mother was *so huge*, her tears were like a calamitous storm in his child's heart. Her suffering became his. And now, it is the same catastrophe that explodes inside when he is the cause of his partner's grief.

In fact, with his hero education, he has learned to be responsible for his companion's moods as he was responsible for this mother's happiness. However, he will never find his freedom or maturation within the relationship without accepting that by expressing his needs he may hinder his partner's needs. He has to accept that she will be hurt, but that he is not responsible for her pain. Symbolically, it is by accepting his power to impose pain and discomfort on his loved ones that a man will begin to conquer the maternal dragon. To overcome his complex, he must withdraw from the sacrosanct image of the good boy.

His decision to be himself, to occupy his rightful space, will no doubt upset and endanger the couple's dynamics. But if *the woman* and *the man* both go through the ordeal, their union will be all the more vitalized. It will cease being an alliance based on principle and formalities; it will be based on the closeness of two authentic individuals. Intimacy is possible only on this condition.

Contempt for Women

It is not all men who hide their weakness under the cover of honeyed overadaptation as does *the man*. Some find self-affirmation so difficult, and fear so much succumbing to a woman's grip, that they decide to control all the home activities. They insist on denigrating and criticizing their partners for fear that they may take too much power. The need to dominate is a reliable witness of the magnitude of an unconscious maternal complex. The man tries to conjure the internal spell by subduing and commanding the woman he lives with. By reducing her to the level of an object, he tries to avenge what he experienced as a child with an overbearing mother; he reveals symbolically that he also was reduced to the rank of a commodity for his mother.

In any case, it seems to me that male animosity toward women expressed in denigrating jokes and in subjugation has only one hidden object in perspective: the negative maternal complex that continues, from the depths of the unconscious, to oppress an ego that has never dared to assert itself. The man casts all his bitterness and helplessness on his companion. Yet, what appears on the outside to be a total contempt for feminine values is intrinsically the only defense system of a disabled little boy who cannot appropriate his power of affirmation.

Forced Sexuality

Sexuality is one of the major modes of human expression. Are we not the product of the merging of two sexed cells? Every fiber of our being is imbued with sexuality, and it is illusory to think of repressing it without expecting all sorts of deviations.

In traditional families, not only was it normal that sexuality had no place in the mother-son relationship, but there was also no place for desire and eroticism. We simply did not talk about these things. Such an austere environment is bound to deeply affect a couple's sex life. As a result, the majority of men are convinced that women have no sexual desires. This is because many mothers have reclaimed their virginity in giving birth. It seems as if their devotion to their children became their main priority, compelling the fathers to be solely responsible for that unspeakable thing, sex.

Negative judgments toward male sexuality are a poor prepara-

tion for men's marital life. On the sexual terrain, more than any-
where else, men must be heroes and take initiatives. They are usually the ones who have to take the risk of being rejected or ignored
by their partner, which can aggravate the wounds already inflicted
on their self-esteem. They have learned to stifle these hurts, and
their companions are usually unsuspecting.

In the bedroom, as elsewhere, men like to perform. But their
sense of duty can often prevent them from being truly present to
their partners. They never learned to relax and share pleasure with
partners, and cannot possibly surrender. At the finale, men feel
obliged to give caress for caress as in a timed ballet. Deep down,
they continue to be good little boys trying once more to please
their mother.

"I'm Sorry, But It Excites Me When I Caress You!"
Men often feel so guilty about their sexuality and their sexual
desires that they end up with quite surprising attitudes. During a
workshop where I was having a discussion with a group of men on
the subject of intimacy in love encounters, one of them told me
about his main problem when making love. He always had an erection at the beginning of foreplay, which he thought indicated a
basic egotism and a form of contempt for women. He had the
impression that he should be completely at the service of his companion, and that he should forget about his own pleasure.

I realized that much like a few other men in our group, he was
ashamed of his inner world of sexual fantasies. He had a problem
with the idea of having pleasure while giving pleasure. He fondled
his partner's breasts and sex, all the time disregarding his pleasure
in doing this. Sexuality had been repressed in his family, to the
extent that his natural drive was greatly inhibited. He could not
believe that his own excitement could arouse and stimulate his
companion.

The Toothed Vagina

My belief is that the popularity of peep shows and erotic phone lines where women take the initiative and men confess their deepest fantasies illustrates quite adequately the type of sexual impasse we are discussing. Also, men need not be heroes to transact with a prostitute, either in person or on the telephone. One pays and owes nothing. By using an easily disposable woman-object, we can avoid commitments and the risk of smothering. One step further away from danger are dolls we can inflate and put away. Escaping interaction with a real woman altogether is another example of the fear of castration that haunts a lot of men. When the maternal figure is not demysticized, the young boy's fear continues into adulthood, since these are different courses men take to resist facing women who remind them of it. This fantasy takes the primitive form of the witch's toothed vagina, which can sever a man's penis. I have met some men in the course of therapy who were afraid of fellatio because they sensed they might lose their organ.

Fantasies and sadomasochistic practices also appropriately express this unresolved aspect of the mother-son dilemma. Tying up a woman, torturing her breasts, making her suffer—all are symbolic expressions of the need to conjure feminine power, that is, maternal imprisonment. The practice in reverse also expresses the same situation. The man who is tied up and humiliated replays, at the sexual level, the psychological atmosphere of his childhood.

It is interesting to note, for example, that the clients of prostitutes who are typically dominating are often men who are in high-powered positions in their business or in society. Sexual masochistic play is a way of expiating before the maternal dragon the sin of having dared to steal its authority.

However, it is not only maternal power that is at stake here. We can also see how the lack of a father or his absence from his children's education leads to a major frailty in the son's sexual identity.

Men suffering from this childhood experience are often not sure of their masculinity and are afraid of entering women, both actually and symbolically. In the actual situation, the result is premature ejaculation or impotence; at the symbolic level it is the fear of intimacy with the woman. As it expresses the need to penetrate all women, Don Juanism can be linked equally to the attempt to escape from the mother's castrating power. Don Juan frantically tries to prove to himself that he is not afraid of his partners.

That is why men can enter their first relationship by unwittingly projecting a shrew onto their partners, a shrew that threatens them with castration. Besides, the fear is based on reality, since, because of the rage of having lacked their father's attention, many women in their relationships are turned into unconscious agents of castration toward their partners. The couple provides the terrain for both men's and women's unconscious vengeance wishes.

The Panic Signal

As I said earlier, the fear of castration is manifested in various ways: indulging in a peep show, viewing pornographic videos, or making love in the virtual reality of one's computer. By abolishing the sense of continuity with others, we avoid getting caught in debts and duties, but the situation still represents castration. We enjoy a form of eroticism in which the other person does not exist, or rather exists as an object serving our satisfaction. There is no loving commitment, and therefore no inherent risk. Moreover, a lot of consumption of pornographic material finally generates a dependency that masks the real need, the need for love. In the long run, a habit like this only brings discontent to the soul in search of an intimate union.

Everyone knows that there is nothing more pleasurable than making love when we are in love, because every strand of our being partakes in sexuality. Those are the moments when differences disappear in deep fusion. Yet, we know what difficulties and rejections had to be negotiated to reach this sometimes brief ecstasy! This is enough to justify solitary pleasures as acceptable substitutes for such a rare and difficult experience.

However, pornography risks to reinforce guilt toward women and to enslave the man even more to the maternal dragon. In fact, as this form of sexuality is usually performed secretly, the man regresses to the rank of a little boy who conceals his libido from his family. Later, as he cannot fully assume his desires in the presence of his partner, he hides his blessed images under the bed, in forgotten drawers, on closet shelves, and in the computer.

A friend confided to me that on one of his computer diskettes he can watch couples making love. The program is equipped with a panic signal that he can use if anyone enters his office without warning. The screen then presents a sheet of accounting figures. Nothing more trite, you might say, but the sheet comes from Mother Teresa's accounting book. I laughed heartily when he told me this. He had just confirmed to what extent the sexuality of men takes place in the wake of a holy mother, virgin, and martyr.

Sexuality is very important in men's lives—much more important than we like to believe. The proliferation of pornography and sexual tourism abundantly confirms this fact. Our attempts to understand the symbolical aspect of sexual habits may give us the opportunity to grasp what is being acted out in these behaviors. We may get an inkling of male emotional suffering, a misery that often has nothing to do with sexuality itself.

For example, I had a patient in therapy who traveled a lot and who, from one hotel room to another, had developed a stock of devices to hear what went on in the next room. His most frenzied and satisfying masturbation sessions occurred when he heard an unknown couple making love. As he had been seriously deprived of his parents' attention when he was a child, he resorted to stealing the intimacy of strangers. This produced the sense of being a nuisance to his parents, especially his father, who had excluded him from the family circle. After listening to his story without judging the behavior, I was able to help him go back to the origin of the problem. The obsession proved to be a disguise. It expressed his rage and his suffering as a child.

Men go into love and romance through sexuality, while women go into sexuality through love and romance, and this creates great differences between masculine and feminine cultures. My impression is that men are able to blossom out in the couple on condition that their sexuality be taken seriously, even in its repugnant aspects. Fantasies must be accepted as an expression of a person's depth. A man will invest himself totally in intimacy only when his sexual vitality is greeted without judgment, and it proves to be the perfect zone for symbolically working out the unresolved maternal and paternal complexes. It is not a question of acting on the fantasies, but to articulate them in order to understand their unconscious motive.

The Voyeur Who Closed His Eyes

As we proceed, we realize that the sexual male drive is still the hostage of silence and timidity. A lot of men are not able to tell their partners what pleases them, to tell her how much they enjoy touching her and looking at her. The whole situation is a paradox, since women wait impatiently to hear themselves valued by the words of men. Women put a lot of effort into making their bodies attractive, their skin soft, and they expect the appreciation of men in return.

On this subject, a thirty-year-old man shared the following anecdote:

He had been married for six months, and he and his wife had rented a new apartment. The living-room window faced the bedroom of a woman who undressed with the light on. For this man with voyeur inclinations ever since his childhood, the situation was wonderful. He started to let his wife go to bed alone after the TV news, so that he could stay in the living room and masturbate while staring at his neighbor.

After a few months of this stratagem, he finally felt rather uneasy and decided to confess to his wife. She responded very tenderly: "How strange, because when we make love you always keep your eyes closed! For someone who enjoys looking so much, you never look at me when I dress up for you or when I enjoy sex. I too need your eyes; I need to hear you say I'm beautiful. I'd like you to tell me that my breasts are beautiful, and that you find my vagina enjoyable. I'd like to see us break away from our prison of conventional sex. I'd like to invent games and scenarios we could play. I don't want us to make love with our eyes closed anymore."

The man had closed his eyes so that his true sexuality would not be seen by his partner. His guilt prevented him from understanding how much his wife needed to be looked at and appreciated. In reality, a lot of men think they cannot carry their desires and pleasures as far as the bedroom. They continue to take pleasure secretly, just as they did in their childhood, and their partner's body remains a forbidden territory, just as in the past when they could not approach their mother's body.

The Triumph of the Spirit of Seriousness (bis)

Whatever the case, our male and female bodies as well as our psyches belong indefinitely to our mothers, to our fathers, and to our whole original milieu. It seems normal that confusion should exist between the individual's ego and the psychic background linking him to the unconscious component of the family. What I just said about men's psychology is not pathological, even if it points to a little boy who is still struggling with his mother. It may become so if pleasure occurs only if we are tied up, or if an erection can be held only when masturbating and not with a real partner. As for the rest, it is only at the cost of sustained efforts that we gain sovereignty over ourselves and are liberated from the past. To become conscious is often a difficult task and leads to choices that are difficult to make, but the outcome warrants improved vitality and creativity in our relationship with life, with others, and with ourselves.

This sexual misery is most distressing because it marks the triumph of the spirit of seriousness. There is no joy or pride in being a man when one's sexuality was adversely greeted by the family. Few people are able to bring their lightness as far as the mattress. Even among the most fantasy-ridden partners, nothing seems to be as serious as making love. Silences, expectations, shyness, and sometimes even shame penetrate our erotic gestures. Our bedrooms are haunted by a colossal number of ghosts: Mommy, Daddy, the Reverend Curate, past or present mistresses and lovers. That is why the real revolution consists in creating a true and unique space for two in an authentic relationship.

Furthermore, a man's fantasies and his playfulness are often dampened when he finds himself in the presence of his partner. One man related that the only times he sensed his father's exuberance was when his mother was absent. It took a flash instant for the house to be transformed into a wonderful playground where his father vivaciously activated treasure hunts and performed tricks of magic. As soon as his mother returned, he became serious again. What is it that prevents a man from revealing his enthusiasm to his partner? Is it because he is still not separated from his mother? Is it the fear of being judged if he dares be spontaneous and vulnerable? Why is it even more difficult to assume joy than to assume sexual desire?

In final analysis, we could say that the real victim of castration in our families is not sexuality, but joy, the simple joy of existing. Enthusiasm and vitality are the real victims; they were sacrificed on the altar of patriarchal puritanism and seriousness. In fact, we cannot recover these gifts without liberating our sexuality.

Joy is the indication that the relationship flourishes and that Eros is alive and well; his assignment is to rally men and women. When we are not able to enjoy this love deity, we surrender to a sad and conventional angel with broken wings and poisoned arrows.

How Men Try to Master Their Fear of Women

Within a relationship, a man uses various strategies to master his interior fear of women. The first, to which I have already alluded, could bear the name *total dependence* toward his partner. In her official position as a substitute mother, she is the one who protects him, who washes him, who chooses his clothes, who loves and pleases him. She allows him to remain in the sweet irresponsibility of childhood, even if his needs of affirmation and independence take a beating.

For the man who is very sensitive to smothering and who cannot tolerate the caring attentions of a woman, the second strategy is to make her pregnant. In this way, she will devote all her attention to someone else and her partner will feel relieved of his emotional responsibilities. In this case, the prime art consists in letting the child sleep in the conjugal bed between the two partners. This assures the continuation of the race of men who suffer from maternal domination and who are afraid of establishing links of intimacy with their partners.

The third strategy involves what I call *counterdependence*. It is a sort of defensive celibacy. Its protagonist might say: "I'm autonomous, I look after myself at every level, I don't need a woman in my life!" In other words, the counterdependent chooses his clothing by himself, eats by himself, and pleases himself! His lot is an empty bed, solitude, and occasional sexual encounters. He represses his need to be united and dependent. His innermost self weeps as he practices self-discipline and austerity.

As a result of the sexual revolution, a fourth strategy seems to have gained popularity. It is a satisfactory method for the man who cannot settle down in dependence or in counterdependence. The practitioner of such an art likes to court *segments of women*. Let me explain: He goes out with one woman because she is good in bed; he courts another because she enjoys the theater; and he hangs on to another because she is interested in mysticism. He is thus able to cater to both his needs, to be united and to be separate.

The fourth strategy basically comprises a postmodern elaboration of the famous split between the virgin and the whore, a vision common to a lot of males. The fifth strategy, then, is *to wed an honest and respectable woman* who pleases the man's family, to confine her to the home, and to have a mistress with whom he can run off. He lives a sort of double life, either to preserve his social image, to let the children grow up, or simply because he does not have the courage to separate. In several ancient cultures, for example, those of China and Japan, this custom is officially accepted. The mistress is even introduced to, and approved by, the wife. However, we must note that in these cultures the status of mothers is the ultimate goal of women, and the men have enormous maternal complexes.

If we consider more closely the range of these strategies, we are aware that it is not really the fear of *women* that conditions their use, but rather the fear of *one woman*. Men fear to be alone in intimate situations with one woman because the phantom of maternal domination forever haunts their psyche.

THE NEED FOR ROMANCE

Why the Couple Is So Important for Women

Men are brought up to be heroes; women are brought up with the dream to live in a couple. If the man's maternal complex usually emerges on the terrain of sexuality, the woman's paternal complex will be replayed on the terrain of love and romance. If men suffer from the *noose syndrome*, we might say that women suffer from the *lasso syndrome*, the wish to capture their man.

As I explained previously, the father's absence leads to a major consequence, that of a wounded self-esteem that affects the woman in her power to relate. While she feels reassured about her identity by the presence of the mother, her sexual difference is not validated by that of the father. There is no recognition of her value as a sexually attractive woman; she cannot love herself as long as she is not loved by a man. She is thus obsessed with the wish to pair up. To confirm her personal value, she seeks at all cost the eyes of a man on her, one who speaks tenderly to her. This is not the voice of love, but rather the cry of her wounded self-esteem. In many cases, the confusion comes from women's psychological heritage, which gives them the impression of being entirely altruistic while their behavior indicates their aim to occupy a central place and to prove that they exist.

The status of womanhood is nonexistent for these women. They feel they cannot be happy or even live without a partner. They believe that love is a solution for everything, that it will fulfill them and compensate for their emptiness. They are convinced that by caring for a man or a child, they will find happiness.

Moreover, the woman who was brought up without fatherly attention may even believe that by applying her control, she will secure the approving gaze of her man. She will thus resort to all kinds of contortions and maneuvers to reach her goal. All methods justify her purpose of provoking her unwary man to give her his undivided attention, and there are no limits: seduction, submission, silent withdrawals, sighs, and tearful tantrums.

This ends up producing the opposite effect, as her attempts to alleviate her insecurity will force the man either to flee or to remain attached for reasons other than love. For example, he may feel guilty about abandoning a woman in distress, and the guilt will be all the more active if he has not conquered his negative maternal complex.

Speak to Me of Love

The sorcery of the Yaquis of northwestern Mexico teaches that men draw their strength from the brain, and that women obtain their energy from the vagina. The Orient professes that men are influenced by Yang, the active creator principle of the universe, while women identify with Yin, the receptive principle. Jung believed that the masculine principle depended on the Logos, or the spirit in general, and that the feminine principle depended on Eros. In brief, *the man* obeys the Law of Reason; *the woman* obeys the Law of Love.

This is universally true: Women in general swear to a manifest love cult. I consciously use the word *cult* because in certain respects it refers to the religion with Venus as its deity. Women renounce much in the name of love; they make offerings and are always ready to celebrate its epiphany. From one love round to the other, they observe a time of rest. When love is present, they give it all the space. The world of Eros has its love potions and its spells, its mysteries and anesthetizing mists. Also, if we consider nature with its gales and tides, thunder and lightning, floods and droughts, we realize it describes this world more adequately than does psychology.

That is why women are sensitive to poetry. It breaks the linear aspect of rational language and expands it to figures of style, metaphors, and moods. Nothing is more satisfying for the feminine soul than to inspire a love poem. I quote the following lyrics of an old song as a fitting expression of this:

> Speak to me of love, repeat the tender words
> My heart will never be weary of hearing your sweet discourse
> As you forever repeat the words supreme:
> "I love you!"

The song is a unique expression of feminine desire. Nothing better reveals the feminine soul than the spirit becoming poetry, than the Logos embracing the adornments of language.

This Ink Is My Blood . . .

In his play *Cyrano de Bergerac,*[2] Edmond Rostand gives a master demonstration of poetry inspiring the expression of feminine desire. The intrepid Cyrano is disfigured by an enormous nose and cannot hope for the favors of his cousin Roxane, whom he loves. She is in love with a handsome but foolish young man. Cyrano offers his poetic talents to the ignorant suitor, so that he may win Roxane with his letters. The first words of love that overturn the Belize's heart are the following: "This paper is my voice. This ink is my blood. This letter is me!" This is how the "word becoming flesh" personifies the feminine animus. When Roxane reads "This letter is me!" she has the impression that she is touching the soul of her beloved.

Also, when she meets her suitor in person, she is all relaxed, receptive to his amorous words; but he can only repeat mechanically, "I love you! I love you!" while attempting to kiss her. Roxane is so disappointed that she repudiates him. This leads to the famous balcony scene where, replacing the young man in the dark, Cyrano reclaims the heart of the young woman by reciting gallant pledges.

For Roxane and for *the woman*, as well as for many others, the love spirit she inspires to her lover is much more important than her physiological reactions. She really wants to kiss him, but the ambience around the kiss is more important than the kiss itself. In the absence of this erotic ambience, when the two persons are not bound by Eros to the same spirit, when the act has no soul, the woman feels reduced to the rank of an object. Sex for the sake of sex does not interest her. This explains the fact that pornography does not attract women very much. What they want from love is the revelation of a complementary soul.

Therefore, just like Roxane's young suitor, *the man* is incapable of love talk. He is imprisoned in silence as was his father. In such a context, *the woman* will try anything to "get her man to speak." Through what appears to be all sorts of caprices and manipulations, she will put him in the situation of an obliging knight in spite of himself. One might think it is essentially a matter of feminine egotism, or the demands of a wounded person who finally reclaims her right share of attention. But the issue goes further.

In her gut feelings, in the twilight zone of things-we-know-without-knowing, *the woman* senses that her fulfillment depends on devoting her whole being to love. She seeks in personal love a way to unlock her strength. If she can convince her companion to give a bit of himself, she will make him happy in return. That is why Roxane demands that her suitor play the romantic hero before surrendering to him.

THE MEANING OF ROMANCE

The Practice of Systematic Error

The world of romantic reverie has also its negative aspect. While it compensates for the pettiness of daily living and prevents suffering, a woman may easily lose herself in such a world. Her fantasies serve as a screen, protecting her from reality; it makes her project on any new partner the prince charming he cannot be. In her imagination, she turns him into a serving knight, and little by little the shock will make her confront herself: The actual man is not what she imagined.

Romance can even influence some women to systematically choose the wrong lover. For instance, a woman may confuse machismo with real strength, believing that she will find security with a partner because he looks strong. The surprise will come when aggression is turned against her. Another woman will interpret silence as wisdom, only to realize later that the man in question simply had nothing to say. Another "falls" for the charming language of a seducer as she mistakes personal interest for devotion. After surrendering body and soul, she will realize that she fell into a trap.

The same applies to the girl who had the tendency to personify her distressed father's anima, to respond to his feelings as a way to place herself between him and the mother. By becoming the confidante of an alcoholic or depressed father, she learned her role as a victim. In the aftermath, her search for a protector will lead her repeatedly to choose a dependent man who will abuse drugs or alcohol, or who will be unable to support himself. She will be tempted to play the savior and bail him out.

The unconscious hope of the woman who marries a man in distress is that she will finally awaken the prince sleeping in his heart. He will then reveal his deep feelings and will confirm her value.

"Someday my prince will come!" is her secret formula. However, if by chance the frog turns into a prince, it is often to abandon the very princess who supported him in his struggle.

The woman must then be conscious of the weak self-esteem she carried over from her childhood and which leads her to choose men who do not respect her. She will one day discover that her capacity to love with such abnegation is simply a compensation for not loving herself adequately. By trying to help her partner to master his dependency problem, she only masks her own.

The Guessing Game

Romance also has other traps. A woman's anticipation of the prince charming leads her to harbor a deep bitterness, constantly stimulated by being disappointed in the man she lives with. This is especially revealed in his incapacity to guess the contents of the feminine world. She would like to find a man who can satisfy her wishes without her having to enunciate them.

This is a paradox. While a woman prides herself on being competent on the emotional terrain of relationships, she very seldom dares to reveal her innermost desires to her man. She is wrong in believing that he knows her right away, and secretly accuses him of being unwilling to respond to her wishes. She considers the game worthless if she must tell him everything, because if she openly expresses her wishes, the gratification will be lessened. The naming of wishes certainly takes away the mystery, but how can the communication between two persons succeed if they are not ready to clarify their true desires?

Women believe that men are like themselves and that they excel in the guessing game, but their partner's intuitive and emotional abilities are often atrophied because their education did not encourage these assets. Men feel more comfortable in obvious situations. I myself prefer to hear my companion say, "I'd like to go out to a restaurant for a tête-à-tête dinner with you," than have her tell me reproachingly, "You never want to be alone with me."

On the other hand, a woman's intuitive sense may also torment her because she believes what she imagines about the man's world. In advance, she puts ideas in his head, feelings in his heart, and words on his lips. She mistrusts him if he ever says anything that does not represent the inner universe she thought was his. No wonder men are silent in such a context. They neither feel heard nor respected for their personal truths. They feel controlled in advance and no longer speak when day-to-day encounters expose them to partners who think they know more about their interior life than themselves.

The Difficulty of Communicating Clearly

To communicate clearly, one must be open to the other's reality and take a bit of distance from oneself. If a woman cries or expresses disappointment every time her companion opens his mouth to talk about his feelings, he will eventually stop communicating. He will feel smothered, rebellious, helpless, and caught in a double bind. She claims she suffers from his silence and invites him to express himself, and then as soon as he opens his mouth, she takes over to talk about herself or to contradict him. Communicating in this style is sure to lead to her unhappiness as well as his.

In such cases, we get the impression that this woman's style of communication aims above all to find out what her companion thinks of her. Her need to be the center of a man's life and conversation indicates a narcissistic wound that may interfere with the sanity of the couple, which is based on mutual respect. It is legitimate to wish hearing what the partner feels about us, but why not clearly state it: "I want to know your real feelings about me!" or even "I need to hear what you think of me." However, we must be willing to greet the response (or no response) as it comes, and act accordingly.

In spite of their ease in navigating on the sea of emotions, women often find it difficult to communicate with clarity. When among other women, they easily express their frustrations, but it is entirely different when they confront a man. Therefore, as long as this attitude is not challenged, chances are that the unexpressed expectations will burden the relationship and make the man run away. Fruitful communications between two beings cannot exist if there is no effort to understand the needs hiding behind emotions and frustrations and if they are not named and expressed as realistic demands.

The woman must understand—and the man also, of course—that there is no magical partner descending from heaven who will understand her needs in advance and who will respond even before they have been said. The prince charming will never come. He is a mythical character whose message conveys a state of interior well-being, but who has little to do with those hairy creatures called men.

The same applies at the sexual level. Most women hate to be treated as a sexual commodity by their partners, and they complain ardently to him about this. Yet, when the man's desire flinches, they no longer feel desired and question the couple's vitality!

This is a double bind that makes togetherness difficult. It would be much better to express one's desires honestly; it would be more beneficial than the incessant complaints that crush the man. A woman tends to complicate relationships, and in so doing discourages the man. Overall, men seem to find it more difficult to express their feelings than women do.

As long as a woman makes no room within herself for the basic divergence of the masculine world, she obstructs the equality she seeks with her partner. Why not accept the man with his differences? If it is true that men are generally more cerebral and women more instinctive, why not use this fact as a basis for communication? Masculine reason contributes a bit of relativity, a useful quality when dealing with wild feminine emotions. Why not laugh at it all instead of taking offense?

THE WAR OF THE SEXES

Creating Infantile Men

Encouraged by patriarchy, our mothers have become women of duty and principle who promoted the spirit of seriousness in the family. Confined to the kitchen and to the children's education, they quickly lost the sense of play and pleasure. Their personal desires were drowned in the bitterness of having been abandoned by their husbands. Viewing life in this perspective, many women ended up having a poor opinion of the men who shared their lives. For a long time, in Quebec, mothers have repeated to the daughter who was about to marry that the first child they would raise would be their companion!

Young women thus learn to control their partners in the same way they witnessed their mother's power over her husband. Through speech, sex, complaints, sighs, and humiliations, they try to teach their companion to relate, and their lengthy monologues on the subject of couples are interpreted as authentic dialogues.

In reality, a lot of women are not aware to what extent they can be "controlling." Indeed, feminine authoritarianism is often unconscious, and this subtle coercion was once called "love" in the couples of preceding generations. When it comes to the education of children and to intimacy in love, women sincerely believe they know what is best for everyone. However, when a woman imposes herself as the only specialist regarding the relationship's emotional situation, she behaves as if in spite of herself, she were still with her father, that is, with a silent and closed-up man. The couple ideal she thus professes, and to which all men should bow (according to her), exerts a real tyranny that crushes instead of rallying.

Many women judge that this coercion is a worthwhile war in the face of men's irresponsibility and oppression toward them. Perhaps. All the same, as a social phenomenon, it perpetuates a power struggle between men and women in their private lives. The attitude hides a secular rage and a contempt toward men. It does not lead to equality. It undermines the unwary couple. The coercion plays on the masculine fear of castration, either leading the man to revolt or to endure the infantile position he is offered. Such leniency does no good, as he loses his partner's respect, and if he revolts, the couple will be caught in endless discussions.

The woman who infantilizes her husband inevitably ends up with a man who resembles the father she had condemned during her youth, a mushy man lacking stability. Consequently, she will feel the gift of herself as an abuse and a servitude.

The Murder of the Patriarch

Men and women do not necessarily take sides in monolithic units as the oppressed or as the oppressors. Social and ideological masculine oppression occasionally finds its counterpart on the private terrain of emotions, where some women exert a form of dictatorship. And since they continue to consider themselves as "victims," they are unaware of their oppressive power.

In this respect, Jung has often emphasized that the opposite of love is not hate, but power. When we no longer love or feel loved, a conflict ensues, and this is particularly true for couples. As love decreases, it is replaced by a war of nerves.

This is equally true for the woman who is disappointed with the relationship with her partner. A mute protestation rises within her in opposition to her husband and her children. This is the voice we discussed earlier, that of the animus imprisoned by a negative paternal complex. However, Jung also saw this dominating attitude as an effect of a negative maternal complex. He said that such a woman had a poor relationship with her mother, and that consequently, she is unable to identify with traditional feminine attitudes and behaviors. She wants to live in a bright world without the darkness of the maternal environment. If she finds a companion who is able to greet the strength and originality of her spirit, her animus thrives. If not, she falls into morosity and is possessed by an animus that does everything to break the man's strength.[3]

The play *The Father*, by the Swedish author August Strindberg,[4] offers an excellent demonstration of the conflict. Strindberg's work sheds light on the unconscious dynamics that exist in a patriarchal couple. The social context of the play is also very interesting, as it was written at the end of the nineteenth century when feminism was making its way in Norway. The women of that time were facing a world where all was under the rule of the father, a world where women rightly exist only in the kitchen or the bedroom. This happy servant must smile continually. Having no space to exert her power, it can break out in the most perverse manner.

The play presents Adolf, an army captain who is passionately interested in scientific research, and his wife, Laura, who drives him insane and has him hospitalized. The wife is bitter, ready to do anything to upset her husband's reason, to free herself of his power. The argument she uses is a terrible one in a realm of patriarchs. To keep their daughter at home when Adolf proposes to send her to study in the city, Laura insinuates that he is not the father. This idea infuriates the captain and finally makes him insane.

At a critical moment in the play, Adolf tells his wife that she is responsible for his insanity, because all she seeks is power. Laura admits to this. She is completely obsessed by her need to dominate, a need that invests her whole intelligence in acquiring the power she has too long been denied.

Looking on from the outside, we can understand her animosity; but inside—as spectators and no doubt as men!—we fear her, because it is the animosity of a wounded and betrayed goddess. Indeed, at a certain moment Adolf declares: "Who then directs life?" Her answer: "God, and God alone." Adolf continues, "The god of war then!" and adds, "Or rather the goddess."[5]

The text is disturbing, since it emphasizes the capacity for violence of an oppressed woman. Laura does not kill her husband with a gun, but rather reaches her goal by killing him psychologically. Strindberg himself used the expression "psychic murder" to describe what he had experienced with his own wife.

Women's Strength, Men's Fragility

There is another moment of terrible truth in the play. As Adolf relates his childhood memories, he finds himself all softened up. His wife, Laura, who is usually stony and implacable, suddenly becomes sweet and tender toward him. She takes his head in her arms, rocks him and caresses his hair, as we do for a child. She confesses that she is never as happy as when they are in this kind of situation and when he appeals to her mothering talents.

For Laura, all men originate from a woman's womb, and in this capacity, all women are their mothers. Men must remain children all their lives. That is how they attract women's love. Laura tells Adolf that it was folly for him to seek the woman in her, since woman is infinitely superior to man; she is stronger and more intelligent. She declares that from the moment he attempted to leave his position of a loving child, there could be nothing but war between them.

THE CAPTAIN: I, who at the barracks or at the head of my men, was always the leader, have been the companion who obeys you. I considered you as a supernatural creature, endowed with all sorts of gifts, and I drank your words like a stupid child.

LAURA: Yes, and that is why I loved you as a child. But, as you were able to notice, every time the nature of your sentiments changed, every time you behaved with me as a lover, I was ashamed, ashamed like a mother caressing her son! How horrible!

THE CAPTAIN: I noticed that, but I didn't understand. As I felt your contempt, I wanted to win you by proving my virility.

LAURA: Well! That's where you were mistaken. The mother was your friend, but the woman was your enemy, because love between the sexes is war and hatred. Don't believe I ever gave myself to you; I gave nothing, I always took what I wanted, that's all.[6]

This part of their dialogue is a powerful statement on the hidden dimension in many man-woman relationships. Patriarchy has held women in a state of inferiority for many centuries, but this is only the surface of the problem. The contrary may be seen if we shift to the twilight zone of the unconscious. By compensation, and as a means to reach some kind of balance, women develop a conviction of their superiority. This applies to every human being. Inferiorization induces us to dream of blatantly showing off our superiority. For women to affirm themselves, they tend to rely on the interior certainty of their superiority. They may even for some time risk a total identification with it and become, like Laura, somewhat blind.

For men, the exact opposite is true, because they believe in their preeminence, a belief they carry from their childhood that has been supported by the patriarchal culture. However, this outward superiority hides an enormous vulnerability. We see how Adolf, who enjoys a good reputation among the military, loses his authority in record time and declares that he is nothing when his wife insinuates that he is not the father of their daughter. The inferiority complex that was hiding in the unconscious has come to surface and has subjugated the conscious personality.

This hidden inferiority also explains why men react to the perplexing love situations by resorting to drugs, alcohol, and sex, behaviors that betray their interior weaknesses. Besides, statistics confirm this interpretation: Three times more men than women suffer from substance abuse.[7] It would seem that male virility is nothing but an appearance masking great dependence.

One may also associate the dependence to the lack of fatherly presence that led to the boy's psychological fragility. The identity wound inflicted by the absence of a masculine model compels the man to compensate by building a rigid armor to hide his feeling of fragility. This is what produces the macho personality that asserts male superiority over women. We may even see in this phenomenon the neurotic roots of patriarchy, which sets out a social and ideological support system to mask a deep wound. The system serves to prove that we are strong when in reality we fear our weaknesses.

Besides, pornography for men as we know it confirms this interpretation. In their suggestive poses, most of the models declare needing at all cost the male sex organ to satisfy their urge. But in real life, this is not always the case; in many couples the lady is tired of the gentleman's expectations. And so pornography serves to reinforce a failing self-esteem and applies a balm on the ailing masculine ego.

As a means to keep their narcissism in balance, men seem to

need a constant reinforcement of their virility. In some respects, the whole culture seems to be built on the maintenance of this reinforcement. It explains why bringing up the issue of patriarchy could only reveal the vulnerability, the frailty, and the helplessness hidden under the male armor.

If women can be possessed by their inner certitude of being right, men in return can be possessed by despair. They react by trying to reestablish their lost superiority—all the time deluding themselves. Often, the news informs us about a maniac who barricades himself in his house, taking wife and children as hostages. This action blatantly stages a condition of internal isolation, the reality of so many men. This violence is the pure product of a society that demands that they shut up, and it tells us how much they are barricaded inside themselves. It is pitiful to see men killing their loved ones because they have no words to express their emotions and because they do not allow themselves to show their vulnerability.

A lot of modern couples function on the basis of a reversal of traditional dynamics. When this newly born reversal is strongly asserted, the man suddenly finds himself nullified without any reason, and communications become extremely difficult. The passionate and angry goddess turns the man into a little boy who fears losing his privileges.

All this occurs as if a surface relationship of the father-daughter type were hiding a deeper relationship of the mother-son type. I am also not convinced that by passing to a surface relationship of the mother-son type and masking a relationship of the father-daughter type in the unconscious would change anything. In each couple, both the man and the woman must struggle to avoid sinking into the archaism of mother-son and father-daughter relationships. This does not mean that we do not regularly go back to these positions. However, the fixation in a given dynamic collides with psychological development, and only heightened vigilance will promote the psychological equality of the partners.

The Rise of the Amazons

Feminism has allowed many women to emphasize their amazonian qualities, to enhance their self-esteem, and to stop expecting from men the confirmation that never comes. At the collective level, this has constructed a factual generation of amazons, and at the individual level, it has led to unexpected reversals in love relationships. In the following theater creation, the German writer Heinrich von Kleist describes this remarkably well. Written two centuries ago, his play *Penthesilea*[8] already foreshadowed contemporary love relationships.

Penthesilea was the queen of the legendary Amazons, who amputated a breast to avoid hindering their handling of arms. They did not tolerate men and either killed male babies at birth or turned them into "love-slaves" to assure their own posterity, a reversal of the patriarchal situation where women were the slaves.

In the play by Kleist, the Amazons start out on a campaign, and on their way, they meet Greek troops headed by the handsome Achilles. The Amazons attack them, and in the fever of the battle, Achilles and Penthesilea fall in love with each other. As Achilles seeks by every means to get closer to his enemy to express his love, he ends up challenging her to a strange duel in the middle of the battlefield. Penthesilea accepts in spite of her sisters' incitement to be prudent, as they realize that her blood is boiling not only from the fever of combat, but also from the much more dangerous fever of love. Yet Penthesilea does not hear their plea. She does not discern her love for Achilles and swears that he will die by her sword.

Halfway through the duel, Achilles has the lead on Penthesilea but cannot bring himself to kill her. He decides to surrender to his lover, bare-chested, and to become her slave to assure his presence at her side. But because of her refusal to surrender to the weakness of love, Penthesilea does not recognize Achilles's gesture and kills him. The victorious queen is carried back to the camp by her sisters, and, intoxicated by the battle, she refuses at first to believe she has killed her lover. The priestess then has the mutilated body of the hero brought before Penthesilea.

> THE PRIESTESS: He loved you! He wanted to be your prisoner! He was ready to follow you to the temple of Artemis. He came to meet you with a heart full of joy . . . and you . . . you have . . .
>
> PENTHESILEA: No! No! No! It isn't I! . . . I would not have disfigured him . . . unless my violent embraces turned into mauls. I was overcome. When we love, we no longer know the difference between biting and embracing. [She kneels before the cadaver.] My poor Achilles! Forgive me! I could not control my amorous lips. I only wished to kiss you . . . [She kisses the cadaver.]
>
> THE PRIESTESS: Take her away from here!
>
> PENTHESILEA: You have all loved enough to want to bite! You have all whispered to your lovers that you wanted to devour them. . . . As for me, I really did so! . . . I am not insane!

Finally, acknowledging that she has murdered the only man she ever loved, Penthesilea kills herself.

There is no doubt that while the romantic author tried to settle some of his own problems by writing this play, he was far from realizing that by bringing to life the mythical Amazons he would portray the love relationships of the future. In fact, the reversal of traditional roles is occurring more and more in our relationships. Young men in increasing numbers are now accusing their same-age partners of being stony and uncompromising: women who lead the dance all the way, women who decide when the relationship should begin, how it should unfold, and when it should end. And men, while being themselves the sons of the first feminists and more openly attentive to women's demands, offer themselves, bare-chested so to speak, as did Achilles, to their ladies. But it so happens that the latter have learned from their mothers not to trust their sentiments. Women have learned to harden themselves and sometimes exaggerate in doing so. Sometimes they kill the relationship and understand only later the unconscious aspect of the tragedy.

The Excessiveness of the Goddesses

It is worth noting that in the play *The Father*, Laura, like Penthesilea, is justified by the goddess. Like these heroines, many women who have rediscovered the goddesses of antiquity let themselves believe that the deities have no *shadow*[9]—as if the goddesses were only generous, fertile, kind, and gentle, as if only peace reigned under their power. They wish with all their might for a speedy passage into a matriarchal society, believing that the world would thus be a welcoming and gentle place. Yet the goddesses of mythology have as much capacity for violence as their male counterparts. For example, the Greeks have their three Graces; but they also have their three Furies. These were totally hysterical women who represented the irrational side of feminine aggressiveness. The beautiful and wild goddess Artemis ordered her dogs against anyone who saw her bathing. She let her animals tear them apart while she looked on impassively.

In fact, mythology is full of the violence of the goddesses. It was even more horrendous as these deities were mostly characterized by a sort of excessiveness, whether it involved devotion, generosity, or malice. The modern Amazon who justifies herself through the goddesses of antiquity may also, like Penthesilea, become a victim of excessiveness. She kills her companion and breaks up the couple, only to realize some time later that she was unyielding and really loved the man.

But because of the atrocities committed by men, the violence of women has become a taboo subject in our society. This has prompted the psychoanalyst Jan Bauer to state that today's women have become untouchable and that they put the entire blame on patriarchy. As they are tired of carrying the collective shadow and of serving as scapegoats for men, they are justified in rejecting this aspect. But they forget the dimension of the individual shadow, the share of evil afflicting all us humans whether we like it or not. That is how, she continues, new hypocrisies and new taboos make their appearance:

> As if women cannot be wrong, as if they only become malevolent when provoked by men, or exceptionally, become demons! They are supposed to be always kind, always victims. Not only is this way of thinking absurd, but it ultimately deprives of all dignity. Self-criticism is essential for whoever seeks to attain wholeness. . . . The major challenge for women is to embrace their entire humanity with its dark side and its bright side.[10]

Every Heart . . . to Love Will Come

In exploring the dynamics of power struggles that take the place of cooperation and enthusiasm when love fails, we finally see that the mute war that rages between the sexes has been going on for a long time. It started well before the arrival of feminism. Yet my impression is that men have started to take it seriously only since they began to have casualties in their camp.

Today, *the woman* and *the man*, like many couples, are paying their dues. How will this war end? Because of a shortage of troops? Because of exhaustion? I sometimes wonder if the artist Leonard Cohen is not right to sing: "Every heart . . . to love will come . . . but like a refugee."[11] War may go on until the battlefield is totally devastated and nothing is saved. Then, perhaps, men and women, having become refugees in exile, will be ready to recognize their need for love. The war will have served to prepare them, to process them. It will have plowed them, tormented them, and torn them to pieces. It will have taught them the illusion of victory and the illusion of defeat. It will have made them live in the shadows of their imprisoned hearts . . . until nothing else matters but the hand reaching out in the dark.

Is it not true that many among us come to love in this manner? Battered and humiliated, we seek a final refuge. Love then appears in its splendor and we reclaim our lives, purged of the enormous pretense of exerting power on another human being. The only power we care to exert is the power of loving, loving with energy and humility, loving without pride or shame, loving like human beings.

That is where we stand. The modern couple has become a battlefield, and headline news is made in the bedrooms, kitchens, and living rooms, and in the cities and countryside. It may well be that the dynamics of domination are in the process of being reversed and that the future belongs to women, as the past belongs to men. The pendulum may be swinging from one extreme to the other. These are the very movements of life. I hope for my part that in passing from the ancient patriarchy to an eventual matriarchy, men and women will enjoy a few generations of walking together side by side in genuine fellowship. Perhaps they will learn to value this path and to abide in it.

Life Is Perfect

Whether we live according to the dynamics of traditional power or the reverse, whether we are the woman who loves too much who lives with a man who can't love, or whether we are a strong and rational woman who loves a very feminine man—we must admit that life is perfect, not in the sense that it is always good and pleasant, granting us what we wish, but rather in the sense that it always gives us what we need for our growth. It thus awakens all our complexes and forces us to outlive them instead of avoiding them. Life does not leave us alone. It constantly pushes us onward, forcing us to discover the dark and bright sides of ourselves, and leading us to realize that we are the first artisans of our joy.

10
Love in Joy

Let us drink to love and liberty, one
not excluding the other!—Julos Beaucarne

LOVE'S LABOR

"Falling in Love" Is Not the Same as Entering a Relationship

As previously discussed, the fact that we ignore our wounds forces us to repeat certain behaviors; these are opportunities to become conscious and to grow. But for the couple to thrive, we must still struggle against certain accepted ideas. This will allow us to evaluate the challenge ahead and to foresee the attitudes that will help us to face it.

Forming a couple starts with two people who fall in love. Passionate love explodes in an empty space where the lovers do not exist. Combustion is spontaneous as desires inflame the forest of fantasies. It takes only one night to organize the parade of dreams come true and to grasp the opportunity we have secretly hoped for, the chance to realize what was impossible because of our needs and shortcomings. We are suddenly transformed, so very open, so very united with life! The new partner we have who appears to be the sine qua non condition for maintaining this expansion must not get away . . . must not be let go . . . must be controlled in his every move. Through our attempts to hold on to it, the barely found joy is lost.

Love cannot save us from ourselves. Our partner cannot take us in charge. He or she takes form only in the fire of passion. In fact, passionate love is based on the needs of each lover. It swiftly becomes a prison because we ask the partner to save us from drowning and to not show his weaknesses. The victims of passion suffer from a huge interior emptiness. They may be compared to the glass beakers used in laboratories to produce a vacuum. As soon as they are set upright, they take in everything around them. Empty and desperate individuals produce the same effect. They attract and fascinate because their inner vacuum is like a magnet. When two empty vessels meet, they passionately weld to each other.

Love is an absolute trauma. We must never forget that Aphrodite, the goddess of love, was born from the testicles of the god Ouranos. The parts were thrown to the sea by Ouranos's son Cronos, who had cut them off upon the insistence of his mother, Gaïa, who was tired of bearing Ouranos's children.[1]

So we must not confuse "falling in love" with entering a relationship. The latter is a conscious and verbalized choice based on the sharing of values as well as on negotiating a common goal. Most of the time, we "fall" into the relationship at the same time as we fall into bed—and there lies part of the problem.

The Narcissistic Stage of Love

The passage from passionate love to an authentic relationship requires the transformation of a narcissistic couple into a couple in which the partners cooperate and help each other. During the narcissistic stage of love, we live in the eyes of the partner as if he or she were an idealizing mirror that forever shows a positive image of ourselves. The eyes prompt us to discover ourselves as beautiful, generous, and seductive people.

The less we have been appreciated and the more frail our identity, the more love will be important in our lives, at least the kind of love that begins in the bliss of ignoring who the other person really is and who serves only as a mirror. This stage has nonetheless the great advantage of allowing us to see our personalty in its best light. It also provides the chance to enjoy a state of fusion where all is love and harmony. These are the impressions that launch the journey, and they will continue to support the couple on its path toward a true relationship.

Contemporary couples do not last because more often than not they do not get beyond the narcissistic stage. They endure only as long as the two partners are able to gaze at each other through the positive reflection they offer each other. But six months later, the mirror has darkened. We then begin to discover ourselves vis-à-vis outside of the projection we had created. His or her reality as a wounded human being shows up, reflecting a much less flattering picture.

"You're no more than a pack of bones; I can't hug you anymore!" These were the words of a young man to his lover after a few months of a torrid affair in which his partner, an older woman, had been the patient initiator. We could restate the lover's words in the following manner: "I can no longer embrace and recognize myself through the image you send back to me!" The ordeal begins for the couple when the partner's eyes no longer reflect so faithfully our sense of perfection.

Why is it so difficult to abandon the dream we have of the couple and of the ideal companion? Simply because abandoning this dream constitutes a loss of virginity at the psychological level. Yet, no complete relationship is real without this loss. We all resist it, men as well as women, because it means approaching someone as he is and not as we would like him to be. It means loving someone even if he does not correspond perfectly to the image of the anima or the animus. A relationship is possible when the two partners both have accepted this loss of virginity.

Real communication is possible when couples are formed on the basis of fewer fantasies. Dreams and ideals can then be shared for their guiding qualities, without entailing compulsive behaviors or rash decisions and by allowing the relationship to blossom on a terrain of mutual respect.

Love Is Like a Battle

We could say that the real labor of love begins when personalities resurface with their array of pride, prudishness, and differences. However, the labor cannot be undertaken without the forceful memory of that first spontaneous outburst of love, that unrestrained emotion expressed in a passionate "I love you," the treasure to be kept as our source and ultimate goal.

Ideally, the path of love begins with "I love you and I can't do without you because in reality I don't love myself and I need you to confirm my value" and then progresses to "I enjoy having you with me, my love, I love the fact that you exist, and I no longer need you to confirm my own existence." For the couple to be a possibility, it must necessarily be based on self-love and self-respect. But we must pass from wanting to absolutely control the partner in fear of losing the love offered, to a more detached point of view whereby we allow the partner his or freedom to live. This can be an intense internal battle.

In this respect, love makes egocentricity tremble most unbearably, the egocentricity that is expressed in petty behavior, susceptibility, jealousy, and intolerance, all betraying a resistance to authentic love. Pride is attacked from all fronts by love, like a demon thrown into blessed waters. In wanting to enjoy passionate effluvia and brilliant insights, the little egocentric character will not allow the partner to cede any territory or transform himself. It will make him fight against love until the relationship falls apart and makes him complain bitterly about the misfortune he unwittingly caused.

The couple is therefore a battlefield, and the war is waged against personal pride. By sacrificing our egocentric claims, we improve our chances for intimacy. The rebellious ego will greatly suffer, and when the sacrifice seems overwhelming, pettiness will once more be the victor. Little by little, however, our consciousness is enlightened. Love finds its way and finally governs the heart.

Love with a Capital "L"

To be united in love and to live together out of love is an undisputed challenge. To make this possible, it is important to question a few accepted ideas. The first involves the belief that to be whole one must be "two." In reality, if we join someone in the hope of finding our *better half*, we are sure to fail. Simply because in a couple there is so much friction between the two partners that it is not an addition ($1/2 + 1/2 = 1$) we are dealing with, but a multiplication. Therefore, if you multiply $1/2 \times 1/2$, you do not obtain a whole unit but rather a quarter. That is where the shoe pinches. When people live together, they rapidly become a quarter of themselves. When you are alone with them, they express their vitality and creativity. When you meet them in the presence of their partner, they seem gloomy and conventional.

As mentioned previously, the ability to live in a couple is also based on the ability to live without being in a couple. Celibacy must be accepted by our society as a valid and serious option, and does not necessarily represent a diminishment or an egocentric choice. It can be viewed as an opportunity for a retreat or a means to renew our strength. It may even be prolonged throughout our entire lives if we decide to devote our energy to values other than the couple or the family. Thank God for the fact that the state of passionate love dodges people in the couple situation. As a matter of fact, extreme solitude intensifies this state.

Since living together still remains an important attraction, it may be helpful if we change our perspective on love. Most of the time, we see it as something we must cultivate. But in reality, we are not the laborers in the field of Love. The true laborer is Love itself, working our soil until it gives its best fruit. As we go along, the obstacles and problems operate on us and beckon us to accept the process. The more we resist, the more we suffer, and this proves how much we intimately participate in this Love. The goal of life is reached when we become One with the divine laborer.

The couple thus serves mainly as an area where love with a capital "L" may grow. As soon as we enter the garden of Love, all our zones of resistance are stimulated. All the acne pimples that did not appear during adolescence will pop out under the intense friction of daily living, so much so that our fears will emerge from everywhere. And they must be manifested so that we may understand and transcend them.

It is entirely normal that men and women should invite and fear Love all at once, because above all, it confirms the ego's receptivity and expansion. Yet intimacy has its purgatory, since there is still the possibility that we may lose ourselves in the partner, or the opposite, that we may withdraw into ourselves and live in the mortal solitude of superficial togetherness. We must never be afraid of intimacy with another person, because what is at stake is our identity.

The Vital Breath of the Couple

The love sentiment is motivated by a need of communion that we seek to realize by being united with another person. Our aim is to cancel differences and to finally hush the sense of aloneness and separation we are so weary of. Unconsciously, we hope to heal the narcissistic wound associated with the fact of being only a man or only a woman. Our wish is that by getting close to someone, this gap will be filled.

However, beyond our attempt to heal the narcissistic wound, we seem to have a craving for life in a couple, as if a deep communion with another person might provide the essential bridge toward resolving the central paradox of our identity that oscillates between individuality and universality. If I am able to remain who I am in another's presence without losing myself totally, if I am able to recognize myself completely in another without losing the sense of who I am, then the paradox is solved. I will know how to be one while being two, instead of being all of one or all of the other.

Happiness lies in respecting two opposite but complementary poles: on one hand, the need to be united and, on the other, the need to be separate. A couple's capacity for regeneration depends on the vital breath between the two poles. The inspiration phase is made of episodes of harmonious togetherness; the expiration phase is made of episodes in which we find ourselves alone and reconnecting with our own individuality.

Of course, our needs of autonomy may challenge the sense of conjugal unity. Quite often we prefer to forget that we still exist as separate individuals. But the model of the symbiotic couple where two people live together day in and day out in the most perfect harmony without quarreling does not stay on the road very long. Besides, this is the model that causes much suffering.

The most fusional couples usually become the most violent ones. Negative affects explode and reveal the unrecognized need for separation. It would be simpler if we could acknowledge anger and irritation as manifestations of our frustrated need of expansion. The need for autonomy could then be expressed realistically and be accommodated within the relationship. When individual demands are not taken seriously, they lead to regrettable actions or to a latent battle that prevents true intimacy between partners.

The autonomy of each partner is the issue that provokes the whole dilemma facing couples. Our primary fears are stimulated by the fear of hurting the other or of being abandoned if we dare take time for ourselves. That is why the issue of individual autonomy, with its limits and possibilities, must be discussed by the couple. It means setting up a scale based on what is tolerable or intolerable for each person. It means risking the emergence of profound differences. Sometimes, the simple idea of raising the issue is intolerable in itself. It will thus be necessary to discuss the internal threats that make the opening difficult.

It is important that each partner set aside a few minutes every day, or a few hours every week, to renew energies and to be able to regenerate the couple. Otherwise, boredom rapidly sets in and the couple flounders in a routine where nothing new ever happens. The long-term result is dryness, and for the union to stay alive, it must be formed of two individuals who never stop meeting and rediscovering each other.

When the members of a couple do not respect their individual needs for temporary isolation, all sorts of negative feelings force them to withdraw and to become the introverts they do not consciously wish to be. And so, each partner ends up in the shelter of his or her bubble; there is no communication, and the couple dies.

Claiming the space we need to grow is the essential ingredient for a viable couple. It stands to reason that the person we love the most is also the one we risk hating the most, because he or she is the one who personifies the greatest threat to our personal identity. When problems appear, we must remember that freedom is no doubt the most precious gift we can offer our partner. For love in its essence is absolute freedom. Love gives itself unconditionally. It does not imprison. The couple provides apprenticeship for this love, in the example of nature that offers itself without our asking.

Are We Able to Tolerate Living Without Controlling Someone Else?

Why must we try to rule those we love? Are we even able to be in an intimate relationship without trying to impose our will over our partner? Or is it even tolerable to live without controlling someone else? Is it at all possible to "drink to liberty and love, one not excluding the other," as proposed by the Belgian poet Julos Beaucarne?

Hardly! It seems as if the moment we find ourselves in a couple, we try to ignore the unavoidable reality of human individuality. It is as if we fought with all our might against the awareness that the other person really exists, with a background, emotions, and needs different from ours. We resist precisely because the reason we are in a couple is to repair the breach of our basic narcissism, the narcissism that affirms that we are the only god or the only goddess in the universe, the only captain on board. That is why the couple in love adopts so easily the attitudes aiming to avoid acknowledging the other person's existence.

The first among these attitudes is the one consisting in *being all for the other*. By becoming totally indispensable, we end up abolishing the reality and the difference represented by our partner. The opposite attitude consists in making sure that *the partner becomes all for us*. So we love the other more than ourselves, so to speak, voluntarily sacrificing our individuality to prevent the love bubble from bursting. The more we confine ourselves to these basic positions, the more our couple will be established on control, possessiveness, and jealousy.

Thus, every time we put a condition on love, a tension develops and causes suffering. Much of the suffering in our lives as couples results from the simple fact that we try to control our partner's life. We control the way he eats, the noises he makes while sleeping, what he thinks, the fantasies he entertains, and, above all, the interests he may pursue outside the relationship.

For example, why do we insist so much on controlling our partner's sexuality? Does it mean for us that sexuality equals intimacy? How is it that entire fates are played out around a bit of skin? Why do we have the impression that if we opened the door to such freedom, it would lead to total debauchery? Does such a fantasy not betray all the frustration we feel toward our sexual needs. Is it because our lives are joyless and that sex is the only area where we find it that we insist so much on controlling our companion's sexuality?

Infidelity

Sexuality is a delicate issue in almost every couple, because what we consider as sexual infidelities and secrets are often part of what cannot be tolerated and possibly lead to breaking up the relationship. We may of course judge the infidelities and sentence them without a trial, but if on the other hand, we agree to learn from them, they may provide an opportunity for work on oneself. They stir up our basic fears and insecurities, whether we commit them or suffer them. It is a matter of remaining in intimate contact with the nature of the experience without slumping into guilt or brutally accusing the partner of the betrayal.

If we view things from this angle, we may discover that we do not respect ourselves if we stay with an unfaithful partner. Or again, we may realize that his or her cheating is the symptom of a flaw in the relationship that puts both partners on the line. We may thus come to expand our limited conception of sexuality or, on the contrary, take leave of the person we love because we feel neither loved nor respected. Both cases will have provided an opportunity for growth.

It is important for the unfaithful partner to question himself. What knowledge of himself or of his partner does he wish to avoid by seeking love outside the couple? What is unsaid, or what is the frustration hiding behind this behavior? What interior venture into creativity has been so circumvented? What deep dissatisfaction has been negated by this? Examining one's conscience in this manner is more productive than torturing oneself with thoughts of how immoral the unfaithful behavior was or modifying one's future behavior solely in reaction to the guilt brought on by the complaints of a partner. It is not a matter of playing the good boy or the good girl, but rather a matter of seizing the opportunity to understand oneself.

During a workshop on the theme of relationships, a man who traveled a lot made the following confession concerning his numerous infidelities:

> I realized that most of the time my running away masked a deep dissatisfaction with my life in a couple, a dissatisfaction I dared not name for fear of destroying everything. Infidelity allowed me to accept a status quo, which otherwise seemed intolerable. This strategy prevented me from having to personify the "bad guy" who induces the crisis, and above all it avoided my having to go through the painful ordeal of separation.
>
> I became aware also that my infidelities sheltered me from being eventually abandoned by my companion. I had aptly buried inside the pain associated with having been cheated a few times, an extreme hurt that made me lose my illusions about love. It's as if I had vowed to never again be faithful to a woman. Besides, this led me to feel

more at ease in affairs where I only half loved, living in a kind of detachment where I could comfortably interpret the question of jealousy.

Yet, the blatant suffering—in all senses of the word—of my companions finally made me understand how, not only that I didn't respect the gift of love offered, but also how I trampled my own love ideal. Love affairs allowed me to escape from the very deep urge I have, the one that desperately seeks to achieve a successful intimate union.

I deeply regret the suffering I may have caused for others. At the same time, I don't collapse under the weight of guilt. This is my story and today it allows me to look forward to the kind of commitment that is free from rigid morality. When the heart has been touched, it recovers its integrity by itself. I know that I'll never be able to live with a partner whose conception of freedom is too narrow. Each intimate dimension must be evaluated in the light of each one's history. I need an open couple where both partners are sufficiently rooted in their personal process to understand that the unfaithful partner is the first to have to face himself.

Obviously, the question of sexual autonomy must be discussed in the light of each partner's need for emotional security. But it is not without interest, if only from a rhetorical point of view, because it brings forth another subject that appears essential if the couple is to have a liberating influence. The subject is friendship between the two partners.

To Love As Friends

How many partners are really able to say that they love each other as friends? When our identities are fused in the couple, we can only hear from our partner a quarter of what our friends might tell us. We do not judge our friends, but we judge our partners because we identify with them. They are "us." Yet, one of the factors contributing the most to the creation of true intimacy is friendship. It allows us to greet the other and to understand him according to his personal life experience, full of stories and issues that are not our own.

Friendship allows the couple to breathe. It is an anchoring factor, more solid and enduring than sex in building a long-term relationship. It is based on authentic communication, which is itself based on language that expresses emotions. In friendship, everything may be said and everything may be received without judgment. Few couples achieve such understanding. Those who do so display an aura of creativity and real love.

Friendship in love is difficult because it binds us to a real task of detachment, not the kind that leads to indifference, but to a "letting go" attitude that lets the partner be who he is. We thus cease to want to control the aspects in our partner that irritate us. We are able to admit that these are components of our own personality for which the partner is not responsible, even if they are activated by his presence. It is possible, however, that without judging him we feel that what he provokes in us is intolerable for the moment. In such cases, it is perhaps best to take different paths.

Things Get Better when They Go Wrong

Each difficulty encountered by a couple is an invitation to face the real questions. Do we honestly believe in the possibility of being happy as individuals and that we deserve this happiness? Do we honestly believe that happiness in a couple is possible? Do we really prefer peace to war?

We are convinced that happiness and love are what we seek, yet they are really what we fear the most. Are there many people who can tolerate more than two or three days of unclouded bliss? When taking holidays, for instance, most couples start off with a smile—unless they have quarreled while packing, a "classic" proof of happiness resisted—but their return is mute and sullen. After a few days of sensual life in paradise, one of them just got up in a bad humor, without any reason, no doubt because happiness has become unbearable.

Another example? Imagine yourself coming home exhausted from work, and your companion has prepared a candlelit dinner. How enticing! How sweet and considerate! But if the next evening you find the candles once more on the table, you begin to think there is something in the wind. On the third day, the same scenario becomes absolutely suffocating. The overromantic spell will have to be broken, and one of you will spill a glass of wine, the roast will burn, or a quarrel will start around a trifle.

Happiness is unbearable; it is a state we have learned to dream about, but not to experience. We therefore need to get used to growing in the midst of positive energies, to cultivate them as we gradually grasp the attitude that stimulates them. This may bring us to forsake certain habits that too often make us heavy and gloomy.

I have the impression that as soon as we leave childhood, most of us forget that we are on earth to play and to celebrate life. We behave as if "things get better when they go wrong," perhaps simply because misery gives us the sense of existing. Sorrow is intense and thrilling! We are thrilled when we have to unravel a difficult situation, when we struggle to win back our partner, when we play the hero in a crisis. When we are unhappy, we are centered on ourselves and on our lives. We exist.

By comparison, our idea of happiness is rather static. It means sitting on a little cloud, contemplating God until the end of time. No more adventures! It means being an angel, contented with the scent of holiness. Such a notion goes against life itself. It is even said that happy people have no story to tell. But who wishes to have no story to tell?

We frequently associate blissful states to rigid asceticism. The idea lacks the force of emotions and creativity, and we are essentially the fabric of emotions and creativity. For happiness to be alive, these angelic notions have to be dusted off and we must embrace the idea that happiness can be thrilling, intriguing, and full of adventure. We must oppose the idea of a static and lukewarm joy to that of a vibrant joy, a joy that utilizes all of a human being's resources.

Our purpose on earth is to be happy. We achieve this by using our senses and all the human possibilities of mind and body. If this were not the case, we would be angels. Every couple and every individual is therefore invited to be in communion with the life force. And now that all the reasons for being together have vanished with the crisis, the only real motivation to be together is the joyful quest for harmony.

THE PSYCHOLOGICAL MARRIAGE CONTRACT

A Liberating Relationship Is Based on a Conscious Choice

In these times when our culture is breaking down, we must plunge deeper and deeper inside ourselves to find our basic solidity. Our present-day marriage contracts can no longer offer a solid base and must be replaced with their psychological equivalents. The new contract may be one based on mutual trust, in which each partner states principles that have personal meaning, and which defines a mode of sharing what the world offers. Couples will benefit altogether from this private contract. It should be officially negotiated and renewed as needed.

Yet we prefer to let things take their course because it is less complicated to do so. We are not accustomed to negotiate together in a solid and honest way when it comes to our inner universe. We have not taken the habit to discuss everything and to set up together a framework for the life we wish to share. For instance, is there enough intimacy between us to avoid building our couple on possessiveness? What are each partner's needs for personal and private time? How can this time be organized? How do we plan to settle inevitable conflicts? All of these issues and many others need to be addressed honestly, because a liberating relationship is based on a voluntary life choice.

It is also a matter of being aware that a relationship exists with its own dynamic that contains two individuals. It represents a symbolic third party whose company cannot be ignored. The union thus becomes a container we can refer to in difficult times. When we are in love, we have no problem with taking out the garbage or running errands. But when tensions arise, the same activities become a problem. We then refuse to do anything for the partner, and a power struggle ensues.

On the other hand, if we have worked together on our idea of the couple and we feel comfortable with it, it is easier to share household duties. The garbage is no longer taken out for the other person, but for "us." Extramarital affairs are not shunned in view of pleasing the partner, but to nurture the relationship.

In my opinion, unless such agreements are arrived at, the couple has still not taken form and does not really exist. By expressing and sharing the ideal, we create a common reference. These values serve as referees in difficult situations and help us to depart from power struggles without completely losing face. It is easier to admit that we did not respect a clause in the contract than to admit our fault to our partner.

The Couple We Dream About

In setting up these common parameters and values, I believe it is equally important for the partners to share their ideas on their future together. In workshops on intimacy, created in Montreal with my colleague Danièle Morneau, we usually proposed the following exercise. Strangers were organized in twos, to form fictitious couples. In the first forty-minute period, the couple had to state their idea of an ideal situation, and then negotiate its realization. Another forty-minute period consisted in planning the ideal vacation to the last detail. The next exercise had a rather dramatic effect, as the moment came for one of the partners to announce that he or she had decided to separate.

This simple role-playing reactivated some very deep traumas. The biggest surprise was to see how people who had known each other for ninety minutes were hanging on to their couples. At each workshop, I could not help seeing the power of the shared dream. I asked myself what would happen if every couple made the effort to seriously plan an ideal situation and to afterward commit themselves to its possible realization.

We do not use the power of dreaming enough. We should imitate politicians and businesspeople who always need a vision to orient their actions. Intimacy needs the sharing of each partner's respective visions as nourishment for the couple. When the couple is able to adjust these visions, it grows with less insurmountable obstacles. In any case, everything grows from the ideal we carry within us. So why not frankly put it on the table, since it will serve as our conscious or unconscious referee.

The Importance of Sensual Games

I also noted during my workshops that to be able to depart from the mental space that carries the judgments and labels we apply to others and ourselves, it is necessary to do body work. My approach is to use all kinds of techniques, from dance to affectionate touching. The latter seems especially effective and may be practiced by the couple in daily life. It simply means to touch the other person with as much honesty and kindness as possible. Our partner makes himself receptive while we express a simple sense of presence. This may last a few minutes or be prolonged. It is not a massage but a silent attention passing through the hands and which has the general effect of reassuring the partner. A climate of trust and love may thus be created outside of active sexuality.[2]

These new attitudes toward the body are absolutely essential because all our tensions and resistance are buried therein. This is particularly true for men whose body structure is often rigid. All during our childhood, we were told not to appear so sensitive or sensual, because it characterized us as effeminate. So we must learn to let go of this defensive rigidity.

To accomplish ourselves as a couple through our bodies requires that we challenge the belief that sexuality leads us away from God. In traditional patriarchal religions, it is the priests and nuns who fulfill themselves and live close to God. Sexuality remains a second choice, and the couple is seen as a sort of weakness for those who are unable to control themselves. Jesus Christ, like other great teachers, had no sex life, and his troops were entirely composed of males. We end up feeling ashamed of our humanity. I often think it would have been easier for us if he had slept with Mary Magdalene and had not been born of a virgin. Even modern spirituality invites us to an abstract communion with the universe in a sort of fusion with the cosmic being by repressing the sexual needs we have as men and women.

Yet desire is a reality, whether heterosexual or homosexual. Men and women are attracted to each other. The reality of this attraction is the very essence of the mystery of love propelling us into the life adventure. We must therefore envisage a radical change in our conception and start reflecting on the possibility that we may get close to God through the celebration of the body and sexuality. Refusing the latter reflects a concealed hatred of life and a limited idea of earthly existence.

In fact, it seems to me that by repressing sexuality, we turn the question upside down, as if we wished to grow a tree from the top. The experience of sexuality in the loving communion of two human beings may provide them with a springboard for an ecstatic experience that may eventually transcend sexuality, but which still needs to begin with sex. Besides, as long as sex remains a point of attraction, it seems to me that it has to be lived out and used as a bridge to joy. It is not sex that is faulty; it is what we do with it.

We Needed the Crisis

The new intimacy presents a huge challenge as it installs itself in the couple like a country that is barely recovering from centuries of dictatorship. To reverse this conditioning and confront the reflexes of domination and submission, it must go through a complete process of learning and deprogramming. Only a fundamental crisis could make us accept such an enormous change. We are living in unique and exceptional times. True communication is trying to be born among men and women. Democracy wishes to take its place in the couple.

I hear men and women say, "Yes, but all this time, our lives are sacrificed." If we think this way, we risk suffering from the crisis without contributing to the solution. This is the creed that proclaims that life makes sense only in a couple. But the issue is to recover the sense of life itself, with or without the couple. We are terribly flawed human beings if we believe our personal happiness depends on the presence of a loving partner. The crucial issue for intimacy is to discover that we can be happy without romantic love. When it becomes an absolute necessity for life's meaning, it poisons all possibilities of a real encounter between a man and a woman. The less we depend on our partner for happiness, the more we can be happy together.

In other words, a man or a woman must be able to transcend the sense of emptiness and depression associated with not being in love. It is only by discovering the joy of living that exists independently from romance that guarantees lasting joy as the basis of an honest and authentic relationship for the couple.

There can be no intimacy with another without intimacy with oneself. That is the magnitude of the love revolution to be accomplished by future generations, a love revolution we can share if we accept the crisis and the lessons it conveys.

11
Intimacy with Oneself

We have the age of our tenderness. What wears
us out is unused love!—Stan Rougier

Healthy Intimacy Begins at Home

I stated in my introduction that I did not know of any other way to leave the love battlefield except by examining ourselves assiduously. It is still the only consideration on which I insist at the end of this long journey. We are placed before the following choices: either there is really a meaning in what we live and encounter, or it is all an absurd comedy; or all these difficulties really reflect our own hidden dimensions, or life is a lottery and we have simply chosen the wrong number, that is, the wrong partner. I believe for my part that the repetitions we go through are absolutely not accidental and that, on the contrary, they reveal our hidden dimensions, which we must not only discover and explore, but transcend.

In other words, intimacy with another sends us back to ourselves, and intimacy with ourselves allows us to improve our intimacy with others. In brief, it is the way of love. Most of the time we confine ourselves to the pole that involves meeting the other person, without ever looking into ourselves. This is equivalent to exposing ourselves to the mercy of events, which sentences us to a state of waiting and dependence. It is true that in reverse, some people confine themselves to the pole of intimacy, sharing their depth but neglecting the actual relationship. This is a delicate position and may lead to a dead end where the interior landscape is dried up.

Love is eminently difficult and will certainly be so forever. It is a constant challenge. But if we accept the proposition that the difficulties it presents are not chance occurrences, we may finally discover their meaning. They will become, through constant attention, the springboard for a deep communion with the partner, with oneself, and with life.

Intimacy with another rests on our capacity to turn inward. The crisis experienced by present-day couples is inevitably forcing us to recognize this fact. When money, children, and the judgments of others are no longer the reasons for staying together, perhaps personal development will be the factor responsible for the union's stability.

The challenge of intimacy is an invitation to work on oneself. It appeals to the capacity of either partner to respond to the couple's emotional needs as conflicts arouse them, instead of waiting for the other person to do so. It is a deep commitment to oneself and to life.

It is no minor task to choose what is best for ourselves by consciously letting go of what belittles us and makes us suffer. We experience a real attachment for the things that destroy and obliterate us, as if a bad habit of hatred and inner conflict prevented us from pursuing what is good for us. For example, we all know that a little bit of physical exercise daily is greatly beneficial. Yet, many are those who know this and who continue to do nothing while hoping that a magic wand will protect them from becoming ill.

In the same way, we prefer to sleep on the illusion that a fantastic love will change everything and will avoid our having to take charge of our lives. Yet the practice of loving ourselves a little every day can go a long way in making us feel better. We need to be present to ourselves, to our pain, to our sadness. Being attentive in a kind and nonjudgmental way can bring about an important change. Our hearts can be healed by granting ourselves some of the care intended for the beloved. This compassion is the secret of self-respect; it is the basis of self-esteem. It takes only a few moments every day to practice.

In reality, no love is possible if we do not love ourselves. It means being good to ourselves and to be lenient instead of being mercilessly demanding. It means passing from the childhood condition where everything happens by chance, to being an adult who is responsible for how he or she feels. Loving ourselves means also to understand that the universe responds to us as if by magnetism and that to be able to give ourselves what is best, we must cultivate internal conditions of goodness. In brief, the best way to avoid being fascinated with partners who do us no good and who induce us to repeat the past is for us to have access to another attraction, that of peace and inner joy.

Loving oneself means to live in the love of what is given rather than in the quest for what is lacking. This also involves cultivating a relationship with what Soufi mysticism names the inner Beloved. When love is within and not only without, when we have taken the responsibility to respond to our own needs, then we cease being victims. We become aware that the love we seek is everywhere around us and that, consequently, we cannot lose it. There is only love. It is simply a matter of recognizing it in the tiniest details and of greeting it. No need to be perfect or imperfect, or to wait until we accomplish this or that. Love is there! It never ceases to wait for us. We have only to grasp it.

The Meaning of Difficulties

Another way of looking after ourselves is to look at every relationship in the light of how it affects our interior life and to decide whether or not we wish to maintain it. We may then have to break certain bonds or recognize that we stay in relationships that are obviously negative because a separation would cause too much suffering. It is important to forgive ourselves for such attachments and to fully live them, so that we might gain emotional knowledge and wisdom from the experience. When separation is too painful, we postpone our exploration of the darkness. It is not a question of transcending the difficulties but to go through them to learn about ourselves and the world.

In romantic love, self-hate is at the center of the dilemma, as we are unable to separate from someone who belittles us. The magic of individual liberty is such that no one will stop us in our predicament, no matter how possessed we may be. In any case, as long as we are inhabited by melancholy, we risk turning any plot against ourselves. We may even ask ourselves if it is desirable in such a context to encounter ideal love. It will only postpone our awareness of our inner misery and will make us live with the illusion that love has been restored. But nothing has been accomplished at the conscious level, and no choice has been made in favor of openness and joy.

When we accept to acknowledge that small or great events are the concealed effects of our desires, those we care not to admit as well as those we cherish, we free others from their responsibility toward us. When it is no longer Daddy's or Mommy's fault, or the government's, when we acknowledge our entire responsibility for what goes on within us, it is then possible to find some meaning in our difficulties.

In reality, from a therapeutic point of view, we may even say that difficulties contribute to understanding ourselves and the universe, whether they are psychological ordeals, accidents, or illnesses. They are not gratuitous. They lead us to ourselves. By accepting them completely, we give them the chance to speak within us and to deliver their precious message. Otherwise, they only repeat themselves until we have the wisdom to pay adequate attention to them.

Seen from this angle, we may even add that from the moment they become conscious, the most difficult relationships are certainly those that bear the most fruits. They require enormous efforts from the individual and compel him to recognize himself completely in a partner who disgusts him. The bigger the shadow integrated, the more rapidly we advance. This is no doubt what the poet Rainer Maria Rilke meant when he wrote, "We know little, except that we must stick to the difficult."

It appears that the real reason for sharing our lives with someone is mutual stimulation. This is what allows each partner's creativity to explode. However, to realize this creativity, the members of a couple must immediately accept that the issue is not what they consider as "positive" or "negative." Life stimulates us in different ways; it strokes sometimes the right way and sometimes the wrong way. Each must judge by himself what is tolerable or not.

Finally, we have to admit that the condition for knowing joy instead of distress is based on our having experienced great suffering. Wisdom demands that we embrace life as it is without judgment. In general, we acquire this ability through repeating the same limiting schemes until our thirst is quenched. By stimulating self-knowledge, the couple's difficulties in daily living become a path toward a more intense communion with the universe and with each partner's life force. This intense communion may be revealed as much in torment as in ecstasy. Life does not discriminate in its methods for awakening us and leading us to discover our basic identity.

What follows does not mean that each must not go his or her own way when the situation is blocked and there is no more creative communication. But in general, it is useful to remain in the critical situation until we are detached enough to separate without accusing the partner for every error. By vigilantly observing a frustrating situation without judgment, we may understand the part of ourselves that led to it and avoid reproducing the same thing in the future.

The Broken Mirror

The passage from seeing ourselves as a victim to concretely perceiving the way we create our own destiny is the most profound revolution an individual can accomplish during his or her life. It is a turning point that no one can do without, even if the majority of people avoid it without batting an eyelid. This is a true passage of initiation and is comparable to the transition from childhood to adulthood. Paradoxically—even if it requires leaving the state of childhood—the spirit of liberty, of play, and of lightness will not prevail without this mutation.

To become conscious of the need to take ourselves in charge because love will not save us is an invitation to release the partner from our demands. It means that we stop asking him or her to bow before the ideal masculine or feminine image we carry within. Withdrawing the animus and anima projections is the only way to recuperate our personal power and touch our basic self. To achieve the knowledge of our essential identity, we must absolutely accept the shadow aspect we carry. No psychological or even spiritual progress is possible if we maintain the illusion of projections.[1]

In order to become conscious of our own essence and thereby the essence of life in the universe, projections must be withdrawn because they prevent us from seeing the other individual as he or she is. It means that everything we recognize in him or her is also part of us. Most of the time, of course, there must be in that other individual a "psychological hook" on which we can hang that projection. But basically, in order to recognize a trait in another person, we must already have it within us.

The following example will serve to illustrate the projection game in a couple. *The woman* finds *the man* very handicapped when it comes to expressing emotions. She suffers from his silence and holds him responsible for the crumbling relationship. Her first attitude is one of accusation. *The woman* maintains her active projecting without having examined her own conscience.

Withdrawing a projection involves several stages and will bring her to realize how she contributes to the dynamic of this situation. For example, does she accept what her partner says when he expressed his feelings? Does she quickly emit judgments without ever letting him say his fill?

The second stage in withdrawing a projection will consist in examining how her own flaws show up when feelings are being shared. *The woman* may then discover that, in certain cases or when it comes to certain feelings, she is quite handicapped herself. By acknowledging a similar wound in herself, she will be able to build a bridge toward *the man* and reach a base of understanding.

The third stage consists in understanding how her vision of things is prefabricated by a previous reality. *The woman* thus becomes aware of the backgrounds of her irritation. If as a little girl she felt responsible for her father's silence and feared his anger, she may well be in the process of applying the same scheme to her situation with *the man*.

Instead of ruthlessly accusing him, she may then share her interior turmoil with him. She may say: "When you're so silent, I feel like a little girl before her father and I'm afraid of your reactions."

The confession of an emotional experience will encourage him to communicate instead of putting him on the defensive as blaming inevitably does. *The man* will understand what *the woman* is going through within herself. She will then be able to talk about her need of emotional security, and even complete her statement with a request such as this: "I need you to reassure me by saying a few words on what you presently feel about us and on what makes it so difficult for you to communicate with me."

Communication Is Indispensable for Living

The preceding stages summarize the nonviolent communication process that was set up by the psychologist Marshall Rosenberg. They may not be helpful in all instances of projection withdrawal, but they still confirm the fact that there is a great advantage in communicating our insights to our partner. We are essentially creatures of communication, meaning that we must transform what goes on within us and offer it to others in a modified form. Through expression, we allow energy to circulate and we stimulate the process. A message provokes me; I react, interpret its contents, and render it in a different form to the communicator, who is stimulated in return. He reacts to my message, resists it, refuses or accepts it, integrates it in a specific manner, and transforms it to express himself once more. And so on and so forth.

Everything that happens or is communicated to us has an effect on us so that we may transform it through our own expression. That is how life stimulates life and how people become themselves. It is not the intensity of a stimulus that causes illness, but the inability to transform it by our own creation. When a need remains frustrated, when an affect remains blocked, vital fluids flow back inward and begin to stagnate. Physical or psychological illnesses are not far away.

Ultimately, it is more important to let the affects circulate than to solve our problems. Even the crude and impulsive discharge of an affect in the absence of transformative actions is healthier than its inhibition. Our reactions to stimuli may of course become more conscious and lead us to a gradual and improved control of our destiny. To achieve this, the withdrawal of projections and the sharing of our insights through communication are still the best tools. We are creatures of language, and in the context of our intimate relationships, verbal communication represents an essential dimension of our lives. We may equally use dancing, drawing, or any other form of expression as ways of transforming our affects and communicating them to others.

The capacity to pass from the transmission that discharges the affect without transforming it to a communication that creates peace and intimacy means basically to pass from a language saying "you" that kills the other person to the language saying "I" that speaks for oneself while respecting the inalienable freedom of the other person.[2]

In the first stage, *the woman* observes a behavior without judging it (*the man's* silence). In the second stage, she must verify how this behavior affects her emotionally (fear and insecurity). The third stage finds her pulling on her emotional strings; she discovers the basic need (security) jostled by *the man's* attitude. In the fourth stage, she is able to adequately express her wish that he respond to her need ("Talk to me a little . . ."). And so, without judging, it is possible to sense and identify the present need and to express a realistic demand. It summarizes a simple process that in practice requires much tact.[3] Obviously, the same process has to be used by *the man* in order to achieve a fruitful exchange.

The task of withdrawing projections relies on authentic communication, one that commits the partners instead of opposing them through blames and judgments. By developing its capacity to communicate, the couple can become a factor of liberation and of self-knowledge. How someone else perceives us and is influenced by us can help us to transcend certain limitations. In one of my therapeutic encounters I recall having been very moved by a man whose wife was rather timid and silent. Both partners were aware of the problem, and the wife decided to seek help in acquiring some new means of expression. Although this had required that both of them abandon their dreams of perfection, the ordeal had brought them together in a very intimate way.

Such incidents appear simple in writing, but they constitute real and sometimes insurmountable trials in a relationship. We all more or less loathe doing this work of withdrawing projections because it is sure to reveal our vulnerability. The challenge for achieving intimacy in a couple is still and always will be to help each other instead of guarding selfish interests. The main principle for such collaboration is nonetheless easy to formulate: Each partner is 100 percent responsible for what happens in the couple. This formulation applies to couples the principle of *global responsibility* professed in Tibetan Buddhism.

Confronting the Shadow[4]

It is difficult for us to own the shadow segment we see in people who in their ignorance caused us harm. Yet, by assenting to recognize the entity within us who is a dictator, a liar, a traitor, and a hypocrite, we acquire power over these forms of expression instead of being their victim when others personify them. The other person very often symbolizes a part of us that we ignore and to which we are bonded as long as we do not claim it. The acknowledgment of the shadow within us opens the way to forgiveness and compassion. These conditions are possible when we admit that other people resemble us in their weakness and malevolence.

Jung gave the label *confrontation* to the encounter with the shadow to indicate how difficult it is. Yet we must recognize that true freedom is won only at this cost. When a human being has liberated his family, his partners, and his friends from the burden of projected shadows by clarifying in his heart the nature of his various relationships, he lightens himself.

Why does integrating the shadow repel us? Because it upsets the illusion we build up every day of our own perfection and the innocence of each of our actions. Nonetheless, working on the shadow does not necessarily lead to a resigned and depressive position. It provides a special space where none existed before because we believed that the power to harm us belonged to others and that we could do nothing about it. When we discover that the power is our own, it becomes possible to behave differently. Instead of complaining about our fate and behaving like an ostrich, why not begin a dialogue with this shadow residing under our roof?

What is it that attracts us irresistibly to be negative when faced with certain situations? What motivates us? What jealousies and envies do we hide? Why do we tend to behave in such a way that events turn against us? Who is this inner character who prefers not to settle anything? Who is this character who indulges in bad moods? Who is it that likes to wage war? What pleasure does he find in solving conflicts by explosive actions that humiliate others and destroy all possibilities of relating? These are the questions that lead directly to our encounter with the shadow.

The perception of this obscure character as it relates to each conflictual situation in our lives will soon convince us that neither our couple quarrels nor the wars occurring on our planet are totally exterior to us. We do not enjoy such self-examination, since it means displacing the battlefield from the exterior to the interior. The negative attitude we constantly criticize in our partner may become the battle against our own negativity. It was just more convenient to project it onto her than to confront it within ourselves.

Finding a scapegoat to carry the burden of our shortcomings is indeed a primordial psychological function in the traditional couple. Since blaming does not solve anything while making us feel somewhat better, it seems that our partners serve this purpose. We need to have someone to accuse! At the collective level, we have Russians, Islamists, women, men, and so on. At the personal level, such are not around to relieve us and the partner fills this role perfectly, especially when a long-term relationship reveals the faults we are more skilled to detect in others than in ourselves.

The projection of the shadow is one of the favorite mechanisms used by the ego to preserve the illusion of its innocence. The weaker our self-esteem, the more we will actively use others as scapegoats. This explains why certain conflicts between lovers absolutely cannot be settled peacefully. The frail self-esteem of one or both partners does not allow this. To admit one's errors and weaknesses to the other would be experienced as yet another failure, a threat too overwhelming for the ego's structure. To avoid losing everything, we prefer to keep a strong image of ourselves and believe that we are victims of our partner's malice.

As mentioned earlier, the shadow does not have only negative aspects. We also project certain aspects of ourselves that are positive but underdeveloped. These attach us just as much to our partner as the negative ones. We must own them also, to free ourselves from attachments that are not beneficial. A person may be convinced of being stupid and fall in love with someone who is gifted intellectually. If a separation occurs, the former will have the impression that a part of herself has been taken away, that she is mutilated more or less. This is exactly what happens psychologically. As long as she neglects to actively develop her intellectual capacities, she will project them on someone else and will repeat the same attachment pattern.

To recover from such a disappointment, part of the mourning task is to withdraw the positive and negative projections. That is how every relationship becomes the terrain for profound self-knowledge. Since the life of the psyche is very active and each of us is a summary of the universe, we need not fear ever running out of projections. However, they become less and less constraining as we go on. And the next time we are fascinated by someone, we may even attain the freedom to explore in advance the kind of projections he or she attracts. This will make it possible for us to decide whether we wish to pursue what presents itself in the guise of love.

Our projections force us to follow our passions. Our unconscious being expresses itself to the conscious being in this matter. That explains why the experience of *falling in love* is usually accompanied by bellyaches and anxiety-ridden nights. Yet we are quite capable of making a choice in situations where blind determination seems to prevail. This freedom is won by accepting to confront the shadow we project, without judging either the other person or ourselves.

The integration of the shadow opens us to universality. By intimately consenting to what we interpret as negative in ourselves, we are able to greet what seems to be faulty in the universe. Without this work on ourselves, we can never achieve Unity. We have a vision that ignores half of the universe, and we exclude it because we want our minds to be untroubled. The path of the shadow is more effective. When we resolve our inner division between the good and the bad, we become united in ourselves and the conflict vanishes. We may then become One with the cosmos. We realize that there is nothing to change. The forces of destruction serve the renewal of life as much as the forces of creation. Integrating the shadow generates detachment, which in turn develops the kind of serenity that transcends pain and pleasure. These still exist, but they become more relative and we take them less seriously. They are part of life within us; they are an opportunity for expression and communication.

We may then experience real joy—at first, through small gushes that increase in frequency and intensity as we are more conscious of the process. This movement continues until we become rooted in lasting peace. It is not an artificial intellectual peace, obtained by renouncing ourselves. On the contrary, it flows from the dynamism generated by our total contentment to life. This vibrant enthusiasm does not require hours of daily meditation, or abstaining from sex, or the unfailing silence of the mind. It needs only to be consciously immersed in the joy of living.

Peace for the Soul and Joy for the Heart

To be in communion with this joy requires freedom in respect to the relationships we have formed in our lives, that is, *all* the relationships and especially those that have remained incomplete and problematic. To be free, we must disengage ourselves from each of them, that is, return to our memories and allow their contents to emerge spontaneously. We follow the strands and untangle the skeins created within us by each of these relationships. It may involve writing some letters, making a few telephone calls, planning meetings for in-depth dialogues. No effort is too great when we need to unburden the heart.

We must leave nothing behind. We must make the rounds of our attachments one by one. We must examine each resentment dwelling within and do everything possible to appease the inner torment. Sometimes it means simply to make a private resolution that does not implicate the other person; sometimes it requires a more concrete contact with someone to resolve certain unfinished conflicts.

This examination makes it possible to be at peace with everything that happened in our lives—with our parents, with unavoidable accidents, with difficult events, and with tormented relationships. We are thus able to evaluate how it all contributed and still contributes to what we are. And it allows us to become conscious of the fact that all of it resembles us.

For instance, my own examination led me to understand that some of my partners had problems expressing themselves. As far as I was concerned, this was the problem that ruined our life together. However, I realize that I am affected by quite the same difficulty when expressing my deep emotions. During many years, my choices of lovers allowed me to unload my personal incapacities on my partners, making them responsible for my unhappiness. This went on until the pain of separations helped me to reconnect with my own story, not only to understand but to actually express my insights. I closed my office. I began to write, to give conferences, and I went back to music and poetry. My entire life seems to be stronger and happier ever since.

This is only a simple example. But, in reviewing our guilt, our resentment, our attachments, and our judgments, we begin to understand ourselves and we become lighter. As we get rid of some of our pieces, lightness comes, and with it a heartfelt joy that becomes more tangible from day to day.

The aim of the exercise is to open ourselves to reality, to be *in the here and now*, according to the trite but appropriate expression. We cannot be present to ourselves, to others, and to the world if our bodies and hearts are tormented by unresolved relationships. They must each be settled and concluded. Then joy will be a peaceful reality in our hearts and minds.

You may object to all this fuss about finding the path to freedom, but when this work is not done, joy is only a chance happening. It is not deeply rooted within and can be swept away by the least adversity. Working on ourselves is the only way to gain any degree of liberty as we deal with the conditioning that imprisons us. Yes, really, a healthy intimacy begins at home. It is the charity that everyone should practice toward himself.

The Path Is Joy

In a rapidly changing world, the only solution lies in interiority, the zone where things do not change so fast. Confronted as we are by surrounding instability, we must seek and cultivate within us what endures, what is permanent. By stabilizing in ourselves the pleasure of living and existing, we begin to connect with our immortal essence. I refer to the experience of being supported deep inside ourselves, an experience that all at once embraces, contains, and transcends the contingencies of our present life.

Our life begins and ends in the simple pleasure of existing. It is therefore important to cultivate this pleasure each day, in the simplest manner, as we accept to orient our choices according to what maintains our vitality. If anyone genuinely dared to use this scale of reference, an incredible stripping would take place in our lives— a painful stripping no doubt—since it would make us part with many habits, obligations, and routines. As a measuring instrument when I evaluate everything I do, I ask myself what revives or lessens my pleasure for life, and this helps me to start behaving in favor of a positive change.

We treat love like a fortunate accident that was bound to happen to us. As mentioned earlier, it is much like a lottery; but few people win the lottery. The lasting solution is not in this direction. We must rather seek to cultivate love within ourselves, independently of the couple's conditions. Then we may be able to offer something to our union and preserve it instead of forever making demands on it. How can something nourish us indefinitely if we do not care for it? At the core of any relationship, the issue is the investment each partner is prepared to make for the sake of saving the couple. The quality of the energies invested is very important. If we always give the couple our exhausted vitality, we will receive only fatigue and irritation in return.

This is the challenge: to pass from a world where I am everything for the other and where the other is everything for me, to a world where I am happy that the other exists and where, finally, I am happy to exist. Sentimental love is a love of reactions and actions, totally marked by passion and jealousy. But the love of the heart is a love based on profound joy, the joy of existing and of seeing the other exist. This love is possible by loving oneself, life, and the other person.

Joy does not imprison, nor does it command or condemn. It is always free and accessible to whoever wants its company. It is the best inner mistress. Consequently, the human being who lives in joy is the best partner possible. The joy experienced in a couple is an apprenticeship for freedom and enhances the soul's capacity for openness and harmony. It culminates in communion with the joy and lightness of living.

The best thing we can do for ourselves and our partners is to install states of joy within us. Slowly, these states abolish the sense of separation from the partner and the universe. We desperately seek joy and harmony in the couple because we do not experience these states within us. How can two beings experience a durable joy together? By which improbable accident will their pleasure of being together last if each one does not sustain the basic joy of existing?

Intimacy with ourselves allows us to greet someone else in a deep communion. This is admirably described in a poem by the Belgian author Émile Verhaeren, entitled *Every Hour I Think of Your Kindness*:[5]

> *Every hour I think of your kindness*
> *So deeply simple*
> *Prayers fuse me towards you.*
>
> *I have come so late*
> *To the sweetness of your gaze*

And from so far away, to your outstretched arms,
Slowly, across the spaces!

The rust within me was so incrusted
Its grasping teeth tormenting
My confidence;

I was so heavy, so exhausted,
Distrust made me so old,
I was so heavy, so exhausted,
Walking a path of vanity.

So little did I merit the joy
Of your footsteps, lighting my path
That I tremble still and weep almost,
Forever humble, meeting happiness.

Conclusion

Because of love, we are together!
—Osho

Love Is Not a Relationship; It Is a State

We are made of raw material, poorly prepared for happiness and the ecstasy of living. The trying experiences of our childhood or as part of a couple serve to cleanse us. They expand us and make us capable of the sublime. They reveal our intimate essence, forcing us to abandon one by one our shells and our limited definitions.

For the alchemists who sought to transform crude lead into gold, the first stage of this purification was called *nigredo*, or the dark stage. Putrefaction, calcination, and dismembering were the main operations of that period, fitting metaphors for our lives together and in general. When something smells, when it starts to burn, when it starts to disintegrate, *nigredo* is doing its work of purification. The danger is that emotions may become too powerful and precipitate the explosion. These are the moments when mothers and sons hurt each other, when fathers crush their daughters, when couples separate. On the other hand, when the fire is too feeble, there is no transformation. People stay together in a sort of indifferent comfort where no communion is possible. The whole art is therefore to make an adequate fire.

This is what happens in a crisis. We should not worry too much about our relationships baking in the ovens of transformation; it is a necessary process. We cannot dispense with the crisis. It allows us to proceed to new values. It is a process of natural purification.

Its aim is to make us abandon the illusion that happiness will be found in someone else, in the right partner, in the perfect human being we may meet and who will solve all our problems. This advent to consciousness is essential because it is the sine qua non condition for realizing something more important, the knowledge that love is not a relationship but a state. The secret aim of this process is to make us realize that love already resides within us. It preexists all relationships, and we can be forever nourished by it.

The ordeal of a relationship provokes a return to the self that promotes, in the long run, the union between two autonomous persons who celebrate together the joy of existing. For the life force calls us to the conscious and shared celebration of the joy of living. Many sages have been able to achieve supreme identification with the One while living in a cave or a monastery. It is now time to expand this realization to life-styles in general and to the life-styles of couples and families.

As long as this goal is not recognized, the earth risks becoming a wasteland. The genuine gifts of sensuality and sexuality are thus useless. They are perceived as temptations delaying the development of the person who indulges in them. But is not the issue simply to celebrate life through sexuality and sensuality? Could it not involve taking pleasure without guilt, and in believing in our capacity to transform physical and psychic matter? Could it not be a simple matter of fully enjoying our capacity to feel pleasure and to respond? Could we not simply share the ecstasy of living with all that exists?

The planet is dying from our absence. Life on earth needs our presence and our total attention. Incarnation is the next paradigm, the next evolution stage, the next challenge to face. The interpretation we gave to the words of sages such as Jesus or the Buddha has led to the neglect of incarnate life for the sake of the spirit. Such a conception of spiritual life is limiting and injurious to the integrity of the human being. The individual who has experienced the Unity of all things knows that there is no other place to go, that the realization we seek exists everywhere, here as well as on other levels of consciousness. Energy is the same everywhere. The energy of love that keeps all things together is akin to itself at every level of existence. What we seek is already here.

We Are Free to Destroy Ourselves

The universe is composed of that undefinable energy that, in its infinite love—how to name it otherwise?—responds to all our whims without ever judging, without ever rejecting. The choice is therefore at our fingertips. Nothing, absolutely nothing, can prevent a human being from destroying himself if he so desires. That is the extent of each one's liberty. There is even no judgment to make on such incidents. And perhaps each one of us needs to partly experience them to gain self-knowledge and connect with the love energy. In the same way, nothing, absolutely nothing, can prevent a human being to strive for his happiness and his liberation by using his personal power.

Life is perfect in its intelligent manifestation; it is conscious of itself and full of joy. It possesses a capacity for self-generation and self-creation. This genius dwells in every living cell, and every human being who recognizes himself in the cosmic mirror achieves his own sovereignty and his ability to use all the possibilities offered by existence to create his own life.

We are in constant communion with the universe. There is no separation. Each fiber of our being participates in it. We are of the same nature. We are made of the same fabric. We are the universe and are able to deeply enjoy it thanks to our consciousness, the consciousness that is, so to speak, its emerging quality. The challenge of intimacy is forever to celebrate this joy, in a twosome, in a threesome, in tens, thousands, or millions. In total awareness, we will become the conscious cocreators of nature's thrilling adventure. Instead of being the victims of the gods and the devils, we will become human beings who are responsible for their destiny.

The Best Way to Be Happy . . .

Eight A.M. . . . I look away from my computer. Outside, spring is everywhere. The tree in front of my office has huge blossoms, waiting only for the heat of the sun to become leaves. The birds are chirping away. The city traffic sounds like an unending sea with its waves clamoring in succession. Spring is also within me. I feel the urge to live, and incredible energy flows through my veins. I am excited, as excited as I was at ten, waking to a sunny morning and jumping on my bicycle to ride off to adventure.

But one last thing before I leave you, the most important, of course. I still hear Vlady, my tai-chi professor, constantly repeating: "The best way to be happy is to be happy!"

Epilogue

The Woman

Finally! Vacation time! As you recall your past experiences with *him*, all goes rather well. A little ocean resort on the East Coast. Haphazard reservations at the last minute. A miserable room above a noisy ventilator. Unappealing food. Enough to irritate you. Strangely, it brings you closer together. There's something in the air, like love renewed. . . . But you're going too fast. . . . There he is, turning his head to watch a girl parading her breasts on the beach. You immediately feel hurt. You're about to retort, but he looks so funny with his guilty little boy demeanor, all ready to swear he wasn't looking, that you burst out laughing. No, really, he'll never get over his mother.

The Man

You were about to run after *her* in that parking lot. The pavement was scorching, and you were holding a Coke and some greasy fries. That's when the goddess walked by. . . . Wow! What breasts! They shouldn't be allowed. You didn't want to look, so as not to hurt *her*. But it was more than you could bear. Suddenly, you feel your legs caving in. No, it's not possible; *she* has come closer, just to trip you and gallop off, yelling loudly at you: "I love you, my love! I love you, my love!" Very nice, but you just dropped all your food on the ground! For a few seconds, you feel invaded by a terrible anger. She never stops bugging you. Really, it's too crazy. The whole situation suddenly appears so ridiculous. And right there, on the hot pavement, your feet all stuck in the fries and the Coke, you feel overwhelmed by a wave of emotions so deep and exquisite that you yell back at her: "I love you, my love! I love you!" This "I love you" is the one she can finally make a recording of. It comes from so deep inside you. You'd been waiting for it for such a long time. It feels so good that you start to cry from joy like a child. You see her smiling through your tears, and *she* takes you in her arms so gently, so gently . . .

The Author

I know . . . I know . . . you thought it only happened in your world. Sorry, it happens everywhere. This is what love is all about. This is love.

Endnotes

Note: The full publishing information for the references is listed in the Sources section.

INTRODUCTION

[1] Psychoanalyst Jan Bauer is the author of an excellent book on love: *Impossible Love: Why the Heart Must Go Wrong*.
[2] Guy Corneau, *Absent Fathers, Lost Sons: In Search of Masculine Identity*. Translated from *"Père Manquant, Fils Manqué, Que Sont les Hommes Devenus?"* by Larry Shouldice.

1. LOVE AT WAR

[1] I am reminded here of the theater play *Lysistrata*, where the women decide to go on a sex strike to claim their rights. The Greek author Aristophanes lived from 445 to 386 B.C.

²This paragraph and the preceding one are largely inspired by an article I wrote entitled "Le défi de l'intimité" [The challenge of intimacy], in *Communiquer pour vivre*, by Jacques Salomé, pp. 65–66.

³Ariane Émond, *Les ponts d'Ariane* (The bridges of Ariane).

2. ON BEING BORN A MAN OR WOMAN

¹Heinz Kohut, *The Analysis of the Self*, pp. 9–45. This concept belongs to a set of theories on the primary narcissism of the child. Kohut has opened the door to what is now called the movement of self-psychology. Through his study of infants, he established a psychology that is not based on the stages of development (oral, anal, genital) defined by Freud, but rather on the needs of the children as clinically observed. Jungian analyst Mario Jacoby saw these theories as a possible bridge to Jung's psychology. He discusses the subject in his book *Individuation and Narcissism: The Psychology of Self in Jung and Kohut.*

²On the subject of the individuation process and its different stages, I suggest reading the second part of the basic book by Jung, "The Relations Between the Ego and the Unconscious" in *Two Essays on Analytical Psychology*, in *The Collected Works of C. G. Jung*, vol. 7.

³The stages are mentioned by Verena Kast in an article entitled "Animus and Anima: Spiritual Growth and Separation," *Harvest: Journal for Jungian Studies*, p. 7.

⁴It was Jung who proposed the word *complex* following his experiments with associations produced spontaneously by the brain. When testing associations, he began to notice what interfered with the response time of the subjects. He concluded that prolonging response time, breaking out in laughter, shyness, refusing to respond, and so on, were indicators that definite emotional centers in subjects had been touched. He had just discovered complexes. For further details see the book by Jolanda Jacobi, *Complex/Archetype/Symbol in the Psychology of C. G. Jung*, pp. 6–32.

⁵For an in-depth understanding of the archetype concept, I suggest reading the excellent book by Anthony Stevens, *Archetypes: A Natural History of the Self*, pp. 21–79.

⁶The *shadow* is a universal archetype justifying our tendency to participate in what is called *evil*. At the personal level, it is the obscure little sibling that we carry within but that we do not want anyone to see. By

extension, the shadow sometimes designates the totality of the unconscious, because it is always hidden. In dreams, the shadow is generally represented by a person of the same sex as the dreamer. Finally, the shadow also represents positive aspects, but which have been repressed or neglected aspects. For further details see the book by Jolanda Jacobi, op. cit., pp. 58, 114.

[7]For a better understanding of the notion of self-esteem, I refer the reader to a book by the Jungian psychoanalyst Mario Jacoby: *Shame and the Origins of Self-Esteem: A Jungian Approach*, pp. 24–26. To trace the origins of shame and poor self-esteem, the author uses the research done on infants as his basis.

[8]"Little Snow White" in *The Complete Grimm's Fairy Tales*, pp. 249–258. In this tale, the heroine's stepmother owns a magic mirror and becomes mortally jealous of the girl, to the point of abandoning her in the forest.

[9]In regard to the theory of organ inferiority, see the chapter written by Henri Ellenberger on Adler, in his book *The Discovery of the Unconscious: The History and Evolution of Dynamic Psychiatry*, pp. 603–606. This remarkable book traces the portraits of the great psychiatrists and psychoanalysts of our time, such as Freud, Jung, and Adler, by situating their theories in the context of their personal biographies and important historical events.

[10]"One-Eye, Two-Eyes, Three-Eyes" in *The Complete Grimm's Fairy Tales*, pp. 585–592. I thank Lucie Richer, Daniel Bordeleau, and Tom Kelly, with whom the story was interpreted in a seminar organized by the Jungian Psychoanalysts of Quebec.

[11]I owe these ideas on sexual identity and its construction to conversations with Tom Kelly and John Desteian. The latter is the author of a book on the couple entitled *Coming Together—Coming Apart: The Union of Opposites in Love Relationships*.

[12]Alfred Charles Kinsey et al., *Sexual Behavior in the Human Male*.

[13]Christiane Olivier, *Les Enfants de Jocaste: L'empreinte de la mère* (The children of Jocasta: The mother's imprint), pp. 53–72. The book is a classic on this theme.

[14]We are so little accustomed to the reality of men taking care of children that the word *mothering*, which means treating children in a motherly way, has no masculine counterpart in the dictionary. I thus introduce the neologism *fathering* to designate the act of treating children in a fatherly way.

[15]In all fairness to Jung, note that the archetypes are not images, but

rather the psychic structures that organize symbolic images. For a better understanding of the nature of archetypes, I refer to the text by Jung entitled "On the Nature of the Psyche" in *The Structure and Dynamics of the Psyche*, in *The Collected Works of C. G. Jung*, vol. 9, pp. 54–71.

For excellent information on the animus and anima, see Jung's "The Relations Between the Ego and the Unconscious," op. cit., pp. 188–211.

[16]Marie-Louise von Franz, "The Process of Individuation," in *Man and His Symbols*, pp. 177–211.

[17]The mask we wear in society or when we are in the presence of someone is what constitutes our *persona*. Jung borrowed the word from Greek. In Greek plays, it was the mask worn by actors for the purpose of making their voices resound in the amphitheater. The *persona* thus symbolizes a bridge to others and a way of adapting our real selves to society. It can become rigid and sickly when it no longer conveys the basic traits of our personality. When there is no harmony between our fundamental *I* and our appearance, we *sound* false and a neurosis is not far away. The *persona* is essential because it makes living in society possible and serves to control instincts. But the individual must not identify with it to the point of letting it represent his whole identity. See Jung's "The Relations Between the Ego and the Unconscious," op. cit., pp. 156–162.

[18]Khalil Gibran, *The Prophet*, p. 22

3. FATHERS AND DAUGHTERS: LOVE IN SILENCE

[1]The label is from Robin Norwood's international best-seller *Women Who Love Too Much: The Need to Be Needed*, pp. 65–66.

[2]The man who is afraid to love has also become a stereotype in popular psychology, mostly on account of the book by Steven Carter and Julia Sokol, *Men Who Can't Love*.

[3]Christiane Olivier, *Les enfants de Jocaste* (Jocasta's children), p. 65.

[4]"The Girl Without Hands" (here called "The Handless Maiden") in *The Complete Grimm's Fairy Tales*, pp. 160–166.

[5]Marie-Louise von Franz, *The Feminine in Fairy Tales*, p. 70.

[6]Ibid.

[7]Réjean Simard, "Au delà de l'inceste: À la recherche de son identité" (Beyond incest: Searching for one's identity).

[8]Gabrielle Lavallée gives witness in the publication *L'alliance de la brebis* (The alliance of the lamb).

[9]There are no official statistics on incest. Michel Dorais, a social worker who intervenes a great deal in the area of prostitution and who has written several books on the subject, believes that there are probably 80 percent of prostitutes who were victims of incest. He is the coauthor of several researches on prostitution, among others: *Les enfants de la prostitution* (The children of prostitution) and *Une enfance trahie: Sans famille, battu, violé* (A betrayed childhood: Deprived of family, beaten, raped).

[10]"En direct" (Live), Société Radio–Canada. Program hosted by Christiane Charette.

[11]Some social workers suggest that the problem of incest is on the rise in reconstituted families, but there are no available statistics on the subject. However, a distribution by percentage of cases of physical aggression and of cases of sexual aggression against children registered by the police in 1992 shows that 45 percent of these are attributable to the mother or the father, 27 percent to a member of the immediate family, and 26 percent to a member of the enlarged family. (Source: Statistics Canada, *Family Violence in Canada*, catalogue no. 89-5 410XPF.)

[12]This thesis was developed by Freud in *Totem and Taboo*, in which a cruel patriarch controls the women and exiles the sons. The latter finally revolt and kill the primordial father. They then decide to establish the interdiction of incest so that there will be no possible rivalry among them for the control of the women who had belonged to the father. They also decide to pay allegiance to the strongest son and to spare his life. Therein seems to be the origin of the two basic taboos of humanity: incest and parricide. Present-day ethnologists are doubtful concerning this story on taboos established by Freud, but it is still nevertheless an interesting psychological myth. See Henri Ellenberger, *The Discovery of the Unconscious: The History and Evolution of Dynamic Psychiatry*, p. 526.

[13]I refer the reader to the excellent work of Jan Bauer, *Impossible Love: Why the Heart Must Go Wrong*, in which she explores the psychological meaning of these passions condemned in advance by social taboos.

[14]Hélène Pedneault, "Mon père à moi" (My own father).

[15]Comments collected from a meeting with French psychologist Dominique Hautreux.

[16]Linda Schierse Leonard, *The Wounded Woman: Healing the Father-Daughter Relationship*, pp. 37–38.

[17]Ibid., p. 39.

[18]Ibid., p. 49.

[19]Ibid., p. 63.

[20]Ibid., p. 66.

[21]Richard Boutet, "Le spasme de vivre" (The spasm of living), documentary on suicide in the young, produced by Vent d'Est, September 1991.

[22]June Singer, *Androgyny*, quoted by Linda Schierse Leonard, *The Wounded Woman*, p. 61.

[23]Linda Schierse Leonard, op. cit., p. 67.

[24]Ibid., p. 71.

[25]Ibid., p. 73.

[26]Ibid., p. 75.

[27]Ibid., p. 74.

[28]Ibid., p. 75.

[29]C. S. Lewis, *Till We Have Faces*, quoted by Linda Schierse Leonard, op. cit., p. 75.

[30]Marie-Louise von Franz, *The Feminine in Fairy Tales*, p. 27.

4. HEALING THE FATHER WOUND

[1]Alice Miller, *The Drama of the Gifted Child: The Search for the True Self*, p. 34.

[2]Marie-Louise von Franz, "The Process of Individuation," in *Man and His Symbols*, p. 191.

[3]Paule Lebrun, "La rage au coeur" (The raging heart), *Guide Ressources*, p. 35.

[4]Ibid.

[5]The following account is based on the remarks of Linda Lagacé in her course entitled "Femmes et relations humaines" (Women and human relations). The course was offered in the context of a certificate in the psychology of human relations at the Université de Sherbrooke.

5. MOTHER AND SON: THE IMPOSSIBLE COUPLE

[1]Boris Cyrulnik, *Sous le signe du lien: Une histoire naturelle de l'attachement* (Marked by the bond: A natural history of attachment), p. 64.

[2]Guy Corneau, *Absent Fathers, Lost Sons*, p. 11. In Canada, at least 20 percent of the children live in single-parent situations; 80 percent of these families are headed by a woman, and 10 percent of the children have never had regular contacts with their father.

[3]Extracted from the book by Elisabeth Badinter, *XY: De l'identité masculine* (On masculine identity), p. 83.

[4]In a 1993 study on violence against women in Canada, "women who, at the time of the survey, were currently in a marriage or common law union for two years or less were more likely than others to report that their spouses had abused them in the year before the survey (8%). In contrast, 1% of women in partnerships that had lasted more than 20 years reported spousal violence." Extracted from "Marital Violence in Canada" by Karen Rodgers, in *Social Tendencies in Canada*, pp. 3–4.

[5]This is also true for fathers who are alone in raising their children. They also risk creating a *fusional* bond with their children. The separating and saving factor will be the new woman in the man's life.

[6]I am not the only one to share this view. The psychoanalyst Christiane Olivier insists on it in all her books, the latest being *Les fils d'Oreste, Ou la question du père* (The sons of Orestes, Or the father question), p. 117.

[7]Quoted from a conversation with the psychologist Lucie Richer.

[8]Jung discusses this abundantly in his book *Symbols of Transformation*, in *The Collected Works of C. G. Jung*, vol. 5, pp. 274–305.

[9]Concerning some rites of passage, see "Betwixt and Between: The Liminal Period in Rites of Passage," by Victor Turner, pp. 3–23, in *Betwixt and Between*.

[10]Gail Sheehy, *New Passages: Mapping Your Life Across Time*, pp. 10–11. The journalist notes an important revolution in longevity. According to her research, adolescence is prolonged into a provisory adulthood spanning from 18 to 30 years; the first adult age is between 30 and 45, and the second adult age, an innovation in the field of psychology, would be from 45 to 60 years.

[11]The data was offered by the psychologist and researcher Camil Bouchard during the program *J'veux de l'amour* (I want some love), a

televised documentary moderated by Claire Lamarche, a broadcast production of Réseau TVA, February 28, 1994.

6. THE PRICE OF EMOTIONAL INCEST

[1]J. D. Lichtenberg, *Psychoanalysis and Infant Research.*
[2]Boris Cyrulnik, *Les nourritures affectives* (Emotional nourishment). These were among the ideas he presented during an interview with Robert Blondin, animator and producer of the radio program "L'Aventure," broadcast May 2, 3, 4, 1994, on Radio-Canada.
[3]Elisabeth Badinter, *XY: De l'identité masculine*, p. 128.
[4]Saint Thomas Aquinas, *Summa Theologiae*, p. 175. I thank the Dominican Father Benoît Lacroix, who provided this reference.
[5]Michel Tremblay, *Les Belles-Soeurs* (The sisters-in-law), p. 101.
[6]Adrienne Rich, *Of Woman Born*, p. 278.
[7]Joëlle de Gravelaine, *La déesse sauvage, les divinités féminines: Mères et prostituées, magiciennes et initiatrices* (The wild goddess, female divinities: Mothers and prostitutes, magicians and initiators), pp. 79–105.

7. THE DRAMA OF THE GOOD BOY

[1]Alejandro Jodorowsky, the film *Santa Sangre.*
[2]Nikos Kazantzaki, *Zorba the Greek*, p. 300.

8. REFLECTIONS ON THE ROLE OF THE MOTHER

[1]The tale is the basis of the work of the American poet Robert Bly, *Iron John: A Book About Men.* See also my interpretation, presented in my book *Absent Fathers, Lost Sons*, pp. 115–117.
[2]See "Fatherhood: Implications for Child and Adult Development," by Henry B. Biller, in *Handbook of Developmental Psychology*, by Benjamin B. Wolman, p. 709.
[3]Carl Gustav Jung, "On the Nature of the Psyche" in *The Structure and Dynamics of the Psyche*, in *The Collected Works of C. G. Jung*, vol. 9, p. 89.

9. LOVE IN DISTRESS

[1]Guilt involves the other person: we feel guilty toward someone. Shame is felt in relationship to more or less conscious representations that serve as reference values for the ego. When the ego is weak, these representations may crush it. It collapses under the weight of shame. The representations coincide with what psychoanalysis calls the *superego* and the *ego ideal*. Mario Jacoby adequately distinguishes guilt from shame in his book *Shame and the Origins of Self-Esteem*, pp. 1–4.

[2]Edmond Rostand, *Cyrano de Bergerac*.

[3]Carl Gustav Jung, "On the Nature of the Psyche" in *The Structure and Dynamics of the Psyche*, in *The Collected Works of C. G. Jung*, vol. 9, p. 98.

[4]August Strindberg, *The Father* in *Three Plays*.

[5]Ibid., p. 73.

[6]Ibid., p. 58.

[7]Huguette O'Neil, "*Santé mentale: Les hommes, ces grands oubliés . . .*" (Mental health: Men, the long-forgotten ones . . .), in *L'Actualité médicale*, p. 27.

[8]Heinrich von Kleist, *Five Plays*.

[9]As I mentioned earlier, for Jung the shadow is an archetypal structure of our psyche, meaning that each human being has the tendency to hide the less shining aspects of his personality. Even if the task is difficult, humans cannot "become whole" without acknowledging this shadow side.

[10]Paule Lebrun, "Face à l'ombre" (Facing the shadow), an interview with the psychoanalyst Jan Bauer, *Guide Ressources*, pp. 37–41.

[11]Leonard Cohen, "Anthem," from the recording *The Future*.

10. LOVE IN JOY

[1]This idea was developed by the psychoanalyst Michel Cautaerts in his presentation entitled "I Love You. Let's Separate!" at the 13th Conference of the International Analytical Psychology Association (IAPA), in Zurich, August 1995. Unpublished.

[2]I wish to thank the kinetic therapist François Dufour for having introduced this exercise in my workshops and initiated me to haptonomy.

11. INTIMACY WITH ONESELF

[1]On the question of withdrawing projections, see the book by Jolanda Jacobi, *Complex/Archetype/Symbol in the Psychology of C. G. Jung*, pp. 13–17.

[2]I suggest reading the book by Jacques Salomé and Sylvie Galland: *Si je m'écoutais . . . je m'entendrais* (If I listened to myself . . . I'd hear myself).

[3]The four stages constitute the basis of the nonviolent communication process set up by the American psychologist Marshall Rosenberg.

[4]Marie-Louise von Franz, "The Process of Individuation," in *Man and His Symbols*, pp. 168–176. See also "The Techniques of Differentiation Between the Ego and the Figures of the Unconscious" in Jung's book *Two Essays on Analytical Psychology*, in *The Collected Works of C. G. Jung*, vol. 7, pp. 212–226.

[5]Émile Verhaeren, *Les heures claires* (The hours of light).

Sources

Aquinas, Saint Thomas. *Summa Theologiae*, vol. 15. London: Black-friars, 1970.

Badinter, Elisabeth. *XY: De l'identité masculine*. Paris: Odile Jacob, 1992.

Bauer, Jan. *Impossible Love: Why the Heart Must Go Wrong*. Dallas, Tex.: Spring Publications, 1993.

Biller, Henry B. "Fatherhood: Implications for Child and Adult Develop-ment." In *Handbook of Developmental Psychology*, by Benjamin B. Wolman. Englewood Cliffs, N.J.: Prentice-Hall, 1982.

Bly, Robert. *Iron John: A Book About Men*. Reading, Mass.: Addison-Wesley, 1990.

Carter, Steven, and Julia Sokol. *Men Who Can't Love*. New York: Berkley, 1988.

Chevalier, Jean, et al. *Dictionnaire des symboles: Mythes, rêves, coutumes, gestes, formes, figures, couleurs, nombres* (Dictionary of symbols: Myths, dreams, forms, figures, colors, numbers). Paris: Robert Laffont et Jupiter, 1969.

Cohen, Leonard. "Anthem" from the recording *The Future*. Columbia Records, 1992.

Corneau, Guy. *Absent Fathers, Lost Sons: In Search of Masculine Identity*. Boston & London: Shambhala, 1991.

———. "Le défi de l'intimité" (The challenge of intimacy). In *Communiquer pour vivre*, pp. 63–69, by Jacques Salomé. Paris: CLÉS et Albin Michel, 1996.

Cyrulnik, Boris. *Les nourritures affectives* (Emotional nourishment). Paris: Odile Jacob, 1993.

———. *Sous le signe du lien: Une histoire naturelle de l'attachement* (Marked by the bond: A natural history of attachment). Paris: Hachette, 1989.

Desteian, John A. *Coming Together—Coming Apart: The Union of Opposites in Love Relationships*. Boston: Sigo Press, 1989.

Dorais, Michel, and Denis Ménard. *Les enfants de la prostitution* (The children of prostitution). Montreal: VLB Éditeur, 1987.

Dorais, Michel, and Christian-André Séguin. *Une enfance trahie: Sans famille, battu, violé* (A betrayed childhood: Deprived of family, beaten, raped). Montreal: VLB Éditeur et Le Jour, 1993.

Ellenberger, Henri. *The Discovery of the Unconscious: The History and Evolution of Dynamic Psychiatry*. New York: Basic Books, 1970.

Émond, Ariane. *Les ponts d'Ariane* (The bridges of Ariane). Montreal: VLB Éditeur, 1994.

Franz, Marie-Louise von. *The Feminine in Fairy Tales*. New York: Spring Publications, 1972.

———. "The Process of Individuation." In *Man and His Symbols*, pp. 158–229. Garden City, N.Y.: Doubleday, 1964.

Gibran, Khalil. *The Prophet*. New York: Arkana Penguin Books, 1992.

Gravelaine, Joëlle de. *La déesse sauvage: Les divinités féminines: Mères et prostituées, magiciennes et initiatrices* (The wild goddess: Female deities: Mothers and prostitutes, magicians and initiators). St. Jean-de-Braye, France: Éditions Dangles, 1993.

Graves, Robert, et al. *New Larousse Encyclopedia of Mythology*. London: Hamlyn, 1983.

Grimm, Jacob and Wilhelm. *The Complete Grimm's Fairy Tales*. New York: Pantheon Books, 1972.

Guggenbühl-Craig, Adolf. *Marriage Dead or Alive*. Dallas, Tex.: Spring Publications, 1981.

Jacobi, Jolanda. *Complex/Archetype/Symbol in the Psychology of C. G. Jung*. New York: Pantheon Books, 1959.

Jacoby, Mario. *Individuation and Narcissism: The Psychology of Self in Jung and Kohut*. London: Routledge, 1990.

———. *Shame and the Origins of Self-Esteem: A Jungian Approach*. London: Routledge, 1996.

Jodorowski, Alejandro. *Santa Sangre* (film), Italy, 1989.

Jung, Carl Gustav. *The Structure and Dynamics of the Psyche*. In *The Collected Works of C. G. Jung*, vol. 9. Translated by R. E. C. Hull, Bollingen Series XX. Princeton, N.J.: Princeton University Press, 1969.

———. *Symbols of Transformation*. In *The Collected Works of C. G. Jung*, vol. 5. Translated by R. E. C. Hull, Bollingen Series XX. Princeton, N.J.: Princeton University Press, 1956.

———. *Two Essays on Analytical Psychology*. In *The Collected Works of C. G. Jung*, vol. 7. Translated by R. E. C. Hull, Bollingen Series XX. Princeton, N.J.: Princeton University Press, 1972.

Jung, Carl Gustav, et al. *Man and His Symbols*. Garden City, N.Y.: Doubleday, 1969.

Kast, Verena. "Animus and Anima: Spiritual Growth and Separation." *Harvest: Journal for Jungian Studies*, no. 39. London: C. G. Jung Analytical Psychology Club, 1993.

Kazantzaki, Nikos. *Zorba the Greek*. New York: Simon & Schuster, 1996.

Kinsey, Alfred Charles, Wardell B. Pomeroy, and Clyde E. Martin. *Sexual Behavior in the Human Female*. The Kinsey Report, 1953.

———. *Sexual Behavior in the Human Male*. The Kinsey Report, 1953.

Kleist, Heinrich von. *Five Plays*. New Haven and London: Yale University Press, 1988.

Kohut, Heinz. *The Analysis of the Self*. New York: International Universities Press, 1971.

Lagacé, Linda. "Femmes et relations humaines" (Women and human relations), a course given at the Université de Sherbrooke in the certificate program in psychology of human relations, unedited course notes, 1994.

Laplanche, J., and J. B. Pontalis. *Vocabulaire de la psychanalyse* (Psychoanalysis vocabulary). Paris: Presses Universitaires de France, 1976.

Lavallée, Gabrielle. *L'alliance de la brebis* (The alliance of the lamb). N.p.: Éd. JCL, 1993.

Lebrun, Paule. "Face à l'ombre" (Facing the shadow), an interview with psychoanalyst Jan Bauer. *Guide Ressources*, 11, no. 8 (May 1996) (Montreal): 37–41.

———. "La rage au coeur" (The raging heart). *Guide Ressources*, 11, no. 8 (May 1996) (Montreal): 32–36.

Leonard, Linda Schierse. *The Wounded Woman: Healing the Father-Daughter Relationship*. Boston: Shambhala Publications, 1985.

Lewis, C. S. *Till We Have Faces*. Grand Rapids, Mich.: W. B. Eerdman, 1956.

Lichtenberg, J. D. *Psychoanalysis and Infant Research*. Hillsdale, N.J.: Analytic Press, 1983.

Miller, Alice. *The Drama of the Gifted Child: The Search for the True Self*. New York: Basic Books, HarperCollins, 1994.

Neuman, Erich. *The Origins and History of Consciousness*. New York: R. E. C. Hull, 1954.

Norwood, Robin. *Women Who Love Too Much: The Need to Be Needed*. New York: Pocket Books, 1986.

Olivier, Christiane. *Les Enfants de Jocaste: L'empreinte de la mère* (The children of Jocasta: The mother's imprint). Paris: Denoël-Gonthier, 1980.

———. *Filles d'Ève* (Daughters of Eve). Paris: Denoël, 1980.

———. *Les fils d'Orestre, Ou la question du père* (The sons of Orestes, Or the father question). Paris: Flammarion, 1994.

O'Neil, Huguette. "Santé mentale: Les hommes, ces grands oubliés . . ." (Mental health: Men, the forgotten ones . . .). *L'actualité médicale* (May 11, 1988).

Pedneault, Hélène. "Mon père à moi" (My own father). *La vie en rose* (March 1985) (Montreal).

Rich, Adrienne. *Of Woman Born*. New York: Norton, 1986.

Rodgers, Karen. "Marital Violence in Canada." In *Social Tendencies in Canada*, catalogue no. 11-008F (Fall 1994), Statistics Canada.

Rostand, Edmond. *Cyrano de Bergerac. An Heroic Comedy in Five Acts*. New York: Bantam Books, 1981.

Salomé, Jacques, and Sylvie Galland. *Si je m'écoutais . . . je m'entendrais* (If I listened to myself . . . I'd hear myself). Paris: Éd. de l'Homme, 1990.

Sheehy, Gail. *New Passages: Mapping Your Life Across Time*. New York: Random House, 1995.

Simard, Réjean. "Au delà de l'inceste: À la recherche de son identité"

(Beyond incest: In search of identity), presented at the 11th Conference on Bioenergetic Analysis, Miami (May 1992).

Singer, June. *Androgyny.* New York: Anchor Books, 1977.

Stevens, Anthony. *Archetypes: A Natural History of the Self.* New York: Quill, 1983.

Strindberg, August. *The Father* in *Three Plays.* Toronto: Penguin Books Canada Ltd., 1958.

Tremblay, Michel. *Les Belles-Soeurs* (The sisters-in-law). Translated by John Van Burek and Bill Glassco. Vancouver, B.C.: Talonbooks, 1991.

Turner, Victor. "Betwixt and Between: The Liminal Period in Rites of Passage." In *Betwixt and Between*, pp. 3–23, by Steven Foster and Meridith Little. La Salle, Ill.: Open Court, 1987.

Verhaeren, Émile. *Les Heures claires* (The hours of light). 1896.